A DEATH IN THE
LUCKY HOLIDAY HOTEL

A **DEATH** IN THE LUCKY HOLIDAY HOTEL

Murder, Money, and an Epic Power Struggle in China

PIN HO AND WENGUANG HUANG

authorized: He, Pin.

PublicAffairs
New York

PublicAffairs books are available at special discounts for bulk purchases in the U.S. by corporations, institutions, and other organizations. For more information, please contact the Special Markets Department at the Perseus Books Group, 2300 Chestnut Street, Suite 200, Philadelphia, PA 19103, call (800) 810–4145, ext. 5000, or e-mail special.markets@perseusbooks.com.

Book Design by Cynthia Young

A record for the printed edition is available at the Library of Congress.

ISBN 978–1-61039–273–0 (HC)

ISBN 978–1-61039–274–7 (EB)

First Edition

10 9 8 7 6 5 4 3 2 1

CONTENTS

AUTHORS' NOTE

This book represents the joint efforts of Ho Pin and Wenguang Huang, who have teamed up to relate a tale of scandal, intrigue, and murder in Chongqing—a tale that has had profound repercussions on China and the world. For the sake of clear and compelling storytelling, however, we have chosen to narrate the story using the voice of Ho Pin—a commentator on Chinese politics, and a magazine/book/website publisher who broke the news about several pivotal events in the Bo Xilai scandal and subsequently, as the scandal unraveled, became part of this sprawling story.

We intend this book to be an insider's take on a political murder that set off a dramatic, behind-the-scenes fight for power at the highest echelons. It has incorporated a significant amount of previously unpublished information as well as the views of many insiders who rarely, if ever, talk publicly to the press and the public. To research the book, we interviewed more than fifty current and former Chinese government officials, well-connected businesspeople, veteran political analysts, and independent journalists—all of whom shared their knowledge about the Bo Xilai case and the inner workings of the Communist Party. Many chose to remain anonymous for fear of political reprisal. In addition to these interviews, we followed the daily postings on Weibo—China's version of Twitter—and various articles posted on overseas Chinese language websites that escaped government censorship and unveiled critical information at the peak of the scandal. Later, in order to get an on-the-ground experience of the locale for this political drama, Wenguang Huang, posing as a tourist, took a week-long trip to Chongqing in November 2012 to interview government officials, police officers, and ordinary people on the street. He also visited and photographed the hotel where British businessman Neil Heywood was killed. The fact-checking trip enabled us to get an exact sense of the drama and its impact locally and nationally.

What has emerged from this endeavor, we hope, is the most comprehensive account of the Neil Heywood murder scandal that shocked and riveted the international community in 2012 as well as a stunning and unsettling portrait of the different intertwined interest groups and political factions within the Chinese Communist Party's top decision-making body.

It is not a pretty picture.

Though, when appearing in public, China's leaders present a uniform picture of total solidarity—an all-male group uniformly clad in dark suits, white shirts, and (often) red ties with dyed, jet-black hair—the group is anything but a solid, unified group of wise men presiding over the fate of roughly a fifth of the world's population. There are fierce internal power struggles, pitting one political faction and economic interest group against another, massive amounts of official and non-official corruption, byzantine intrigues, and hardball tactics that stop at nothing. The rules of engagement more closely resemble those of warring mafia families than anything else, with princeling tangling with princeling over turf and territory.

And this time, there are some new ingredients in this Chinese hotpot. In the past, the Communist Party monopolized the flow of information and political scandals were kept secret. The public didn't learn about events until months, or years, later. However, as more Chinese are becoming fluent English readers, they use many different means to translate the foreign media reports and transmit them back to China via the Internet.

Realizing that the public craved Chinese news from overseas, and considering Western media outlets to be more reliable sources of information than the state-controlled propaganda machine, the political and business elite as well as friends and relatives of senior Communist leaders have often used secret means to feed Western journalists and political analysts with "exclusives." Some had their friends post banned information on Weibo. Thanks to these political insiders, the world was able to receive real-time coverage as the scandal unfolded, enabling the foreign media to create a small fissure in the secret maneuverings of the Communist Party. Many blog postings and overseas media reports were castigated by government as "vicious rumors," but the majority of them proved to be close to the truth. The government official media, on the contrary, turned out to be the biggest rumormonger of all.

However, the foreign media have also learned a valuable lesson from the Bo Xilai coverage. Knowing the challenges Western media face in obtaining news via regular channels, some political insiders, often with tacit approvals from the Communist leadership, manipulated the international media, leaking information that was a mélange of truth, lies, and pure speculation to advance a specific political agenda. As a consequence, many media outlets, including *Mingjing News* (one of Ho Pin's Chinese-language news sites), carried stories that subsequently proved to be inaccurate or wrong. For example, based on an insider's tip, we posted a story that Bo Xilai's trial would take place in October 2012 in the city of Changsha, but it never panned out. In addition, before Bo Xilai was officially charged, Western reporters, acting on tips from insiders, published lurid allegations against him, suggesting that the Bo Xilai case was a fight between reformists and an extreme and corrupt Maoist. As a consequence, the overseas media played a role, in a way that the state media could never have, in a massive government smear campaign against Bo.

As more sources are becoming available in China, Western media organizations are better able to verify each story to improve accuracy and independence. Since this book was written over a period of six months, we were able to work with Chen Xiaoping, a US-based legal scholar and journalist, to check our sources in China, verify details, incorporate the most up-to-date information, and modify any inaccuracies that had occurred in earlier news reports. Despite these efforts, some errors and misjudgments may remain and we take responsibility for them. We hope that other writers, journalists, and historians who follow in our footsteps will be able to further clarify the historical record.

At the time of this writing (January 2013), Bloomberg and the *New York Times* released a series of investigative reports that shed light on the family finances of senior Chinese leaders. With their aggressive coverage of China, Western media giants such as the Bloomberg, *The Guardian*, the *Daily Telegraph*, the *Economist*, *The Financial Times*, the *New York Times*, and the *Wall Street Journal*, as well as Chinese-language media outlets operating outside of China, are directly influencing Chinese politics more than ever before. Their coverage is being filtered back to mainland China, forcing the government to respond and making events more transparent. We expect this will continue in the future. As different factions compete to leak information to the Western media and air their opponent's dirty laundry, their actions may intensify power struggles in the short-term, but in the long-run will hasten changes within the Communist Party.

Ho Pin and *Wen Huang*
January 2013

CAST OF CHARACTERS*

Neil Heywood—Former British business consultant in China.

Wáng Lùlu—Neil Heywood's Chinese wife.

Wáng Lìjūn—Former police chief and deputy mayor of Chongqing.

Guo Weiguo—Former deputy police chief of Chongqing.

Bó Xīlái (bo-shee-lai)—Former party chief of Chongqing and a Politburo member.

Bó Yìbó—Bo Xilai's father and a revolutionary veteran who was a Politburo member and served as China's vice premier before his death in 2007.

Bo Guāguā—Bo Xilai's son, who now resides in the US.

Gǔ Kāilái—Bo Xilai's wife and a former lawyer.

Gǔ Jǐngshēng—Gu Kailai's father and a former military general before his death in 2004.

Fan Chengxiu—Gu Kailai's mother and a retired Communist Party official.

Li Danyu—Bo Xilai's ex-wife and an army doctor.

---

* We follow the Chinese tradition by placing family names first.

Wen Qiang—Former deputy police chief of Chongqing who was executed on corruption charges in 2010.

Zhou Yongkang—Close ally of Bo Xilai and former member of the Politburo Standing Committee who was dubbed China's security czar.

Xu Ming (sh-yu-ming)—Billionaire businessman in the city of Dalian and close friend of Bo Xilai and Gu Kailai.

Xi Jinping (shee-jeen-ping)—Princeling and current Communist Party general secretary and president of China.

Xi Zhongxun—Xi Jinping's father and a revolutionary veteran who was governor of Guangdong province before his death in 2002.

Hu Jintao—Former Communist Party general secretary (2002–2012) and president of China (2003–2013).

Ling Jihua—Hu Jintao's former chief of staff and Bo Xilai's "deep throat" who now heads the United Front Work Department.

Wen Jiabao—Former premier of China (2003–2013).

Jiang Zemin—Former Communist Party general secretary (1989–2002) and president of China (1993–2003).

Li Keqiang—Current premier of China.

PROLOGUE

AN ENGLISHMAN'S BODY was found in Room 1605 of the Nanshan Lijing Holiday Hotel, or Lucky Holiday Hotel. Nestled atop the densely-wooded South Mountain, the three-star resort is about eight kilometers from downtown Chóngqìng. The clear mountain air provides a welcome change from the smog-shrouded, fast-growing municipality of more than 30 million. Its secluded location overlooking the sprawling city that straddles the Yangtze River below makes it a popular venue for weddings, holiday parties, government conferences, and leadership retreats. In the spring and summer, the hotel accommodates tourists who visit the nearby botanical garden or worship in the Tushan Temple built around 700 CE.

During the off-season month of November, the hotel compound looks eerily deserted. Inside the empty lobby of the main building, two thick wooden ceiling beams, painted in bright red, tower over a big glass fish tank. It feels like entering a gaudy Chinese restaurant. Two young female attendants staffing the registration desk reluctantly stop their computer games to greet guests who either arrive to check in or inquire about the special winter rates.

The hotel registration shows that a *lao wai,* or foreigner, checked into a private villa suite on November 13, 2011. His name was Neil Heywood. He was forty-one, an Englishman with a British passport and a Beijing address. He was last seen with a middle-age Chinese woman who, before she left the suite, flipped on the door's "Do Not Disturb" sign and told the villa supervisor not to bother the foreign guest because he'd had "too much to drink."

Two days later, the cleaning staff, noticing that the guest in Room 1605 had not stepped out of his room the whole time and suspecting something had gone awry, notified the villa supervisor. On receiving no answer to his knocks and calls, he opened the door and discovered the foreigner dead on his bed. The hotel's general manager contacted the police.

Wang Lijun, the police chief of Chongqing, was the first to show up at the scene with the vice chief of his criminal investigation team, whom government papers identified by his last name, Huang. After getting details from the hotel manager, villa supervisor, and cleaning staff and examining the room, Wang Lijun sent Huang away and assigned the case to four of his trusted senior police officers—his deputy police director, the chief of the criminal investigation section, the chief of technical detection, and the chief of the Shapingba District.

The initial police report shows the investigative team interviewed the hotel staff, took a blood sample from the victim's heart, and conducted a CT scan on the body. The next morning, the team declared that Heywood had experienced "sudden death after drinking alcohol" and reported the results to Wang Lijun, who later testified that he "did not oppose their conclusion." Police located Heywood's family in Beijing—he was married to Wang Lulu, a Chinese national, and had two children. Based on a British report several months later, Heywood's mother in London was grief-stricken after receiving notice of her son's death. Her husband, Heywood's father, had just died of a heart attack at the age of sixty-three after drinks over dinner at their London home.

The Chongqing Public Security Bureau persuaded Heywood's family members to accept its conclusion on the cause of death and, with their approval, cremated Heywood's body. No autopsy was conducted. Heywood's friends said he was "not a serious drinker," but neither the family nor the British Consulate raised any objections to the investigation and its conclusions.

On November 18, three days after Heywood's body was found, the case was closed. With so many foreigners living in China, Heywood's death went largely unnoticed by the media and the public. But in Chinese mythology, the spirit of the dead does not dissolve if he or she has unfinished business in this world. The ghost lingers, clinging to its enemies, manipulating their minds, and causing havoc in their lives. So it would prove for those who had come into contact with the dead man from Room 1605, including the most elite members of the Chinese Communist Party. The crisis triggered by Heywood's death reveals more about the scandalous state of corruption in China than any dissident or journalist could ever manage.

PART I

Ku

Li

The Fate of a *Kuli* (ruthless)

K*uli*, pronounced "cool-lee," is an ancient term referring to an official or police officer who relied on extreme means of torture and brutality to help his master maintain power.

THE STRANGER'S PHONE CALL

LUNAR NEW YEAR PREDICTIONS are taken seriously in China, if only in the hope that the coming year will be better than the one just passed. At midnight on January 23, 2012, Chinese people around the world ushered in the Year of the Dragon. Though the mythical creature symbolizes strength, power, and good fortune, many were wary of its fiery nature, which heralds volatility and change. "China will have some political surprises," a newspaper in Hong Kong quoted a fortune-teller as saying. "In the second half of the year, a scandalous corruption case will be exposed in China. A number of high-ranking officials will be forced to step down. Some may be thrown behind bars, or even pass away."

"Political surprises" was a fairly safe bet and was glossed over amid the celebrations in mainland China, where the government-controlled media hyped up the dragon's auspicious associations,

3

such as "harmony" and "grand takeoff of the Chinese economy." In private, many in the leadership would have shared the fortune-teller's foreboding. The 18th Party Congress was scheduled for the fall, when a new generation of thoroughly vetted leaders who had won fierce power struggles would take over. Leadership transitions historically have been times of political intrigue and conspiracy, and during the past two decades a common and effective way to eliminate a challenger or political opponent was to link a rival with a corruption scandal. President Jiang Zemin employed the trick to consolidate his power, as did his successor, President Hu Jintao. In a one-party state such as China, jockeying for influence is a raw reality of the political system. There is nowhere else to go, so all fighting must be infighting. However, nobody, not even the fortune-teller, expected that the first political surprise of the new year would come even before the fifteen-day celebration was completed. And I was an unwitting messenger.

On February 2, I was in Taiwan. While I waited in the lobby of the Grand Hyatt in Taipei for an early morning meeting, my cell phone rang. "Are you the publisher of *Mingjing News*?" asked a low, nervous voice, referring to one of my US-based Chinese-language news sites specializing in exclusive coverage of Chinese politics. When I said yes, the voice whispered, "Please give me a private number. I have something important to share with you." Intrigue is everywhere in greater China and I'd encountered similar situations before. I gave the man, who sounded middle-aged, a colleague's cell phone number. The conversation was brief. The caller identified himself as an official at the Communist Party's Municipal Committee for Discipline Inspection in Chongqing. The caller disclosed that Wang Lijun, the city's police chief, had just been sacked and was under internal investigation and charged with corruption. I was skeptical. The caller noticed and raised his voice in agitation: "Trust me. It's 10,000 percent correct!"

Wang Lijun had made a name for himself in the city's much-publicized campaign to crack down on corruption and organized crime. He was said to have been seriously wounded more than twenty times fighting gangs, and the local and national media played him up as the "Iron Blooded Police Spirit." More important, he was the right-hand man of Bo Xilai, the party chief of Chongqing and a rising political star.

If Wang was under arrest, it was a significant story. I rescheduled my appointment and contacted a source, a senior official with the Chongqing municipal government, to verify the information. Though the source confirmed that Wang would no longer head the public security bureau, he was not aware of any internal investigation against Wang, adding, "Don't forget, he's still the deputy mayor."

But I knew that even if Wang were allowed to keep the title of deputy mayor, he was obviously on his way out, because the public security department had been the real base of his power.

As a journalist and writer, I have covered Chinese politics for more than twenty-five years, first for the government media in mainland China and subsequently for numerous newspapers in Taiwan and Hong Kong. In the 1990s, I started an overseas independent publishing company, aiming to provide a free forum for writers in and out of China, where such opportunities are not available. Even though the books and magazines I have published remain banned in mainland China, tourists smuggle them in from Hong Kong and Taiwan. Moreover, a large number of Chinese Internet users employ proxy servers to access the content on *Mingjing News*. Over the years, I have received a steady stream of news tips and article submissions from senior officials and their friends—well-connected businesspeople, Chinese journalists, and scholars, all of whom represent different political factions and viewpoints. Some attempt to fight the government propaganda machine by revealing the true stories behind certain political decisions, or exposing corruption scandals within the party and the government out of a sense of justice, whereas others have no such noble intent, aiming to smear their political opponents with a mixture of truth and rumor or to advance certain political agendas. These "deep throats" understand that they can effectively influence public opinions. With the explosion of Internet technology, news in the overseas media is available in China in seconds—despite the government's firewalls.

Based on the anonymous tip and my own research, I dictated the Wang Lijun story to a colleague, who posted it on *Mingjing News* at eleven o'clock in the morning China time. In the story, I mentioned Wang could be under investigation for alleged corruption.

I had no idea that the one hundred-word news item, which soon spread across the Internet, would become the prelude to a political drama that contains all the elements of what the Chinese call *da pian,* or Hollywood tent-pole production—raw ambitions, secret succession plots, historical feuds, shifting alliances, murder, espionage, power marriages, and sexual trysts. The cast would include some of the most influential politicians, business moguls, army generals, and TV celebrities, whose formal photographic portraits often appear on the front pages of Chinese and Western newspapers, and the faceless women who supposedly control their men "behind the bamboo curtains." The locales for the drama would include tiny, winding streets in the mountain city of Chongqing and an idyllic seaside resort in the UK. The events that have been unfolding in China since February 2, 2012, are not part of what the director or directors of the movie led us to believe: a battle between the good and evil, or a conflict between Maoist radicals and moderate reformists. What we are seeing is political intrigue and power struggle—different cliques competing for the top positions—many driven as much by personal loyalties and generational ties as they are by ideological differences.

TWO HOURS AFTER my website posted the news of Wang's sacking, press officers at the Chongqing municipal government, which administers some 30 million people, released a short announcement on Weibo, China's equivalent of Twitter and Facebook:

> The Chongqing Municipal Party Committee has recently decided that Comrade Wang Lijun will no longer serve as the chief and Party secretary of the Municipal Public Security Bureau. As the deputy mayor, he will be in charge of science research, education and environment.

The "deputy mayor" reference reminded me of an article in the Hong Kong–based *New Century Magazine,* which reported on the staged mayoral election in March 2011 at Chongqing's People's Congress, the equivalent of a state legislature in the US. All the mayoral candidates on the ballot were preselected by the party and delegates merely rubber-stamped every name. Wang's name was on the ballot. Even though the city had just awarded him the "People's Protector" honor, several delegates abstained from voting for Wang. Embarrassed, the head of the Congress annulled the vote and initiated several more rounds of voting until every delegate voted yes; the government media wanted to state Wang had been chosen unanimously.

A year later, the same people who had given him "unanimous" support were plotting his exit. Wang was allowed to remain as deputy mayor, but his responsibilities had shifted from his areas of expertise—public security, national security, judiciary, citizen petitions, and political stabilities—to fields about which he knew nothing. It was the first sure sign that Wang had really done something wrong.

The anonymous caller's tip that Wang might be under investigation for corruption charges sounded credible and did not surprise me or other political analysts overseas. In a country plagued with rampant corruption, no Communist official is immune. In 2009, Wang's predecessor, Wen Qiang, who had held the deputy police chief's position in Chongqing for sixteen years and cracked several of China's high-profile criminal cases, was executed for bribery and ties with organized crime.

However, the Chongqing government seemed to go out of its way to dispel the rumor that Wang Lijun was under such investigation. Soon after the city's short statement was posted, a copy of Wang's "performance evaluation" surfaced on the Internet. In the review, which had been prepared by Chongqing party chief Bo Xilai's office for the mayoral election the year before, the former police chief was characterized as being "politically firm and reliable, principled and possessing a strong sense of responsibility." He was a "tough and impartial" cop who "enjoys a high reputation among the masses." Occasionally, the review said, Wang "displays impatience at work and lacks diplomacy when criticizing others."

On the surface, it seemed Wang's temperament and confrontational style were the cause of his job change and there was no hidden agenda. A Hong Kong newspaper went so far as to cite a source in Chongqing as saying that by assigning him to new areas, his boss, Bo Xilai, hoped Wang could expand his experience and prepare for "bigger things" in the future.

Behind such bland assurances, the Chongqing government was in crisis control mode, trying to downplay Wang's firing. Meanwhile, political insiders in Chongqing and Beijing were busy contacting overseas media via secure mobile channels, churning out completely different stories.

The following day, the same anonymous caller reached me once again, with a "Didn't I tell you it's 10,000 percent true" tone. Self-congratulation was not the only purpose of his call. He wanted to share still more startling revelations. In an encrypted e-mail he sent subsequently, he wrote:

Several business people bribed Wang by buying him houses in Beijing, Dalian and Chongqing. Wang was also implicated in a corruption scandal in the city of Tieling, where he served as police chief for twenty-two years. Three senior police officers, all of whom were Wang's friends, had been convicted of taking bribes and embezzling government construction funds.

In addition, the Central Commission for Discipline Inspection charged Wang with colluding with organized crime syndicates to monopolize the sale and production of minerals in early 2000 when he was deputy mayor in the city of Jinzhou. After Wang was transferred to Chongqing, he had awarded profitable contracts to his friends, pocketing thousands of yuan in commissions and depositing the money abroad. For example, a clothing factory tailored uniforms for the public security bureau in Chongqing. Each set cost about two hundred yuan but they were sold at four thousand yuan per set. Lastly, Wang changed the name of the Chongqing Public Security Bureau to "Police Administration" and altered the police uniform design. All of these were done without the approval of the central government. The leadership in Beijing was shocked and outraged. At the moment, several of Wang's business partners and friends, including his driver, are being detained for investigation.

In the face of these corruption allegations, Bo Xilai decided to act fast to distance himself by sacking Wang from the police chief's position.

In retaliation, Wang had sent a thick letter by express mail to the Central Commission for Discipline Inspection, accusing Bo and his wife of taking bribes and transferring a large sum of assets abroad.

The allegations were shocking, but some, such as "colluding with organized crime syndicates to monopolize the sale and production of minerals," sounded far-fetched and lacked proof. Because I had no time to e-mail or call my contacts to corroborate the details, I put the story aside until I could check the claims.

Two hours later, a colleague in the US informed me of an "exclusive" insider's story on Boxun, a popular user-generated Chinese-language news site in the US. I skimmed through it and realized it was the same story that the anonymous caller had provided to me. The Boxun "exclusive" sparked a slew of reactions in the overseas Chinese media. "The newly released reports about Wang's accusation against Bo and his wife have added elements of uncertainties to Bo Xilai's blatant attempt to join the Politburo Standing Committee at the upcoming party congress," broadcast Voice of America.

The next day, as I was pondering the accuracy of Wang's claims against Bo Xilai, the same persistent caller got ahold of me, expressing his disappointment that I had not yet published the information he had e-mailed. He teased me with more anecdotes:

Wang acted like he had been possessed by an angry ghost. When two officials showed up at Wang's office to inform him that he would no longer be the police chief and urge him to hand over his weapons, Wang was so confrontational that he pulled out his handgun and subsequently smashed his water glass in anger. He threatened to expose the illegal activities of Bo and his wife if anyone dared harm him. Wang even requested a transfer back to Beijing or Liaoning province, claiming that his life was in danger.

Meanwhile, a "princeling"—as children of senior Communist officials are known—e-mailed me through a secure mobile channel from Beijing. He offered a similar version, but with a twist:

Wang became emotional after Bo took away his police chief's position and locked himself up in an office on the fifteenth floor of the Municipal Public Security Bureau building, one level below the department's ammunition warehouse. Worrying that Wang would get out of control and access the warehouse, officials there put him under surveillance. Wang was tipped off. He thought the surveillance [team] was meant to assassinate him.

Boxun and *Mingjing* posted the unverified stories. By then it had become clear to me that some invisible hands were out to destroy not only Wang but also, by association, the Chongqing party chief, Bo Xilai, and that the deliberate leaks or rumors could further antagonize Bo and Wang, pushing them to take extreme action against each other.

Bo Xilai had definitely seen the overseas coverage. On February 3, he emerged. At a conference on publicity and culture work, Bo remarked, "Each time something happens in our city, the hostile forces painstakingly make up stories and spread vicious rumors. Their intent is to cause chaos. This is an invisible battle, but the fight is fierce. . . . We cannot neglect our propaganda front. This is a hard job. Information itself might be soft and invisible, but its results are concrete and hard. We should provide a large amount of healthy and uplifting information to the press. We should focus on our strengths and build our steely stamina."

Wang resurfaced on February 5. He acted very cooperatively in public, as if he were busy adapting to his new role. A TV clip showed him visiting the Chongqing municipal education department and then the Chongqing Normal University, where he looked poised and listened attentively to reports from the school authorities. When commenting on his new assignment, Wang said with apparent sincerity, "This is a new challenge for me and a great learning opportunity." Wang and Bo had presented a seemingly unified front, suggesting that the rumors were malicious and that each man would be continuing as normal, although Wang had been assigned new duties. The pretense lasted barely forty-eight hours.

THE UNEXPECTED VISITOR

NO. 4 CONSULATE ROAD is a sprawling white cinder-block building in the southwestern city of Chengdu, reached by a tree-lined street south of the crowded city center. It is the US Consulate, where thirty or so American officials handle mostly visa applications and commercial affairs for southwestern China.

Students and residents applying for visas to study and visit the US come to the consulate from Sichuan, Guizhou, Yunnan, and Tibet. In the past, the line for visa interviews would begin forming around midnight, made up mostly of young college graduates. On a normal day, the visa line was up to two blocks long by the time the doors opened in the morning. "It looked like every young person with family connections and money wanted to go to America," a local resident recalled.

Appointments these days are arranged online and via telephone, the line in front of the consulate is rarely more than a sizeable gaggle, and the street scene is serene. Even as China gradually emerged as an economic powerhouse, enthusiasm about studying or living in the US never waned. Many young Chinese still see the consulate as holder of the key to an exciting and free life in the home of Microsoft and Apple, Hollywood movies, and multinational investment banks. Others see it as an expression of American imperialism, especially when China and the US spar over human rights or trade issues. On the Google satellite map, beneath the address of the consulate, was a comment in Chinese: "The place looks ominous. People come here to betray their country and surrender to our enemy."

For ordinary residents, the consulate, guarded by frozen-faced Chinese police, looked mysterious and inaccessible, a place that bore little relevance to their lives. The perception changed on the cold, windy evening of February 7, 2012.

Many commuters found themselves stuck in the area near the US Consulate, which was suddenly cordoned off. Dozens of police cars with flashing lights lined the street. Checkpoints were set up on every cross street. Police directed traffic and yelled at pedestrians who attempted to slip past. Frustrated commuters posted pictures on Weibo trying to figure out what had happened, and people in the city and around the country soon learned about the news.

A person with the alias "Gray Wolf in the Desert" tweeted:

Does anyone know which VIP is visiting the US Consulate? There are about several hundred policemen surrounding the US Consulate—armed police, traffic police, ranger police, you name it.

Another posting stated:

Police are everywhere. I've been waiting in the cold for an hour and can't go home. Lights on the streets have been turned off. Fully armed police are posted around the Friendship Hotel next to the US Consulate. If they are not making a movie, it means something major has happened.

As questions swirled around cyberspace, another Weibo user noticed that the police were towing an SUV that had been parked in front of the consulate. Judging from the license plate number, the car belonged to a government official in the city of Chongqing. By midnight, Wei Jiuru, a lawyer in Beijing, cited a government source as saying, "Wang Lijun, the deputy mayor of Chongqing, has escaped into the US Consulate to seek asylum."

The news quickly circulated, touching off a tidal wave of speculation. A person with the alias of "Koki-Wong" added more details: "Wang Lijun claims that Bo Xilai is out to assassinate him. So he is now hiding inside the US Consulate. At the moment, the US Consulate is under siege. A large number of armed police from Chongqing are there to get Wang Lijun. I think he will evaporate from this world soon!"

By the time offices opened on the morning of February 8, Internet censors had deleted every posting about the incident, but by then everyone knew about Wang's attempted defection.

In a country where the government operates in secrecy and the media serves as the "mouthpiece" of the party, Weibo is tearing down the walls that block the information flow across the country. When anything major happens in China, netizens ignore state TV, radio, and newspapers and look to Weibo for their information. This is especially true for controversial events when regular media outlets are restricted and required to keep quiet and follow official lines. More than 300 million people subscribe to Weibo on Sina, one of China's largest Internet search portals, with daily posts exceeding 100 million. The popularity of Weibo has posed a major problem for Beijing, which finds it difficult to shut down or simply ignore a Weibo site. Oftentimes the government has to respond to reports on Weibo, such has been the pressure of posts.

The Chongqing municipal government turned to its Weibo shortly before eleven o'clock on the morning of February 8 and issued a ludicrous one-line comment:

> Chongqing deputy mayor and former police chief Wang Lijun, 52, is undergoing "vacation-style treatment" due to his heavy workload and stress.

That merely fueled further speculation and ridicule. In a matter of hours, "vacation-style treatment" became the most popular political buzzword online.

One sarcastic posting stated, "Getting a vacation-style treatment in the US Consulate? Did he defect or seek vacation-style treatment? What a blatant lie, unheard of in Chinese history!"

Realizing the absurdity of its statement, the Chongqing municipal government removed it from its Weibo but reposted it an hour later, then removed it again. To many, it was an indication that local officials had lost direction and did not know what to do.

Wang's defection had caught Beijing off guard. While senior leaders were mulling over a solution, government censors were left without directions. They waited for instructions, unsure what they should be blocking and what could go through; their inaction allowed comments and news leaks to flood the network. Wang Xing, a journalist with China's *Southern Metropolis Daily* newspaper, found out from a contact at the Chengdu Municipal Public Security Bureau that Wang Lijun had left Chengdu. His newspaper spiked the story, so he posted it on Weibo: "Wang Lijun was taken away [from the US Consulate] this morning in a car provided by the Sichuan Provincial Public Security Department. He then flew to Beijing." The posting proved to be true.

Western media outlets, such as *Forbes, Reuters,* the *New York Times,* and Voice of America, contacted the US Embassy in Beijing to verify the details. Richard Buangan, US Embassy spokesman, said he was "not in a position to comment regarding reported requests for asylum." On the night of February 8, under intense media pressure, US State Department spokeswoman Victoria Nuland confirmed in Washington that Wang had requested a meeting with the Chengdu consul two days earlier, then "left of his own volition." Nuland declined to comment on whether Wang had requested asylum.

The lack of details prompted many of Wang's supporters to question claims that their patriotic anticrime hero would seek political asylum at the US Consulate. One Weibo posting quoted an inside source as saying Wang was the unwitting victim of a trap by his enemies within the party—in this version of events, the US consul general had invited Wang to go in for an urgent antiterrorism meeting.

On February 9, political insiders bombarded *Mingjing News* and Boxun with details and speculation. Despite years of government control, ordinary people have stopped trusting the state-run media. News from overseas is considered more credible than a report in the *People's Daily*. Knowing that antifirewall software enables overseas news to filter back to China, different political factions have learned to use overseas Chinese media to influence public opinion and embarrass their opponents by supplying them with inside scoops. Not all of the information I had received was reliable—there were many elements of deliberate fabrication—but as the events unfolded in the following months, the majority proved to be true, or at least close to the truth.

On the morning of February 9, an article on Boxun, which quoted an official from Beijing, shed more light on Wang's "defection":

On the afternoon of February 6, after attending several activities at a university in Chongqing, Wang Lijun left in disguise and entered the US Consulate in Chengdu to seek political asylum.

Authorities in Chongqing sent troops to the consulate and surrounded the building for twenty-four hours. During his stay, Wang Lijun had long conversations with American intelligence officials and divulged political information relating to power struggles within the Chinese leadership. He also applied for political asylum. Due to pressure from the Chinese government and to the fact that Wang was disturbed and emotionally unstable, American officials turned him over to the Ministry of State Security early in the morning of February 8. At the moment, he is being held for questioning at a secure location in Beijing.

Before leaving the US Consulate, Wang was heard talking to officials of the State Security Ministry: "I'm Bo Xilai's victim. Bo Xilai is a conspirator. I'm going to fight him until my death. My evidence against him has been transferred overseas."

Wang's attempted defection made Bo and his wife, Gu Kailai, very nervous. Gu hasn't been able to sleep for several days.

When the Boxun story came out, I was still in Taiwan. My skepticism remained: the melodramatic descriptions seemed to have been taken from a bad Hollywood action movie, leaving too many questions unanswered. What prompted a nationally known police chief to seek shelter at the US Consulate? How could the Chinese government ignore international law and send troops to block the US Consulate for twenty-four hours? I could not think of any precedent that would suggest that the series of amazing events described in Boxun was authentic. With poor telephone reception, I felt reluctant to verify a story I suspected had been embellished with many fictional elements.

However, as insider e-mails poured in with similar details about Wang and Bo over the following two days, I became convinced that most of what had been reported was authentic.

On February 12, a letter supposedly written by Wang Lijun on the day after he had been fired appeared on many overseas Chinese news sites.

When everyone sees this letter, I'll either be dead or have lost my freedom. I want to explain to the whole world the reasons behind my actions. In short: I don't want to see the Party's biggest hypocrite Bo Xilai carry on performing: When such evil officials rule the state, it will lead to calamity for China and disaster for our nation. . . . Bo Xilai is a despot who makes arbitrary decisions, hateful and ruthless. If you go along with him you'll prosper, go against him and you'll perish. He always forces his subordinates to use any means possible to do all kinds of unspeakable things on his behalf. If you don't comply you are dealt with ruthlessly. He treats people like chewing gum: after a little chew, he just throws you away, and he doesn't care whose feet you end up under. . . . Bo Xilai has the reputation of being honest and upright, but he is actually corrupt to the core, conniving with his family members getting outrageously rich. I have documented these matters, and have already submitted reports to the relevant parties and I also ask that friends abroad help to circulate this letter to the world. Everybody's got to die, I am willing to use my life to expose Bo Xilai. For the sake of ridding the Chinese system of this scourge on the people, this brazen careerist, I am willing to sacrifice everything!

Zhou Lijun, a scriptwriter who befriended Wang while doing research for a TV series based on the renowned police chief's life in 1999, considered the letter credible because he had heard the chewing gum reference from Wang before. The letter made me realize a political earthquake was rumbling to a head before the 18th Party Congress. I assembled a news team to monitor the constant flow of news tips from inside China and to cover, after verification, developments relating to Wang.

"THE IRON BLOODED POLICE SPIRIT"

GENETIC SCIENTISTS BELIEVE that 17 million people in Asia are direct descendants of Genghis Khan. Wang Lijun liked to brag at the height of his fame that he is a product of that fearsome thirteenth-century Mongolian warrior.

Born in Arxan, Inner Mongolia, on December 26, 1959, Wang shared the same birthday as another formidable figure, Mao Zedong, who led the Communist revolution to victory in 1949 and ruled China with brutality for twenty-seven years. At the height of Wang's career, a local newspaper in the northeastern city of Tieling described Wang's birth in a style once reserved only for Mao:

> When the glowing sun broke through the clouds and rose slowly on the horizon, spewing golden rays, a crying baby boy was born in a house at the foot of the Arxon Mountain. By Mongolian tradition, a newborn's name is based on the specific time and the natural environment of his birth. Wang's father, well versed in Mongolian culture, bestowed upon him a romantic name—"Ünen Bayatar," which means "A True Hero." Ünen Bayatar's Chinese name is Wang Lijun, which means "Finding your call in the military." As a little boy, Wang inherited the heroic styles of his famous ancestor Genghis Khan, and began practicing horse-riding and archery.

Not everyone was prepared to buy into the Mongolian-warrior angle; Wang Licheng, a lawyer and blog writer in China's northeastern province of Liaoning, disputed Wang's ethnicity. Though he was born in Inner Mongolia, the lawyer, who has closely monitored the official's career path over the past decade, claims Wang is 100 percent Han—the largest ethnic group in China. His ancestors lived in the northeastern province of Liaoning. In an application form that Wang submitted to the army in 1978, he listed his ethnicity as Han.

"Why did Wang change his ethnicity from Han to Mongolian?" asked the lawyer in his blog. "At the 14th Communist Party Congress in 1992, Wang Lijun, who was then the deputy police chief in Tieling city, was contending for a delegate spot, which could put him on a fast track to the top. Knowing that the Party always allocated token seats for members of the minority groups, Wang changed his ethnicity to Mongolian."

Whether Mongolian or Han, Wang was brought up in the Mongolian tradition. As a teenager, he was a member of a Mongolian youth boxing team and commanded superb martial arts skills. After high school in 1977, he was assigned a job at a state farm in northeastern China and a year later joined the army. According to a childhood friend, Wang always dreamed of becoming a military officer. While stationed in Tieling, a northeastern city with a population of 3 million people, he twice took the rigorous national college entrance exam hoping to get into a military academy, but he never passed. In 1982, a year after his compulsory military service ended, Wang married Xiao Shuli, who was a switchboard operator in the army. Four months after their marriage, the two settled in Tieling, where, through the connections of his father-in-law, an army officer, Wang obtained a job as a truck driver at the municipal commerce bureau. His wife also left the military and was employed at the local police department.

Wang's police career started in 1983, when the local public security bureau enlisted him as a volunteer in a neighborhood watch group. Wang took the assignment seriously and trained a group of young people who diligently patrolled the streets and coal mining facilities. In 1984, a friend at a local mining company introduced him to the Tieling deputy police chief, who later recommended Wang join the police force when the Tieling Municipal Public Security Bureau began recruiting in 1984. Despite his lack of a college education, which was required of other candidates, he got the job.

Three years later, at the age of twenty-eight, Wang was promoted to head a police station in Xiaonan township at the southern-most tip of the city, where robberies and gang-related killings were rampant. A month before he assumed the position, a young police officer there was ambushed and stabbed to death. The assailant was never caught. An article in the *Law Weekend* described vividly Wang's first week at his new job there:

> Wang received a phone call while he was on duty one night. "Are you the new police chief? Do you know how your predecessor died? You will end up like him. If you don't believe me, come see me at the train station." Wang slammed the phone down, holstered his

handgun and headed directly to the train station. In the icy cold wind, he searched for the gang leader and shouted, "If you have the guts, come out to meet me!" Wang waited until dawn, but the gang leader never showed up.

Thus, Wang's reputation as a brave and fearless officer soared. The new police chief was not only brave, but also smart. In his spare time, he invented an automatic alarm system, connecting all public security offices nearby. He had the alarm system installed in factories and government offices. Each time someone broke in, the red lights in the public security bureau would flash. Police could be on site within minutes.

The crime rate plummeted in Wang's district and within three years, the state media said he solved 281 criminal cases and the township was being cited as a model in the province. In 1991, he was transferred to another branch, where he practically lived in the office. Wang created a record by busting ten criminal groups in nine days. In January 1992, he was honored by the Ministry of Public Security as one of "China's Ten Most Remarkable Policemen" and traveled to Beijing to meet many of China's senior leaders. Upon his return, Wang was appointed the deputy director of the Tieling Public Security Bureau and sent to receive training at the Chinese People's Security University. At the beginning of his tenure in Tieling, the city was infested with organized-crime gangs that controlled the city's nightclubs, hair salons, and restaurants, engaging in prostitution and blackmail. Gun shootings were rampant and gang members even planted bombs outside government buildings. In winter, many farmworkers were largely unemployed and engaged in drinking, pickpocketing, and street fighting. Ordinary residents suffered at the hands of mafia leaders and street gangs.

As an important new initiative, Wang launched an anti–organized crime campaign in September 1994. He set up a forty-member work team and turned a three-level office building into a temporary jail, detaining and interrogating suspects. Over the next four days, he cracked more than 800 cases, arresting 923 people in connection with the 87 gangs, or mafia groups, that controlled the city. At subsequent trials, seven ringleaders received the death penalty. Nineteen police officers were found to be corrupt and were jailed or sacked on charges that they had colluded with criminals.

Many legal experts, including Wang Licheng, the lawyer who disputed Wang's ethnicity, criticized the campaign for denying due process to the accused, but dissenting voices fell on deaf ears. The authorities were pleased with the results and Wang was hailed as a tough crime fighter. The local government commissioned a book, *The Legends of the Northeastern Tiger,* to chronicle his heroic acts. In one chapter, Chen Xiaodoing, the author of the biography, described how Wang captured the two mafia leaders:

> On September 19, 1994, Wang was tipped off by an informant that Yang, a local mafia leader, was hiding at a nearby hotel. Wang took a small police squad there and they took up positions in an employee meeting room on the hotel's first floor. The informant went to see Yang, whispering to the mafia head that he had something urgent to share. The informant brought Yang to the employee room on the first floor. Barely had Yang entered the room than Wang leapt on him like a tiger on his prey and subdued him. "Do you know who I am?" Wang shouted. Yang looked up and stammered, as if waking up from a dream. "Oh, you, you are Wang Lijun. It's totally worth it." Wang asked, "What do you mean by that?" Yang answered, "It's worth it, dying by your hand."

Another triad leader, Ho Jing, was a kung fu master. He fled after hearing police were after him. A month later, Wang received news that Ho had returned to the city and was hiding in his company headquarters. Wang, not wanting to arouse suspicion, took with him a single assistant, but as they arrived at the headquarters, Ho was spotted getting into his Peugeot 605. Ho recognized Wang and sped off and a car chase ensued. As Wang almost caught up with Ho, a tractor inadvertently blocked Wang's car and Ho had the chance of a clear escape. Wang was furious. But Ho's car got only a few meters' advantage before it stalled. Wang leaped at the opportunity and dragged Ho from the Peugeot as he struggled to restart it. As the story goes, kung fu master Ho and lone cop Wang fought for twenty minutes, Ho managing a choke hold on Wang that should have killed him, but Wang broke his grip and followed through by slamming Ho's head into the roadway, knocking him unconscious. Police reinforcements completed the arrest. Wang's face was covered with blood and deep cuts.

Wang's bravery earned him a number of accolades and his uniform was covered with medals. In 1995, he went on a nationwide lecture tour, touting the success of his anticrime programs in Tieling and explaining how a more alert and aggressive police crackdown could achieve good results. On the day he made his presentation to senior leaders at the Great Hall of the People in Beijing, he was told by the local court that the mafia leaders he had captured would be executed. A government newspaper described Wang's reaction to the news:

> Wang was eager to hear the gunshots of justice. When he finished his talk at the Great Hall, he quietly left the stage and stood in the hallway, where he called Ji Lianke, deputy director of the criminal investigation unit. "Director Wang, can you hear the gunshots? We are shooting the fourth one now," Ji reported to Wang, who held his phone tightly to his ear. "Bam!" Wang could hear the sound of gunshot through his phone. After the execution, several hundred residents spontaneously showed up in front of the city hall, carrying a twenty-meter-long banner to thank Wang Lijun.

During his tenure as deputy director and then director of public security in Tieling, Wang gained a nickname, "Biaozi," which in the local dialect means "a pigheaded and fearless person." For example, an officer who worked alongside Wang at the criminal investigation team said Wang used to forbid forensic experts from wearing masks and gloves, which he believed "impeded the expert's senses of smell and touch." At one time, he jumped into a waist-deep pond and dragged out a rotting corpse.

Although a tough fighter, Wang was also depicted by the local media as a man with a soft heart. According to one online story, Wang raided a house he believed harbored an escaped prisoner. After Wang kicked the door open, the prisoner dashed toward him brandishing a cleaver. Wang dodged the attack but, though he had a clean shot, holstered his weapon and instead wrestled the man to the ground and disarmed him. He had seen a baby wriggling in the room's only bed. "You should thank your child for saving your life," he said. "I didn't want to traumatize the baby with gunshots."

Another story involved a mob leader who refused to cooperate with police during interrogation. Wang realized that the mafia leader's wife had also been detained and nobody was looking after his two children. Wang lobbied the court to grant parole to the leader's wife, allowing her to care for their children. At the same time, he hired a special chef to prepare halal food for the mafia leader, a Muslim, who was allegedly touched by Wang's compassion and freely answered Wang's questions and confessed to his crimes. Wang ordered a new suit for the mafia leader before sending him to the execution ground: "You used to be a somebody in the city," Wang was quoted as saying. "I want you to look decent when you leave this world."

Wang's life stories were later adapted into a nationally broadcast TV series, *The Iron-Blooded Police Spirit*. The director, who invited Wang to the set, described to a Chinese newspaper his first impression of Wang: "When he appeared, the room suddenly became smaller because of his physique and powerful presence. He sucked the air out of the room."

Initially, Wang was cast to play himself in the TV drama, but many did not feel it appropriate. Zhou Lijun, who penned the movie, said Wang was a born performer who had a flair for drama. As part of his research, Zhou followed Wang for ten days and went on an antipornography sweep with Wang one night:

> Wang put me on the passenger seat of his Mitsubishi jeep and he personally drove me over to Tieling. The jeep looked very unique. Large characters—"Chinese Criminal Police"—were painted on both sides of the jeep. Wang told me the characters were copies of his own calligraphy and he had applied for a patent for those handwritten characters. The top of the jeep was equipped with eight high-voltage search lights, four in the front and four at the back. The jeep sped through the darkness and Wang didn't even bother to

slow down when we crossed a railway track. My head bumped against the top of the vehicle several times as I held on tightly. His colleagues lagged way behind. Upon arrival, Wang issued some simple instructions and within minutes, his subordinates dispersed and went directly to their targets—hair salons, karaoke bars and massage parlors. While raiding a hair salon, police found no sign of anything shady. But Wang ordered the detention of a young man with dyed yellow hair. "A man with hair like that can't be any good," he barked.

Wang's high-profile anticrime campaigns worked. Official statistics showed that crime rates went down dramatically in Tieling. According to a police officer in Tieling, Wang enjoyed tremendous support from the lower ranks of society, such as the tricycle cabdrivers, many of whom were laid-off state workers and were easy targets for gang members who extorted protection money from them. Wang initiated a citywide crackdown and each time a gang member was caught bullying a cabdriver, the offender would be asked to pay a heavy fine and police would distribute the money on the spot to tricycle cabdrivers as compensation. A popular story has it that Wang walked home one night and one tricycle cabdriver recognized him and insisted on driving him home. Wang politely declined and kept on. A few minutes later, he noticed that a dozen tricycles were silently escorting him.

There is a tendency toward propaganda among China's officialdom, and public stories about Wang were probably embellished by the state media, if they happened at all, or by his supporters who aimed to bolster his populist appeal. Still, there is no denying that many ordinary people in Tieling revered him. In an article posted on 360doc.com, the author, who identified himself as a resident from Tieling, compared Wang Lijun to Bao Zheng, a legendary official and judge in China's Song Dynasty, who was known for defending the rights of the ordinary people and who used a guillotine given to him by the emperor to execute criminals.

Wang's tough tactics against mobsters made him many enemies among local crime syndicates, which at one time were said to have put a bounty on his head and allegedly threatened his wife and daughter. On his blog, Wang posted a line frequently quoted by the media: "Fellow fighters and comrades, if I die someday, don't shed tears or feel sad for me. A policeman's profession means death and sacrifice."

Wang's enemies were not limited to gang members; he also had many detractors among his colleagues, including the deputy director, who had first brought him into the police force.

In March 1999, a tricycle cab driver was struck by Wang's car and claimed that Wang beat him up—after the cab driver and his passenger laid the blame on the police chief. He later sued Wang for assault. The court dismissed the case for lack of evidence. Four months later, Wang was taken to court again on charges that he had used torture during an interrogation, causing the death of a woman who had been caught selling fake watches on the street. Even though this case was also dropped for lack of evidence, the Municipal Committee for Inspection Discipline received anonymous letters accusing Wang of systematically using torture to extract confessions. Similar complaints also reached the Ministry of Public Security, which was planning to award Wang a medal. The award was postponed until Wang cleared his name four months later.

Wang dug around and found out that his close friend and former mentor, the deputy director of the public security bureau, was behind the anonymous-letter campaigns against him. He struck back and had his mentor arrested and jailed for two years.

By the end of 2002, Wang's reputation had soared. The provincial police department offered Wang a temporary assignment in Panjin, an oil-producing city, to tackle "oil rats"—organized-crime rings that stole crude oil from the production facilities and were causing the government huge economic losses.

During his investigation, Wang realized that the real enemies lay within the party and the government. Different crime rings sought political and legal protection by bribing senior party officials, judges, and public security officials with money and luxury cars. Oftentimes the local police bureau became the security branch of certain mafia groups. Law enforcement officers engaged in drug trafficking, gun sales, prostitution, and extortion. In one instance, the deputy chief of a local public security bureau tipped off his own brother, who was a notorious oil rat, and helped him escape when police closed in on him. In addition, government officials received bribes and awarded lucrative construction contracts to companies with mafia connections.

To root out the problem, Wang transferred police officers from other regions and organized special teams to conduct internal investigations, purging eight officials with mafia connections, including the city's deputy police director, several local bureau chiefs, and heads of the special criminal investigation unit. Once the bad apples were cleared out, Wang began focusing on the external enemies, and within a short time, he broke up six key crime organizations, arresting 211 suspects.

It was in Panjin that Wang became acquainted with Zhou Yongkang, one of his mentors who would play a decisive role in his political career. Zhou had served as mayor of Panjin before becoming a powerful Politburo Standing Committee member and chairman of the Party's Central Politics and Law Commission, which oversees China's law enforcement and judicial activities. One unsubstantiated story has it that many of Zhou's former friends, who were targeted by Wang for their involvement in the "oil rat" scandals, reached out to Zhou for help. Zhou intervened, urging Wang to end the campaign before implicating more people. Wang is said to have agreed and stopped pursuing Zhou's former friends. As a gesture of gratitude, Zhou's godson allegedly invited Wang to Zhou's home in Beijing, where he befriended many of Zhou's close friends.

Such powerful political connections further boosted his confidence. In May 2003, the provincial government ordered police chiefs to swap cities. Wang left Tieling—where he had worked for twenty-two years, cracking approximately 8,300 criminal cases and arresting nearly 3,000 criminals—and assumed the top post in public security in Jinzhou, a similar-size city about 190 miles away. Two weeks after his arrival, a grisly murder case occurred: a serial rapist broke into residences and over the course of four months raped five women, brutally murdering two of them. Wang mobilized nearly 2,000 people to work on the case and set up a process that held each policeman accountable for each phase of the investigation. Fifty-three days later, a suspect with a prior criminal history was caught and confessed to the crimes.

At a ceremony on the morning of July 23, the city honored the policemen who helped crack the case. In the afternoon, Wang gathered all the officers together for another ceremony, where he announced penalties for thirteen officers accused of negligence. A local bureau chief was fired for failure to locate the suspect, who lived only a few hundred yards from the branch office. While police officers cried foul, residents applauded Wang's efficiency. He soon became a household name in Jinzhou and was elected deputy mayor the next year. Ironically, both in Tieling and Jinzhou, police officers who had been fired or jailed gained back their jobs soon after Wang Lijun left. His reform programs, such as combining patrol and traffic police into one unit to improve police efficiency, were rolled back. His successors saw his sweeping measures as too radical.

In June 2008, Wang was transferred from the city of Jinzhou to Chongqing, one of the four mega cities that fall under the direct control of the central government. He took up the deputy police chief's position. For Wang, it was a career milestone.

"PROFESSOR WANG LIJUN"

IN CHONGQING, known in the West as Chungking, Wang's political career took a meteoric rise. He moved from a city of 3 million people to one with 32 million, and within three years he jumped three bureaucratic levels: from deputy police chief to police chief and deputy mayor.

How did Wang end up in the politically important Chongqing in the first place? Who made the connection between Wang and Bo? There are several competing narratives, I found; this detail is critical to understanding the Bo–Wang partnership in Chongqing and their eventual break.

A popular version indicates that Wang came to Bo Xilai's attention in 2007, when his wife, Gu Kailai, suspected that someone had slipped a mix of lead and mercury into the capsule of her daily herbal medicine and attempted to poison her. Xu Ming, a billionaire businessman in Dalian and a friend of the Bos, contacted Wang Lijun, who had by then become a celebrity in China's northeast due to the popular TV drama based on his life. Xu invited Wang to handle the investigation. Wang solved the case in a matter of days and had Bo's family driver and a helper arrested. In 2008, one year after Bo's appointment as the party secretary of Chongqing, he was concerned that organized crime was rampant and considered the then-police chief, a protégé of President Hu Jintao, untrustworthy and incompetent. As an outsider without many local connections, he needed to boost his team with his own people. Bo's wife strongly recommended Wang Lijun.

A businessperson well connected with the Ministry of Public Security argued that Zhou Yongkang, chairman of the party's Central Politics and Law Commission, was the one who made the official connection between Wang and Bo. Zhou Yongkang, who is featured later in the book, owed Wang a favor—the anti-crime hero released several of Zhou's friends who had been arrested during the 2002 crackdown on "oil rats" in Panjin. The two became close friends after Zhou was made minister of public security. "All the key personnel changes had to be approved by Zhou," said the businessman. "Otherwise, it would have been administratively impossible for Wang to make that big career leap."

Regardless of how the two met, officials in Chongqing say Bo and Wang hit it off. Bo, on multiple private and public occasions, played up Wang's credentials and his fearlessness. For Wang, the son of a railway worker, one would assume he cherished the honor of working with a prominent princeling and a rising political star capable of opening up a new world for him.

The honeymoon was sweet. Wang started out as deputy chief of the city's public security bureau. Nine months later, Bo made good on his initial promise and appointed Wang bureau chief.

Wang did not disappoint either. In the first year, he embarked on what he called a "thorough social investigation." He disguised himself as a cabdriver, visiting different neighborhoods and talking to residents. As in other parts of China, Chongqing was plagued with rising crime rates. In some areas, prostitution and illegal gambling dens were operating just a short distance from police stations.

On the early morning of June 3, 2009, a forty-four-year-old man named Li Minghang—neighbors described him to police as a polite and mysterious renter in a dilapidated housing development with a fancy Scottish name, Edinburg—was gunned down outside his apartment. Subsequent police investigations revealed the tenant, who drove a BMW, was a drug trafficker. He had been killed by a mobster in a dispute over illicit profit. The incident grabbed national headlines and posed a challenge for the Bo administration.

Wang's special investigative team soon captured three suspects who had allegedly plotted the shooting in Edinburg. Based on the suspects' confessions and tips provided by residents, Wang arrested more than fifty suspected of gunrunning, drug trafficking, and gambling. The two chief suspects were found guilty and executed in six months. The swift resolution proved to be politically popular. Riding on the success of the case, Wang also mobilized hundreds of armed policemen to wipe out several illegal ammunition and gun manufacturing facilities hidden inside the mountains outside Chongqing. In response to the overwhelming public support for such initiatives, Bo instructed Wang to launch a citywide *da hei,* or "Smashing Black" campaign against the mobsters terrorizing the city. At a conference for police, Wang declared in his usual dramatic style, "We'll stir up a storm and generate an avalanche."

Wang's yearlong campaign targeting mafia organizations involved 10,000 police broken up into 329 investigative teams. State media reported that nearly 5,000 people were taken into police custody and among them, 3,273 of them were prosecuted. The court convicted 520 people, with 65 executed or given life imprisonment. In the same time period, police successfully cracked 4,172 previously unsolved cases and broke up 128 crime rings. However, a recently released Chongqing government white paper showed a much smaller number of arrests. The media's exaggerated figures probably spooked many senior leaders in Beijing, who feared that Bo could expand his program nationwide—and threaten their political and financial interests—if he joined the Politburo Standing Committee.

Over the course of the campaign, Wang also targeted police officers who, he said, were working with criminals. "We are supposed to attack the underworld, but some in the police force are more corrupt and dangerous than the mobsters," Wang told the Chinese state media. In addition, a policeman in Chongqing remembered receiving a short notice about a meeting one morning:

> We walked into the auditorium and saw the entrance guarded by fully armed policemen. People could smell blood. Wang stood on the stage and read off the names from a list. Most of the people on the list were in leadership positions and have been found taking bribes or collaborating with criminals. Each time a name was called, Wang would announce the charges and follow them with an order, "You are under arrest." At the end of the meeting, seven officers were handcuffed and taken away on the spot.

By the end of 2010, more than 1,000 police officers and government officials had been charged with corruption and abuse of power, including many high-ranking officials, such as Zhang Tao, vice president of the Chongqing People's High Court, who received the death penalty, later commuted, and Wu Xiaoqing, a senior court official; prison officials claimed he committed suicide while in jail awaiting trial.

The arrest and trial of Wen Qiang, the head of Chongqing's justice bureau, galvanized the nation. Wen, a veteran police officer of thirty-eight years, was deputy chief of the Chongqing public security bureau before Wang. Ironically, Wang and Wen, who are three years apart in age, shared oddly parallel lives. Born in 1956, Wen grew up in Sichuan's Bai county—a poverty-stricken region—and farmed rice paddies as a teenager. He was recruited by the Luzhou Police Academy in 1977 and became a junior police officer in his hometown. As with Wang, Wen was said to be dedicated and fearless, and was promoted to deputy chief of the Chongqing public security bureau at the age of thirty-eight. He had received numerous medals and awards for cracking difficult criminal cases. In 2000, while Wang was hailed in the north as an anticrime hero, Wen earned a similar title in the southwest after capturing Zhang Jun, who was dubbed as China's number-one "bandit" and "monstrous murderer." Zhang had traversed the country for eight years with three partners, stealing 6 million yuan in jewelry and cash and killing twenty-eight people. Despite the nationwide manhunt, Zhang and his partners, who were well-trained in special military skills, evaded police.

Wen was under tremendous pressure to capture Zhang after the bandit and his two partners seized an armored truck in front of a bank in Changde city in the nearby Hunan province on September 1, 2000, killing two guards and two cashiers while snatching two micro-submachine guns. A witness inside the bank pushed the alarm, forcing them to flee, so Zhang stopped a taxi, shot the driver, and fled empty-handed. Despite his indiscriminate killing sprees, the seemingly invincible Zhang was deemed a hero by many, who applauded him for killing mostly corrupt officials. Some female college students even wrote him love letters.

Wen had studied and tracked Zhang for six years. Two weeks after the failed armored car heist, Wen zeroed in and captured him with a girlfriend at his hideout in a small town not far from Chongqing. After Zhang was wrestled to the ground, Wen had a picture taken, with one foot ostensibly trampling Zhang's face. On April 21, 2001, Zhang was executed. A novelist wrote a book about Wen's legendary career, much as Wang's story had been told to the wider populace of China through a TV drama.

WANG AND WEN, two legendary anticrime heroes, met on June 26, 2008. As the Chinese saying goes, "Two tigers cannot coexist on one mountain." Wang took over the deputy police chief's position that Wen had held for sixteen years, and Wen was transferred to what was regarded as a less important post: chief of the justice bureau. At the handover ceremony, an official recalled, Wen shook hands with Wang and went on to express support for the party's decision in his farewell speech. Over the next year, the two remained amicable. But Wang was secretly plotting—he had heard stories about Wen's cozy relations with leaders of the mafia and his multiple young mistresses. Besides, the impetuous Wen, favored by the city's previous party chief, was said to have defied orders from Bo.

Wang made his move on August 7, 2009, sending police to arrest Wen at a conference in Beijing. He was flown back to Chongqing, where Wang was waiting at the airport with one hundred fully armed police officers. Police raided Wen's home and discovered a plastic bag containing 20 million yuan hidden under a pond in his courtyard. Over the next few days, local and national newspapers carried a series of salacious stories based on information provided by the public security bureau. Wen was portrayed as a godfather figure who had shielded mobsters from the authorities. One article said Wen had attended the birthday party of a mafia leader's daughter and accepted a huge amount of money. Another article alleged that Wen had asked his subordinates to get him a young girl who was virgin, at the cost of 100,000 yuan. Wen's sister-in-law had been arrested and detained two weeks before he was, allegedly for running a gambling and drug ring. She was depicted as a nymphomaniac who kept sixteen young men as sex slaves.

The public outcry against Wen Qiang generated by the lurid media reports effectively blocked any attempts by his supporters in Beijing to intervene. In the end, Wen was charged with accepting bribes up to 12 million yuan and raping a college student. In April 2010, eight months after his arrest, the court sentenced Wen to death. His wife and his sister-in-law got eighteen years respectively for taking bribes, operating illegal gambling dens, and harboring drug users.

Wen was awakened in his jail cell early on the morning of July 7, 2011, and told he would be executed. Two hours later, he met with his sister and his teenage son for ten minutes. Reportedly his last words to his son, words many believe were concocted by Wang, were, "Daddy ends up like this today because I have committed crimes. Don't hate society. Be an honest person. If others give you money, don't accept it."

Wen was executed by lethal injection early that morning. In the afternoon, his relatives were called to the crematorium and were handed a plastic bag containing his ashes.

Wang bragged about Wen's swift conviction, calling it "Chongqing speed," though critics claimed that Wen's conviction was politically motivated and that some of the charges, such as raping a young woman who later became his mistress, were fabricated to justify the death penalty. When Wen Qiang initially refused to admit guilt, Wang detained his son for ten months. During interrogations, Wen was tortured and denied due process. In December 2012, a Hong Kong newspaper disclosed that Wang had allegedly planted the bag of cash under a pond in Wen Qiang's outdoor courtyard.

Following Wen's death, Wang restructured the police force. He set up a "talent retraining center"—where police officers he considered incompetent or disobedient were sent to reflect on their "mistakes" and get brainwashed. In the next two years, Wang fired, detained, and imprisoned nearly 1,800 police officers. All the leaders within the police force, more than 3,000 of them, lost their jobs but were free to reapply for their positions, as could anyone else. Wang took the opportunity to install nearly seventy of his former colleagues from northeast China in leadership positions to boost his power base.

Another of Wang's populist restructuring programs was to merge the traffic and foot-patrol police units, putting 800 to 1,000 police on the city streets every day, with a policeman no more than three minutes away from a crime taking place. The move made Chongqing one of the best-patrolled cities in the world.

In November 2012, a police officer in Chongqing posted the following observation online about Wang:

> [He] was stubborn and strove to do everything in a speedy manner. He was tough on those who failed to follow his instructions. For example, Wang required those in managerial positions to work fourteen-hour days and would constantly make midnight phone calls to local branches. If the officer on duty did not answer, the branch chief could be in trouble for dereliction of duty. People worked under constant fear. Some could no longer handle the pressure and invented excuses [or simply] left the police force.

In 2011, Wang's popularity was high. In January, he was elected as a delegate to the National People's Congress. In May, he was appointed deputy mayor and many residents called for making Wang China's minister of public security.

Wang had not attended college after graduating from high school. In a country where academic degrees are valued, his lack of education was a defect, which he set about correcting. His official résumé indicates that he obtained a master's degree in business administration through a one-year correspondence education program at something called "California University," though an Internet search for the institution produces no results. Wang also obtained an eMBA from the China Northeastern Finance University between 2004 and 2006, when he was deputy mayor of Jinzhou. A professor at Beijing University said Wang's eMBA degree has no academic value because the program is a revenue-generating engine for the university. According to the professor, decorative titles are sold to officials and businesspeople who need an academic degree but have no desire to study.

Despite his lack of higher education, more than ten of China's prestigious universities have made Wang an adjunct professor and doctoral supervisor. In December 2011, the president of Beijing University of Post and Telecommunications invited Wang to be a part-time professor. In a grand ceremony attended by several hundred students, the university president addressed Wang as Dr. Wang, saying that Wang had a PhD in law. In a newsletter called *Police Salon*, published by the Chongqing Municipal Police Bureau, Wang was frequently addressed as Professor Wang Lijun and his photos were prominently displayed in every issue. The Chinese state media reported that Wang was an expert on forensics, criminal psychology, and law; had written five books on law; and had presided over eighteen legal-research projects. Wang was also listed as an inventor and fashion designer. On China's State Intellectual Property Office website, one can find more than 119 patents filed by Wang, from police equipment and alarm systems to police raincoats and policewomen's boots.

Over the years Wang had meticulously cultivated an image of a scholarly policeman. During an interview with the *Sichuan Legal Daily*, he said, "I have a special respect for intellectuals. I worship culture." Inside the public security bureau building in Chongqing, he set aside a room called the "Reading Salon" and encouraged his officers to read during lunch breaks.

To further heighten his cultural status, Wang promoted his calligraphy and painting skills. In China, calligraphy is a hobby for many senior Chinese officials, who practice it and secretly compete with one another. Many collect works from famous calligraphers and mount them on silk scrolls they hang on their office walls to create a refined and distinguished atmosphere. According to the state media, Wang won fifth place during a province-wide calligraphy contest in Liaoning and one of his watercolor paintings was once on display at a museum in Mongolia. On his office desk, he insisted on using old-fashioned ink brushes to write and used a regular pen only to sign documents. Soon, other officials started to follow suit. Wang's flowery handwriting was used to decorate several public security bureau buildings and office walls in Chongqing.

He was said to have many idiosyncrasies, which the official propaganda machine used to humanize him. One story has it that Wang never used a key to open his door at home because he believed that keys should be for hotel rooms only. "When you get home, you press the doorbell and your family members embrace you at the door. That's called family," he was quoted as saying. "The feelings and the atmosphere are sublime." He was also depicted as a doting father who missed a tour of the Eiffel Tower, which he had particularly wanted to see during a business trip to Paris, because he was running around the city trying to buy his daughter toys.

There was a widely publicized story that Wang found a little boy who was lost on the streets of Chongqing. He could have left the boy at a shelter. Instead, he took the boy home and cared for him. When the boy's parents were located three months later, the boy didn't want to leave his new "daddy."

These tear-jerking tales could be true, but they failed to soften Wang's image inside the police department, where officers categorized him as tyrannical.

In July 2009, a police officer in a Chongqing suburb—carrying a hunting rifle—accidentally killed a civilian. On seeing media reports, Wang held the entire local leadership accountable and summarily stripped them of their positions.

In July 2010, a police officer who was out on his lunch break got into an argument with a security guard who refused to let him back in without an ID. The officer was subsequently exiled to a smaller branch in a remote region for allegedly calling the security guard "Wang Lijun's lackey."

On August 30, 2010, six police officers complained and made some unfavorable comments about Wang during lunch. A colleague sitting nearby recorded their conversation and reported it to Wang. A week later, the six officers were interrogated and later demoted.

Such incidents created fear in the police force—each time the topic of Wang Lijun came up during casual conversations, officers would ask each other to take the batteries out of their cellphones to prevent taping. And they avoided mentioning Wang by name, referring to him as "the professor" or "W."

At the office, if Wang happened to encounter an officer who dressed sloppily, or talked too loudly in the mess hall, or chatted on the phone in the hallway, or slung his bag casually over his shoulder, or failed to greet him properly, he would scold the officer or demote him on the spot.

Shortly after his arrival in Chongqing, Wang organized a five hundred–strong team to solve more than 28,000 open cases that had built up over the previous ten years. He made it a priority to improve the crime resolution rate for each branch by setting annual quotas. Fearing they could be punished if the quota was not met, many police officers would report only the cases they had solved and left many unreported. There were also stories about policemen deliberately sending gang members to commit petty crimes in the market so they could easily catch them and fulfill their quotas for "solved crimes."

After Wang's fall, his former assistant Xin Jianwei disclosed that Wang had gone through fifty-one assistants during his two-year tenure in Chongqing—one man was sacked on his first day. Xin himself served as Wang's secretary and personal assistant for four months before he was locked up in jail for talking back to Wang over a trivial matter. Based on Xin's account, Wang had ordered Xin to book him a hotel room during a police conference in the spring of 2010. Because

Wang did not check out on time, his room key had automatically expired. "Wang Lijun was furious because he couldn't get into his room. He got hold of me and began swearing at me, calling me all kinds of names," Xin was quoted in an online article in December 2012. "When I vigorously explained that it was not my fault, Wang yelled, 'Get the hell out of here' and fired me the next day."

A month later, Xin, arrested on charges that he had provided "protection for mafia leaders," was held in a tiny cell with two guards watching him twenty-four hours a day for three hundred days. During his incarceration, Xin was forced to confess that he had been hired by several municipal leaders to spy on Wang and block his promotion. When Xin refused, he was tied down to a wooden bench and beaten up numerous times. He suffered severe head injuries. At one time, Xin said he collected the mosquitoes he had killed in the cell and stuck them on the wall to form a character, "injustices."

An officer who worked in the publicity department of the Chongqing Public Security Bureau also described Wang Lijun as a narcissist who had an entourage of more than twenty camera-carrying assistants. Known as "blue spirits" for the blue jackets they wore, Wang's assistants followed him everywhere—their job was to record every word Wang uttered and take pictures and videos of him, capturing what he called "his most moving and breathtaking moments." If any pictures were not up to Wang's standards, the photographer had to Photoshop them until Wang was happy. Each time Wang delivered a speech, he pressured other police officers to write down their comments. Then, all of Wang's speeches would be compiled into a book which included lavish praise from his subordinates—items such as "Professor Wang Lijun is a saint, a police hero, and a model teacher. Each time I savor Professor Wang's words, my heart surges with passion and my blood is boiling."

The state media, which had helped create a legend out of Wang, also fell victim to his tyranny. In recent years, driven particularly by commercial interests and journalistic sensibility, many media outlets would occasionally push the envelope and run stories critical of the government or the police. Wang had no tolerance for any criticism. At a conference for Chongqing police officers in October 2010, Wang said:

In the future, if the newspapers distort the truth and attack our municipal public security bureau and individual police, we will sue both the media organization and the writer. If the news article mentions a certain individual policeman and caused negative consequences, the policeman will gather evidence and take the journalist to court. The bureau where the policeman works and other related organizations should coordinate and support the lawsuit. I call this practice "double lawsuits"—the public security organizations sue the newspaper and the policeman sues the reporter. Once we turn this into a lawsuit, the reporter will be a helpless spectator.

During Wang's reign, the police department recruited 12,000 new officers and expanded the police force to 70,000, the largest in Asia. Wang also attempted to gain influence over the judicial process. In January 2011, he read a news report about the trial of an official with mafia ties. He wrote a comment on the margins of the article and sent it to the court, recommending capital punishment. Four months later, the official received the death penalty during the first trial.

Wang raised an uproar among legal scholars across China after he imprisoned a defense lawyer, charging him with fabricating testimony in favor of a mobster during the crackdown on organized crimes.

This is how it happened. In June 2009, an alleged crime boss was arrested by Chongqing police for murder, illegal weapons trade, drug dealing, and leading a criminal organization. On November 22, 2009, the defendant's wife retained Li Zhuang, a well-known lawyer who worked for a prestigious law firm headed by a powerful princeling and who had defended many similar cases. During his research, Li found that Wang Lijun had established an interrogation center with a deceptive name, "The Militia Training Camp," inside a mountain. Police used extensive torture while investigating defendants, including his client. Li raised the issue with the police.

Li's legal work made him a target of persecution by Wang Lijun. On December 10, 2009, Chongqing police sent a telegram to the Beijing judiciary bureau, claiming that the Chongqing Detention Center's audio and video records showed that Li had tried to entice his client to give false testimony by conveying his enticement through "winks."

Meanwhile, Li's client also confessed to prosecutors that his lawyer had advised him to falsely testify that he had been beaten for eight days and nights and that he had become incontinent.

On the night of December 12, Li was secretly arrested in Beijing, and police escorted him back to Chongqing.

> At the airport, Wang Lijun, flanked by more than one hundred police and journalists, waited for me on the tarmac. The plane was surrounded by ten light-flashing police cars. The policemen, armed with anti-riot gear, were dressed in camouflage uniforms, wearing helmets and black boots and carrying micro machine guns. Then, Wang pointed at me and shouted at his assistants. "You can do your job now." The assistant came up and handcuffed me. Then, I heard him whisper to another policeman. "Be aware, he is someone who is a legal expert." The policeman nodded, "Understood."

He was thrown in a police car and the whole entourage followed them to the detention center, which was about four miles from the airport. The road was completely blocked by police. Li said Wang was, by nature, "melodramatic and a showoff," but admitted that he was intimidated by the "welcome ceremony." During the investigative process, Wang hired legal experts to advise the police department, teaching them how to skirt laws and regulations.

Li was tried, and in January 2010, the Chongqing People's Intermediate Court sentenced him to two and a half years in prison and barred him from practicing law for life. Li filed an appeal and in its second review, the court reduced the sentence to eighteen months, citing that Li had cooperated with the court. However, at the sentencing, Li claimed he had been deceived by leaders within the Chongqing government, who promised to release him if he admitted guilt.

Li's assertion about confessions made under duress and other abuses was later corroborated by another lawyer, who released videotapes of his client, a wealthy thirty-nine-year-old construction contractor charged with running a crime syndicate and murdering one of his rivals. In the video, the contractor claimed police had coerced him to confess and implicate others—he had been subjected to severe beatings and sleep deprivation for six months. During his incarceration, he tried to kill himself twice and bit off his own tongue in protest. Medical reports back up these claims. Despite mounting evidence, the court rejected the contractor's appeal and he was executed in July 2010.

Even with Li's imprisonment, Wang was still unhappy. He sent investigators to other cities to collect more evidence against Li. Three months later, Li was prosecuted again on a charge of obstruction during a case that Li had handled in Shanghai two years before. When Li entered the courthouse, a crowd, allegedly brought in by the Chongqing government, chanted, "Clear out all the bad lawyers." Despite Wang's pressure, the prosecution eventually withdrew the charge for lack of evidence.

Fang Hong, an employee in Chongqing's Fuling district, posted a satirical Weibo comment, calling the lawsuit against Li a "pile of shit." Police detained Fang and sent him to a Reeducation through Labor Camp for one year. According to Fang's lawyer, more than 10,000 Chongqing residents had been sent to labor camps by Wang Lijun.

Between 2009 and 2011, court papers say Wang used the anticrime campaign to terrorize the business community by branding legitimate private businesspeople as mobsters. "The party needs to tie a timed bomb around your waist to make sure you obey orders," Wang said to a private entrepreneur who was a delegate to the Municipal People's Congress and vowed to collect petitions calling for Wang to resign. Wang had him arrested on charges that he colluded with organized crime, and his assets were confiscated. "I could have him executed if I want," Wang remarked. In May 2011, one of Wang's friends held a fundraiser for a scholarship that sponsored policemen's studies abroad. Wang advised his subordinates to gather some local entrepreneurs at police headquarters for a "meeting" and blatantly solicited money from them. At the end of the meeting, the officer collected 30 million yuan. Wang called this practice "robbing the rich to help the poor." Using Russian president Vladimir Putin as an example, Wang was quoted as saying, "If there are ten people, four are wealthy and six poor. We only need to get rid of two wealthy ones. The other two would be intimidated and voluntarily give their money away. The six poor folks would applaud our actions."

The *Washington Post* reported that the public security bureau confiscated the assets—estimated at US $700 million—of Li Jun, once one of the richest men in Chongqing. Li now lives as an exile in Canada. Eight of his relatives are languishing in a Chinese jail and his business empire is under police control.

The businessman, originally from Hubei province, moved to Chongqing in 1984 as a soldier in the army and after five years of service, set up a small trading business and then a petrol station. Other ventures followed, including a restaurant, a karaoke parlor, and a sauna, all of which, police said, were connected with organized crime.

Li stated that his arrest was related to a real estate transaction. In 2008, he had purchased a plot of undeveloped military land in Chongqing. The deal had supposedly offended a senior military officer who was a friend of Bo Xilai and had intended to sell the property to a relative. In December 2009, Li was picked up by police, who beat him repeatedly during questioning. Li said he was kept chained for days to a "tiger bench"—a metal chair specially designed to maximize pain— and his arms and legs were shackled while security agents pummeled him and demanded he confess. Held for three months at the secret "Militia Training Camp," Li was released after agreeing to pay US $6.3 million in penalties. In October 2010, while on a business trip to Chengdu, Li was tipped off that he was about to be arrested again. He fled the next morning to Hong Kong, then later to Canada.

Meanwhile, Wang was accused of sexually abusing female police officers. In 2010, as he sought to reform the image of the police in Chongqing, he formed a "special police patrol unit" consisting of eighty young female university graduates, whose average age was twenty-four and average height was 5 feet 7 inches. They drove Volvo cars and dressed up in uniforms designed by Wang. Court papers indicated that Wang had sexually assaulted eight of the female officers. In addition, a police officer in Tieling claimed on the Internet in April 2012 that Wang had raped a policewoman while he worked in his home city. The policewoman, who subsequently became pregnant from the rape, filed a lawsuit against Wang but the local court refused to handle the case out of fear of Wang Lijun.

In 2011, a former police officer in Chongqing said Wang seemed invincible, "His ego ballooned. With Bo on his side, Wang Lijun was ready to attack anyone who dared criticize him."

With such unchecked power vested in him and so many police officers, government officials, and businesspeople he had unfairly targeted, Wang's downfall was inevitable. As the Chinese proverb says, "The mantis seizes the locust but does not see the yellow bird which is ready to snatch him from behind."

THE SLAP IN THE FACE

IN MAY 2011, Bo Xilai made Wang Lijun Chongqing's deputy mayor, but Wang knew that the position carried no substantial power unless he joined the Municipal Party Standing Committee, the city's highest decision-making body. He actively lobbied both of the Bos for a promotion. He also invited visiting senior leaders to tour his "Smashing Black Campaign Victory Exhibition" and aggressively sought their praises, which he later used lavishly in his police newsletters.

Senior leaders in Beijing might feel obligated to utter positive remarks about the "Smashing Black" campaign, but many were wary, and shuddered at the prospect that Bo's program could expand nationally and jeopardize their business interests. By the summer of 2011, more than 5,000 people had been detained or arrested. Several victims' relatives had sent petitions to senior leaders recounting horror stories about the practices of torture, forced confessions, and confiscated assets. Many of the complaints and petitions reached Wang Yang, the party secretary of Guangdong province, and He Guoqiang, head of the Central Commission for Discipline Inspection, both predecessors of Bo in Chongqing. Many officials whom Wang had purged, imprisoned, or executed were also protégés or former colleagues of Wang Yang and He Guoqiang. However, the two senior leaders felt constrained and helpless because Bo Xilai was too powerful to tackle. They quietly bided their time.

An opportunity came in 2011 when the Central Commission for Discipline Inspection received anonymous letters from citizens in Tieling accusing Wang and his friends of embezzling public funds. One letter alleged that 450,000 yuan budgeted for construction were unaccounted for when Wang was police chief in Tieling.

He Guoqiang gave permission to his staff to act, and the move was carefully calculated—investigation would specifically target Wang's friends. Because Wang was far removed from Tieling, he wouldn't be able to intervene easily. If Wang's friends were found guilty—very few survived an extensive investigation by the commission—the convictions would send a warning to Wang so he would think twice before going after his political opponents in Chongqing. The source called the strategy "striking at the mountain to scare the tigers." But nobody expected the mountain would collapse, burying the tigers alive.

In June 2011, a friend from Tieling called Wang to say that "fires" had broken out in his backyard. The word "fire" was used figuratively to indicate trouble; a corruption scandal had erupted in Wang's home city. The Tieling police chief had been taken away earlier in the month by officials from Beijing. The detention was based on allegations that the Tieling police chief had taken bribes and embezzled funds allocated for a new office building for the Tieling public security department. A week later, six other officials, all of whom were Wang's friends and loyal supporters, were also under investigation.

The office building was designed under Wang's supervision, but the actual construction work started after Wang's departure in 2003. Even though Wang received reassurance from his friends in Tieling and Beijing that it was an isolated case and he was not implicated, Wang felt insecure and became concerned, especially after relatives of his detained friends arrived in Chongqing seeking his help.

Wang inevitably thought of Bo Xilai and expressed his concern. With the princeling's extensive support network in Beijing, Wang was certain that Bo could exert his influence to reverse the situation in his hometown and rescue his friends. Moreover, Wang felt Bo owed him. He had worked wholeheartedly to advance Bo's political career; it was because of his association with Bo that the head of the Central Commission for Discipline Inspection was against him.

What Wang didn't know was that Bo rarely stuck out his own neck for friends, especially someone like Wang, who was simply a lackey, not his equal. More important, Bo did not want to be involved in messy deals that could stand in the way of his upcoming bid for the Politburo Standing Committee. Sources in Chongqing said Bo remained uncommitted to Wang's request.

Wang was deeply disappointed and hurt. Growing up in a northern culture, which places friendship above sibling love, Wang saw his inability to save his friends in Tieling as a tremendous loss of face, and this drew attention to his waning influence. At the same time, he saw Bo's rebuff as a sign of distrust in him.

In July 2011, Wang watched the deepening investigation in Tieling helplessly from afar—more police officers were arrested and detained. Meanwhile, in several of the official news reports about senior leaders' visits to Chongqing, there was only brief mention of the "Smashing Black" campaign. Sensing that many in Beijing might have taken offense at his signature programs in Chongqing, Wang became paranoid. One of his colleagues said Wang suffered from severe insomnia. Adding insult to injury, Bo Xilai led a "Red Song Singing" troupe to Beijing, and no one from the Politburo Standing Committee showed up. The cold shoulder confirmed Wang's suspicion that Bo's policies lacked support in Beijing and that Bo's political future might not be as secure he had anticipated. Wang was said to be secretly concerned that Bo Xilai could eventually shift all the blame on him, making him a sacrificial lamb if mounting complaints about the excesses and abuses during Wang's anti-crime initiatives jeopardized Bo's bid for the Politburo Standing Committee. Wang felt the urgent need to secure his political future and protect the more than sixty police officers he had transferred from northeast China to Chongqing.

Wang reached out to cultivate relations with other senior leaders, including Li Keqiang, China's premier-in-waiting who belonged to a different political faction. A princeling who is now a businessman in Beijing said Wang had met Li Keqiang when the latter was party secretary in Liaoning province in 2004.

Knowing that Li Keqiang and several Politburo members felt threatened by Bo's soaring political ambition, Wang secretly taped many of Bo's private meetings where he discussed his political plans. Wang allegedly fed them to some senior leaders.

In one conversation, Bo compared the current Chinese president to a weak and spoiled emperor in the Han Dynasty, called former president Jiang Zemin the dowager in the Qing Dynasty, who had ruled China behind the bamboo curtain until the dynasty collapsed, and the president-in-waiting as an incompetent crown prince in the Han Dynasty. The actual existence of this conversation cannot be verified but Bo Xilai's alleged remarks were widely distributed on the Web, souring Bo's relations with his peers in Beijing and fueling speculation that Bo was conspiring to usurp power from the senior leadership.

On November 15, the death of English businessman Neil Heywood offered a wisp of hope for Wang Lijun. Based on initial media reports in April 2012, Wang had rushed over to the Lucky Holiday Hotel after receiving a call from the hotel's general manager and had briefly examined Heywood's body. Given that the deceased was a foreigner, Wang had assigned four of his trusted police officers to investigate the case. From evidence collected at the hotel room, Wang Lijun said investigators concluded that it was a homicide and Bo's wife was a key suspect. "After coming to Chongqing, I visited Gu Kailai's home often, and I thought she treated me quite well," said Wang Lijun in his testimony. "I knew if the case was treated as a homicide, it would be devastating to her. However, to avoid antagonism with Gu Kailai, I shunned the case." With Wang's approval, police investigators covered up Gu's involvement in Heywood's death.

On November 16, the Chongqing public security bureau ruled the cause of Heywood's death as alcohol overdose and persuaded Heywood's widow to accept the verdict. Thus, Heywood was cremated without an autopsy. Before the cremation, an official at the Central Commission for Discipline Inspection said Wang had secretly drawn some blood from Heywood's body and told his aide to store the sample at a secure location.

As the case was settled, a source familiar with Wang's investigation said Wang began to press Gu Kailai, urging her to lobby Bo Xilai for help with Wang's friends in Tieling as payback for his cover-up and silence on Heywood's death. Gu willingly complied and lied to Wang, telling him that Bo had promised to give him a promotion. As a matter of fact, Gu did pester her husband with Wang's request, but Bo refused and even became angry with Wang.

In December 2011, Wang found out about Gu Kailai's lie. At the same time, the Central Disciplinary Inspection Commission had completed the investigation of Wang's Tieling friends and turned them over to the local court. The news unnerved him. Wang probably saw that his enemies at the commission were using the trials to eventually get at him. Realizing that Gu held no sway over Bo, he needed to come up with a new plan to salvage the situation.

A top Hong Kong businessman who lives in Chongqing disclosed to me that Wang had actually disguised himself as an old man and sneaked into the visa section of the British Consulate in the southern city of Guangzhou in early December 2011 to inquire about the possibility of political asylum, but consulate officials ignored him. The businessman, who claimed to have heard the news from a reliable source inside the Chongqing government, did not know if Wang had revealed his true identity at the consulate. "Wang was fearful that his political enemies would get him and he probably wanted to use Heywood's death as a ticket for asylum."

In mid-December, Gu Kailai, worried that Wang Lijun could betray her, reached out to the deputy police chief, asking him to destroy evidence without Wang's knowledge. Gu's unilateral move upset Wang. When their relations worsened, Wang decided to take a gamble. Revealing Gu Kailai's murder of Heywood to Bo, Wang forced Bo to deal with him. Wang was certain that Bo would consent to his previous request for help with his friends in Tieling. He would also demand a promotion. According to court papers, Wang shared his plan with members of his inner circle—officers and sworn brothers he had brought from his home city—before his meeting with Bo. They pledged ultimate loyalty to Wang, addressing him as "Teacher."

On January 28, the last day of the weeklong Chinese New Year celebration, Wang held a private meeting with Bo. According to leaked testimony by Xu Ming, a close friend of Bo's, Wang presented Bo with evidence that would link Gu Kailai to Heywood's death. Wang also said officers on the investigative team had submitted their resignations because of the pressure to hide the truth. To protect Bo Xilai's political future, Wang said he was willing to bend his principles and help out. He allegedly told Bo, "As far as I'm concerned, the case is over." Bo was reportedly shocked by the news. At the end of the meeting, Bo said he was thankful and praised Wang for his "loyalty." Wang later told his friends that his talk with Bo had gone "very well."

After Wang Lijun left, Bo immediately went to his wife to confirm the story. Gu reportedly denied poisoning Heywood, claiming that Wang Lijun had framed her for murder. She also confided in Bo that Wang Lijun had repeatedly pressured her to talk Bo into helping with his friends in Tieling and granting him a spot on the Municipal Party Standing Committee.

The next day, Bo called Wang and the deputy chief into his office. Calling Wang an "ungrateful bastard," he accused the former police chief of plotting against his wife as well as against him. When Wang argued back, Bo flew into a rage and slapped Wang in the face, ordering him to leave the room. Wang left with blood on his lips.

Wang was said to be deeply hurt and mortified by the face slap, which in Chinese culture is considered the worst insult to a person's dignity, made even worse by the fact that it was delivered in front of a junior colleague, the deputy police chief.

According to a police officer in Chongqing during a phone interview:

> Wang Lijun, a man of humble origins, was sensitive to how others, especially princelings like Bo Xilai, treated him. Over the years, as he gradually built his career, Wang meticulously cultivated his image as a national hero. He cherished his image like a peacock does its plumes. The unexpected slap from Bo Xilai was a terrible affront to a tough Mongolian man.
>
> The slap was a wake-up call and a reality check. He saw clearly that he was merely Bo Xilai's hound dog. When he is no longer of any value or becomes a liability for his master, he could be kicked out and put to death to be served at someone else's dinner table. The slap shattered the last shreds of his illusions about dignity.

After leaving Bo's office, Wang Lijun immediately ordered the four police investigators to re-create Neil Heywood's case file. A police officer later testified in court:

> We were asked to re-obtain testimonies from witnesses; properly protect key material evidence, including the blood extracted from Neil Heywood's heart; and reorganize the evidence and documents regarding the suspicion that Gu Kailai may have murdered Neil Heywood. We spent several days making the file. Wang Lijun asked us to keep the file separately and store it in a safe place. I knew something had gone wrong and he had a personal purpose in starting the case.

Realizing that they were up against the party chief of Chongqing, one of the most influential politicians in China, two investigators suggested that Wang Lijun inform the Ministry of Public Security in Beijing about Heywood's murder. Wang adamantly declined, citing that he had other plans in mind.

As a shrewd politician, Wang did not want to lose what he had accomplished over the past twenty-eight years. He suppressed his anger from the humiliating slap and wrote a letter of apology to both Bo and Gu, pledging his loyalty. Wang also blamed Bo's chief of staff, who was said to dislike Wang intensely, for instigating the conflicts. However, the apology letter did not help and the situation soon became irreversible.

On January 30, Bo called a few senior municipal leaders for an emergency meeting and declared his intention to sack Wang. However, Huang Qifan, the mayor of Chongqing, dissented on the grounds that firing the police chief of Chongqing, the largest city under the direct administration of the central government, needed approval from the Ministry of Public Security. Bo ignored his advice and responded angrily that he knew how to handle Beijing.

On January 31, Wang was informed that his Tieling friends had been convicted—the former Tieling police chief was sentenced to twelve years in jail on corruption charges and the court confiscated 9.8

million yuan. Two of his former colleagues received sixteen and four-teen years, respectively.

The following afternoon, Bo convened an expanded meeting attended by members of the standing committee of the Municipal Communist Party, and announced that Wang would leave the public security bureau but would stay on as deputy mayor. Bo explained that Wang needed to become familiar with other areas of the government so he could be ready for more challenging tasks ahead; those at the meeting speculated that Wang was the subject of a corruption-related investigation.

On February 2, the city announced Wang's job change to members of the police department. Concurrently, Bo Xilai probed four of the police officers who had been assigned to work on the Neil Heywood case. Court documents said Bo forced the investigators to destroy evidence relating to Gu Kailai's involvement in Heywood's death and sign confessions stating that Wang Lijun had made false allegations against Bo's wife. Three investigators cooperated and wrote allegiance letters. But Wang Pengfei refused to hand over the blood sample that Wang Lijun had drawn from Heywood's body before his cremation and managed to transport the sample to Beijing, storing it in a friend's refrigerator. When Bo found out, he kidnapped Wang Pengfei and detained him for nearly a month.

Also in early February, Bo ordered the detention of three of Wang's personal assistants, including his driver, for secret interrogations. They told Bo about Wang's secret tapings of both Bo's private conversations and his numerous rendezvous with young women. Bo realized that Wang had been conspiring against him and he put Wang under surveillance.

On February 4, a journalist with Southern Weekend got in touch with Wang, seeking to confirm the rumor that he was under investigation. Wang responded tersely, "I'm still free." When the reporter asked if it was true that his driver had been arrested, Wang snapped before hanging up, "Let them arrest anyone they want."

Following the detention of his personal assistants, Wang instructed a close confidante to write and sign with the person's real name a letter to the commission and the Politburo, reporting on Bo's connection to the Heywood murder and Bo's past transfers of money overseas, according to a source at the Central Commission for Discipline Inspection. Under normal circumstances, the majority of the letters to the commission are sent anonymously. However, Wang understood that a letter signed with a real name carried more weight and credibility, and could easily attract attention. After the letter was completed, he sent it via express mail to Beijing.

Wang also planned to travel to Beijing and seek meetings with either Zhou Yongkang or Li Keqiang, both Politburo Standing Committee members. There is no verification of whether Wang got to meet either of them. But a source inside the Public Security Ministry indicated that some of Wang's friends in Beijing dissuaded him from pressing for the meetings. They warned Wang that Bo had a vast network of powerful supporters and he was untouchable. If Bo found out about Wang's petition, Wang could disappear without a trace, like the people he himself had secretly imprisoned in the past. An article in the Hong Kong–based *Wai Can* magazine maintained that one of Bo's opponents in Beijing might have encouraged or given tacit approval to Wang's escape to the US Consulate: creating an international incident would be an effective way, perhaps the only way, to shake up Bo Xilai and save his own life. This article, whose claims have not been substantiated, highlighted what one analyst said: "A sad reality in China—unless a citizen enlists the help of Western powers, the system cannot protect him."

As Wang contemplated his next move, Bo Xilai plotted to have Wang killed, at least according to an official in Chongqing: Bo's aides designed three alternative plans to get rid of Wang. In the first, Wang would die a martyr's death—Bo Xilai would have him shot to death, making it look as though Wang was killed by a criminal organization that had "retaliated" against Wang's tough anticrime initiatives. In the second, Wang would die as a corrupt official who "killed himself" after the city launched an investigation into his personal finances. In the third, Wang would commit suicide due to severe depression from job-related stress. Of the three options, the third one allegedly gained the most votes.

Suicide from depression is common among leaders at all levels of the Chinese government. The Hong Kong–based *Oriental Daily* said more than 120 officials killed themselves while under investigation on corruption-related charges in 2003 alone. Ai Weiwei, the prominent Chinese artist and dissident, questioned the suicide phenomena. In a 2009 blog, Ai wrote, "Officials dying during investigations left no wills. The government sees no need to publicize the will or to conduct an autopsy. They always rule out homicide. Since there are so many gray areas, the circumstances leading to the deaths are murky."

Wang himself was very familiar with the practice of using mental disorder to get rid of political opponents. Human rights organizations claim that more than 1,300 people were locked up in mental institutions during Wang's reign. Although some detainees were religious activists or political dissidents, many were ordinary residents who had made negative comments on the Internet about Bo's anticrime initiatives or public welfare projects.

On February 4, a website posted an unnamed "doctor's diagnosis" of Wang's mental condition at a hospital attached to the Chongqing No. 3 Military Medical University. In the document, the doctor wrote that Wang had complained about "tremendous stress at work and long-term sleep deprivation" since 2011. He had to remain alert all the time and didn't dare sleep with the lights off. The doctor examined Wang and noticed he was lethargic and sometimes lacked coherence in his conversations. The diagnosis was severe depression. The document, dated February 4, two days after his removal, had neither a doctor's signature nor a file number. A day later, officials at the hospital openly denied the existence of such a diagnosis.

The hospital's denial did nothing to stop the speculation. During an interview, Su Tiecheng, a retired historian and the son of a Chinese military general, was quoted as saying:

> Based on reliable information I have obtained from Chongqing, the real reason for removing him from his position was his mental illness. . . . As the police chief of Chongqing, he has been under a lot of pressure and has received many death threats. He couldn't sleep for days. This lasted for quite a while. When he had a cold or fever, he refused to take the medicine that doctors prescribed for fear that he could be poisoned. He said frequently that people around him want

to kill him. He sometimes became suspicious when he saw a car with an unfamiliar license plate—thinking they were there to follow and assassinate him. At one time, he held a gun to his head for several minutes.

Seeing these online reports about his mental illness, Wang was said to fear for his life. He sensed that Bo was attempting to eliminate him by creating circumstances in which Wang's death would be unremarkable. He had to act fast and wisely to protect himself.

US CONSULATE UNDER SIEGE

SUN TZU, the ancient Chinese military general and strategist, once advised, "Of the thirty-six top stratagems, fleeing is the best." However, no matter where he ran in the vast country, Wang knew he would be caught. Bo had already ordered a watch on airports and railway stations. To save himself, and to turn the tables on Bo, he started to consider the foreign consulates in Chengdu.

Ironically, escaping to foreign embassies and consulates is a time-honored tradition in China, for both the persecuted and the persecutor. In the early days of the Communist movement in China, many leaders, who fiercely repudiated Western colonialists, constantly ran to the English and French concessions for help when they were being hunted by the Nationalist government. In most cases, asylum seekers succeeded because authorities were afraid of offending the Western powers with direct intervention.

After the Communists took over China in 1949, most Western democratic countries severed diplomatic ties with Beijing, and none existed except through back channels until China entered the United Nations and President Richard Nixon visited Beijing in the early 1970s. In the absence of foreign embassies and consulates, dissidents and those who had been persecuted during the Cultural Revolution had only one escape route, Hong Kong, which was British controlled and hosted foreign consulates from around the globe. But there was no guarantee of sanctuary. Many caught by the British were sent back to China. Ma Sicong, a famous violinist, escaped to the West with the help of the US Consulate in Hong Kong after his family was tortured by the Red Guards in 1967. One year later, Shen Yuan, a scholar in Beijing, disguised himself as an African and sneaked into the embassy of the Soviet Union, which had broken up with China in the early 1960s when Chairman Mao Zedong and Premier Nikita Khrushchev openly clashed over their interpretations of the Marxist ideology. The Soviet Embassy turned Shen over to the Chinese government, and Shen was executed.

On June 5, 1989, the day after the Chinese government brutally cracked down on protesters, a small but vocal prodemocracy movement drawn from Beijing's universities demanded an end to corruption and the abuses of power by party cadres; many fearing reprisals sought asylum. Fang Lizhi, an astrophysicist and vocal critic of the government, entered the US Embassy in Beijing and sought asylum for fear of political reprisal. But Fang's request was initially turned down. US officials feared that granting asylum to those on the Chinese government's most wanted list could complicate US–China relations. At the urging of senior officials at the State Department and the White House, the embassy changed its initial decision and granted Fang's request. Fang and his wife remained in the US Embassy for more than a year before they were allowed to leave China.

The US Embassy and its consulates are considered the last resort for political dissidents who face arrest and imprisonment from officials such as Wang. The dissidents believed that the US government had the clout to resist Chinese pressure and any such attempts could also trigger international media attention. Nobody expected that Wang would seek asylum with the Americans.

Over the years, Wang regularly issued harsh statements against the US and regularly persecuted pro-democracy activists in Chongqing. In October 2011, he referred to the US contemptuously as a country without history or friends, and strongly condemned those who betrayed their country, their (Communist) faith, and ethnicity.

However, in private, Wang had a secret fascination with the US. He displayed an MBA certificate from a US university in his office, even though the university was an unlicensed educational institution. In addition, a police officer in Tieling told the Chinese state media recently that Wang had harbored ideas of seeking asylum in the US Consulate in 1999, when he served as police chief of Tieling. At that time, he was facing two lawsuits from local residents. Several colleagues, including a close friend, had written multiple letters to Beijing, accusing him of using torture to extract confessions. The frustrated Wang Lijun pouted to his friends, "This country is hopeless. I want to seek asylum at the US Consulate."

That probably explained why Wang Lijun thought of the US Consulate again twelve years later. The timing couldn't have been better. Vice President Xi Jinping would be visiting the US within days and Wang figured the escape would attract major media attention to his case. With his flair for drama, Wang wanted a grand exit. Besides, he had already attempted—without success—to contact the British Consulate in Guangzhou in November 2011 to inform them of Neil Heywood's murder. He believed he would have a better chance at the US Consulate because he could provide valuable information to the US government.

On the morning of February 6, Wang phoned a close friend, Wang Pengfei, a district police chief. Pengfei had attended the prestigious China Criminal Police University and, on graduation, was assigned a job in Tieling. Under Wang's tutelage, Pengfei rose in the ranks and established himself as a top expert in criminal investigation. In 2011, Wang brought him to Chongqing to head the criminal investigation unit. It is not clear whether Wang ever briefed Pengfei on his escape plan. After Wang's defection, Bo kidnapped Pengfei, trying to find out what type of information Wang had delivered to the US Consulate.

A source in Beijing said Wang asked Pengfei to arrange a driver and an SUV, and to bring three new cell phones. In China, it is common for an official to carry multiple phones for different functions: for example, one specifically for the boss, one for the family, and one for his mistress and to keep in touch with sensitive contacts.

Wang wanted the phones for a very specific purpose. He typed up different messages exposing Bo's role in Heywood's death and stored them in each phone. In the event that his escape plan failed and he was abruptly killed, Wang urged his friend to give each phone to a trusted individual, who would release the messages at different times in the following week. A reporter with the *Southern Metropolis Daily* received a phone note from Wang three days after his defection that said, "Bo Xilai and his wife are connected with the murder of British businessman Neil Heywood."

Wang left with the driver Pengfei provided, and headed directly to Chengdu, the capital of Sichuan province. On the highway, he phoned a deputy director of the Sichuan provincial public security, saying that he needed a face-to-face meeting to discuss something very important. The deputy director drove to the highway exit to greet Wang. The two had lunch and Wang claimed he had been asked to brief American officials at the consulate about an urgent joint US–China antiterrorism program. Because he hadn't set up an appointment, Wang asked if the deputy director, a designated liaison with the US Consulate, could make the connection. The deputy director willingly obliged and phoned the consulate. At 2:30 P.M., Wang had walked into the American mission on Consulate Road in Chengdu. Consul General Peter Haymond was out of town. Two senior consulate officials greeted Wang. Without realizing the political storm that was about to erupt around them, US diplomats took Wang to the consulate's library rather than a safe room designed to block Chinese surveillance. The initial conversation centered on promoting further exchanges on antiterrorism initiatives. Then the political asylum request came up.

Western media and anonymous sources in Beijing and Chongqing provided more details. *Newsweek* reported:

> The American ambassador Gary Locke was at an afternoon meeting in Beijing, away from his office at the American Embassy, when he received a cryptic email on his BlackBerry: "Return to the embassy's secure communications area immediately." The ambassador rushed back. It was Feb. 6, and Locke was stunned to learn that a senior Chinese policeman had arrived at the U.S. Consulate in the southwestern city of Chengdu, telling officials there that he wanted to go to the U.S. because he feared for his life.
>
> Wang Lijun, known as the Eliot Ness of China for his ruthless campaign against organized crime, told a riveting story of how his

one-time mentor, a local party secretary by the name of Bo Xilai, was out to kill him because he knew too much about the alleged poisoning and murder of a British businessman, Neil Heywood, who had known Bo and his wife. It was "fascinating, eye-popping revelations," Locke said. "My first reaction was 'oh, my God,' I mean 'OH, MY GOD!'"

Bill Gertz with the *Washington Free Beacon,* a conservative online news service in the US, quoted a US official as saying that Wang had divulged information about the power struggle within the Politburo Standing Committee. Wang claimed that Zhou Yongkang and Bo Xilai had conspired to "upset the smooth succession of Xi Jinping," who was designated to be the party general secretary later in the year.

According to the *New York Times,* Wang sounded "agitated" and "incoherent" during the conversations, and "the American diplomats who oversaw his brief, bizarre stay pre-empted any formal application for asylum because of the difficulties of spiriting him out of the country and questions about his eligibility."

The US State Department and the White House might have underestimated the potential impact of Wang's action, mistakenly thinking that he was a mere regional official and that the information he offered held little value. More important, it happened a week before Xi Jinping's much-publicized visit to the US. "Granting asylum to Mr. Wang could have soured or scuttled Mr. Xi's trip," said the *New York Times.*

As a courtesy, a source said that US officials notified the Chinese Foreign Ministry of Wang's presence at the US Consulate.

In the end, Wang agreed that the best option was to hand himself over to authorities in Beijing. Consulate officials did allow Wang to use his phone to contact his friends in Beijing so he wouldn't end up in the hands of Bo Xilai's security forces. Wang reportedly got ahold of Zhou Yongkang, who informed Wang that a delegation had been dispatched from Beijing to meet him.

A Chinese official briefed on Wang's investigation claimed Wang had brought a suitcase containing documents detailing his own investigation of Neil Heywood's murder and the Bo family's attempts to transfer assets overseas. On learning his asylum request would not be granted, the paper said Wang did not hand over the documents. However, the *Wall Street Journal,* which quoted US officials who witnessed what had happened, reported that Wang might not have brought the documents. Before he left the consulate, Wang "slipped US diplomats the cell phone number of an accomplice" who could help produce the evidence about Heywood's murder:

> The US handed the cell phone number over to British diplomats and gave them instructions on how to track down the information from Wang's mysterious accomplice. The instructions included setting up an e-mail account under a designated name with a popular Chinese e-mail and messaging service. The British set up the account and texted the cell phone number. People involved gave conflicting accounts of the timing and whether the accomplice responded. For reasons that are unclear, the British never received the promised documents.

As Wang Lijun was spilling out the astonishing details about how Heywood was allegedly murdered, an equally captivating drama was unfolding outside the US Consulate.

The minute Wang had walked into the consulate, Chinese staff inside reported the information to officials at the Sichuan provincial State Security Department, who immediately alerted senior officials in Beijing, including Zhou Yongkang, who headed the Central Politics and Law Commission. Zhou telephoned Bo Xilai, urging Bo to "get Wang out at any cost."

The deputy director of the Sichuan provincial police department, who helped arrange Wang's meeting with US Consulate officials, also sensed that something had gone wrong after Wang failed to emerge from his private meeting after four hours. He reported Wang's activity to Liu Qibao, the Sichuan provincial party secretary, who promptly contacted senior leaders in Beijing. President Hu Jintao instructed Liu to send armed police to the US Consulate to prevent Wang Lijun from slipping away.

Meanwhile, the exasperated Bo Xilai decided to resolve the situation before Beijing could get its hands on the documents in Wang's possession. He first sent Huang Qifan, the mayor of Chongqing, to the consulate to bring Wang back. Huang hurried over with an assistant and requested a meeting with Wang inside. The mayor talked to Wang for nearly an hour, trying to persuade him to leave the consulate building, but Wang refused. No matter what promises the mayor made, Wang wouldn't return to Chongqing.

After sending the mayor to Chongqing, the hotheaded Bo also dispatched what many witnesses claimed were seventy cars carrying armed policemen to Chengdu, but the provincial armed police intercepted Bo's people five blocks away from the US Consulate. The two sides got into fierce arguments. A Chongqing police officer who witnessed the incident said Bo Xilai was sitting in one of the police cars. When Bo learned that the mayor failed to get Wang out, he turned hostile. With the excuse that the Chongqing police had received tips that terrorists had planted a bomb inside the US Consulate, Bo ordered his men to break the blockade set by the provincial police, force their way into the American mission, and seize Wang. As the confrontation was escalating, members of the US Marine Corps Embassy Security Group set up a line of defense inside. Three armed forces, each answering to a different command, buzzed around the consulate.

News of possible attacks on the US Consulate quickly reached President Hu Jintao, who was said to be alarmed by what he called an "armed revolt." He was also embarrassed and angry at Bo's reckless behavior, which had broken international laws and exposed the Communist Party's internal division to the outside world. President Hu personally phoned Liu Qibao, the Sichuan party secretary, requesting that he use whatever means possible to protect the US mission. Liu first ordered the provincial armed police to take up positions in front of the US Consulate, facing Bo's policemen. Then he cobbled together additional members of the armed police and the provincial State Security Department in Chengdu to keep Bo's police at bay. A retired US official who was briefed on the situation told me that about seven hundred police officers were outside the US Consulate that night.

To defuse tension, the Sichuan provincial policemen stationed in Chengdu even offered their counterparts in Chongqing local snacks and persuaded them not to act irrationally. The confrontation lasted five hours.

Around midnight on February 7, a small delegation, led by the deputy minister of state security, flew in to Chengdu and immediately headed to the consulate. They handed Wang a letter from Zhou Yongkang, who promised, "Your political career won't be affected and we'll protect your safety and conduct a fair investigation if you voluntarily leave." With asylum becoming a remote possibility, Wang saw Zhou's offer as his only choice. Before his departure, consular officials emphasized the US government would closely monitor his situation.

As Wang stepped out with officials from the State Security Ministry, China's intelligence agency, he caught a glimpse of the fully armed US Marines deployed inside the consulate walls and a large number of Chinese armed police outside. Wang must have realized the grave consequences of his action. As he was about to get in the car, Chongqing mayor Huang Qifan rushed over, trying to wrestle Wang away. The deputy minister from Beijing stopped him and in the process, the two men got into a scuffle. At one point, they parted and stood on opposite sides of the street, each contacting his respective boss. The deputy minister reached Zhou Yongkang, who in turn called Bo Xilai, asking him to withdraw. Bo ignored him. President Hu Jintao finally stepped in and phoned Bo, assuring him that Wang's attempted defection was an isolated incident and Wang's investigation would in no way affect Bo's work in Chongqing. Bo gave in and ordered his men to withdraw.

On the early morning of February 8, Wang left Consulate Road with officials from the State Security Ministry. Because the airport was closed, they stayed in a nearby hotel guarded by armed police from Sichuan province, and flew out when the airport opened.

In the afternoon, an airline insider posted online the scanned boarding passes of Wang and his handlers at the State Security Ministry, including the deputy minister. This revealed that Wang had taken China Airlines Flight 4113 for Beijing.

News about Wang's botched defection shocked his supporters. His trip to the consulate prompted Wei Ke, a well-known cartoonist, to post a sarcastic comment online:

In the future, if any of those damn officials wish to escape, don't go to the US Consulate. Didn't you all hate Americans? Haven't you deceived a large number of young pigheaded lackeys to rally around your anti-American causes? Why don't you run to your North Korean friends? I advise US officials to kick out any bastards who show up in the future.

After Wang was taken away to Beijing, his friends and foes continued to battle fiercely in the blogosphere. Insiders in Beijing fed startling information to overseas media to dispel the myth of Wang as a national anti-crime hero and silence his supporters.

For example, on April 11, both Boxun and Hong Kong-based *Wai Can* carried articles on Wang's surveillance programs. In the name of combating crime, an insider said Wang had partnered with the president of the Beijing University of Post and Telecommunications, one of the architects of China's notorious Internet censoring system—the "Great Firewall"—and set up an extensive surveillance system that involved wiretaps and monitoring of Internet communications in 2009. Wang had bugged the phones of several senior leaders during their visits to Chongqing.

Wang found out that President Hu Jintao communicated regularly via a secure hotline with his friend Liu Guanglei, who served on the Chongqing Municipal Party Standing Committee. He began to wiretap their conversations. The surveillance device was later uncovered by the technical staff at the Central Party Committee's general office. Tapping leadership phones is considered the number-one taboo in Beijing. In the Mao era, Yang Shangkun, who served as Mao's chief of staff in the 1960s, installed listening devices in Mao's train cars and recorded Mao's many womanizing activities. Yang ended up with severe punishment during the Cultural Revolution. The source who supplied the story surmised that Wang would be dealt with similarly.

After the story was released, I interviewed an IT expert, who did not think the surveillance was technically possible. So, I posted his comments as a follow-up to Wang's wiretapping story, questioning the authenticity of what had been reported. However, the subsequent indictment against Wang Lijun showed that the insider's information was largely accurate. According to the court, Wang had violated the country's laws and regulations "by using technical reconnaissance measures on a number of people since 2010, either without the approval of authorities or by forging approval documents."

In an article by *Nandu Weekly*, a popular newspaper owned by the one of the most liberal newspaper chains in Guangzhou, the Chongqing police department, under Wang Lijun, budgeted more than US $300 million to purchase surveillance equipment from Germany and Israel, and to construct what Wang describes as the "Big Intelligence Center." At a conference in January 2010, Wang bragged that his "Big Intelligence Center" could check the whole population in China in 12.5 minutes. In addition, if a targeted person surfed the Internet, bought an airline ticket, or shopped with credit cards, police would have that information immediately. The Chongqing police could also use GPS technology to monitor the activities of criminals and political dissidents. During the Chinese New Year celebration in 2010, about 4,000 out-of-towners with criminal records entered the city of Chongqing. Within six hours, police tracked down 3,400 of them and advised them to leave Chongqing.

In addition, an official in Chongqing told *Mingjing News* that Wang lived a decadent lifestyle: he wore a watch that cost 500,000 yuan (US $80,000), and he collected limited editions of name-brand suits, with one costing 200,000 yuan (US $32,000). When workers moved him out of the police chief's office, they had prepared forty boxes to package his personal belongings but ended up using eighty, the majority of those boxes containing expensive gifts. In 2010, Wang set up the "Heroes and Martyrs Fund" with money he had confiscated or extorted from private businesspeople and relatives of those who had been arrested or detained. The foundation, which was supposed to provide financial subsidies for families of police officers who had been killed in the line of duty, sometimes sponsored Wang's pet projects. One time he purchased hundreds of tickets with the foundation money for a concert given by a singer who was known to be former president Jiang Zemin's favorite. Many of these corruption-related claims, which were initially discarded as rumors, appeared in Wang's indictment. However, Bo supporters also dished out bogus claims to discredit his records.

On February 13, I received an e-mail from a source in Chongqing, who rehashed the story that Wang suffered from intermittent delusional disorder. He said Wang was neurotic and paranoid, and had become obsessed with his security matters. Each time he went on an inspection, he would use a helicopter, even for trips of less than thirty kilometers. When he moved around in the city, he would be escorted by a large contingent of police cars. When he stayed at a hotel, his bodyguards, most of whom were female in red uniforms, were stationed in the hallway.

Another source provided a similar example to illustrate Wang's mental disorder. On January 6, 2012, a thief killed a customer in front of a bank in the southern city of Nanjing, snatching 200,000 yuan. Subsequent investigation found that the same person had perpetrated similar crimes in two other cities, including Chongqing, killing seven people, injuring two, and stealing 480,000 yuan in cash. The Ministry of Public Security ordered police chiefs in the three cities to coordinate their investigations and capture the criminal before he killed again. Over the course of the investigation, the police chief in Nanjing received a call from Wang, who claimed to have caught the suspect. Excited by the news, the Nanjing police chief flew over to Chongqing, only to find that it was only Wang's fantasy.

"If he truly suffered from a mental disorder, why would the leadership cover up his medical condition and continue to allow him to work in such an important law enforcement position?" I asked.

My source didn't answer.

These mental disorder claims were said to have prompted Hu Jintao's chief of staff to order doctors at a psychiatric hospital to assess Wang's mental fitness after he arrived in Beijing. But, from his meticulously planned escape to his calculated testimony at his subsequent trial, one could see that Wang Lijun was not only mentally competent, but also possessed the acumen of a seasoned politician who, when cornered, successfully created an international incident to destroy his enemy and save his life.

"INVITING THE GENTLEMAN TO THE URN"

IN 700 CE, when China was under the reign of Empress Wu Zetian, there lived a man called Lai Shijun, who served as the imperial censor, in today's terms the minister of justice. A devoted supporter of the empress, Lai used extreme means to torture and persecute political opponents or outspoken court officials who dared challenge the empress.

Lai's power grew significantly and he was said to have personally retained a staff of several hundred men whose jobs were to make false reports against other officials. Lai even cowrote a book known as the *Classic of Accusation*, teaching his subordinates how to accuse people of crimes and how to create details to make an alleged plot appear logical and likely.

Legend has it that Lai invited a senior military officer to dinner one day. Over the course of the meal, Lai posed a seemingly innocuous question: "It is very hard nowadays to get criminals to confess. Do you have an idea on how to get them to open their mouths?" The general responded, "That's easy. Find a big urn, gather a pile of wooden sticks, set them on fire, and put the urn on top of the fire. Then you put the accused in the urn. I'm sure it will get them to talk." Lai nodded and beckoned to his assistants. Soon they brought in a big urn and put it on top of the stove. Lai turned to the general: "Her Majesty has received reports that you are plotting against her. What do you say if I ask you to get into the urn?" The general trembled in fear, knelt, and confessed.

In later years, Lai became more emboldened and began to target the crown prince and the empress's daughters, charging them with treason. His blatant accusations angered other royal family members who felt threatened and decided to ally themselves against Lai. Using the same schemes that Lai outlined in his book, several members of the royal family reported that Lai was planning a coup and eventually convinced the empress to condemn Lai to death. Following Lai's execution, people on the street celebrated and Lai's former victims were said to have cut out his flesh and organs, consuming them in retaliation.

Lai's story gave rise to the Chinese proverb "Invite the gentleman into the urn"—meaning put a person into the trap he himself had set.

In addition to Lai, another often-cited *kuli* was Shang Yang, who lived in the kingdom of Qin around 395 BCE. As an adviser to the king, Shang encouraged economic development and implemented tough legal measures, including torture and severe physical punishment, to keep law and order. He specifically targeted the old aristocratic families. A prince's nose was cut off after he was found violating the law. Shang's policies helped rejuvenate morale and the economy. However, after the king died, Shang lost favor with the new ruler. His former political enemies retaliated by ordering the execution of Shang and his family, on the charge that he had attempted to foment rebellion. Shang tried to hide at a hotel, but the hotel owner refused to take him in because it was against the law to admit a guest without proper identification, a law Shang himself had promulgated. Shang was executed by dismemberment—he was fastened to five chariots and his body was torn into pieces, and his whole family was killed or buried alive.

As people started to reflect on the fates of Wang and Wen, several Chinese political commentators compared Wang with Lai and Shang, who were known in history as *kulis*—an ancient term referring to imperial officials or police officers who employed extreme means of torture and brutality to help their masters maintain power. The word was coined by a Chinese historian, Sima Qian, 2,000 years ago when he compiled a biographical sketch of ten notorious *kulis* in the Han Dynasty.

In his blog, contemporary historian Li Xianzheng described what he called "three common characteristics" of *kulis*:

First, *kulis* flourished under the authoritarian political system. Rulers employed cruel and extreme means to intimidate the public and maintain their control without regard for the law. During political struggles, which were common under a totalitarian system, different political factions hired *kulis* to protect their interests by torturing and randomly assassinating opponents.

Second, *kulis* were closely associated with despotic kings or political leaders. For example, notorious *kulis* emerged during the time of

Emperor Wu in the Han Dynasty and Empress Wu Zetian in the Tang Dynasty, both of whom were notorious for their tyrannical, cruel, and suspicious nature. On their way to the throne, they both hired *kulis* to help them consolidate power. During the reigns of Emperor Wu and Wu Zetian, thousands of innocent officials died in the hands of *kulis*.

Third, most *kulis* met tragic endings. The majority of them had risen from humble origins and acquired power through their attachment and loyalty to an influential political figure. As enforcers of the law, they were known for their uprightness and uncanny problem-solving abilities. They made their names by fighting the wealthy and the powerful, and bullies. However, they soon became assimilated into the system and turned into bullies themselves. To their victims, they were conniving, corrupt, ruthless, and misanthropic. Their brutality and corruption caused deep enmity, which ultimately contributed to their fall. Throughout history, notorious *kulis* in China were either discarded by their masters when they became a liability or persecuted by a stronger *kuli* with more power.

China's emperors were deposed and the monarchic system was abolished a hundred years ago, but the totalitarian system remains the same. Communist officials such as Bo Xilai rule like emperors. It is not surprising that *kulis* continue to flourish and fall.

IN THE CASE OF WANG LIJUN, author Ji Weiren, who wrote *China Coup*, a book published in Hong Kong about Bo Xilai, noted:

> There is no doubt that Wang Lijun used to be a cop hero. He battled against organized crimes in society and fought his own internal demons. However, he did not realize that he gradually turned into one of the people he had executed. For years, Wang Lijun acted like he had unlimited power. He could file a criminal case or dismiss one as he wished. He could put surveillance on anyone as he wished. He could detain or release anyone as he wished. When he imprisoned other officials for embezzling public funds, he himself took hundreds of thousands of dollars in bribes. When he learned that the

wife of his protector had perpetrated a murder, he felt no qualms about covering up and destroying evidence.

In July 2010, the day before Wang put Wen Qiang, his predecessor at the Chongqing Municipal Public Security Bureau and an anticrime hero like him, on death row, Wang held an hourlong conversation during which Wen was said to have told Wang, "In a few years, you'll end up like me. I know it."

Upon hearing Wen's words posted posthumously online, Professor He Weifang with Beijing University also posted an open letter to Wang Lijun in April 2011. He warned:

> If the government employs means that are illegal, such as extraction of confession by torture, violating suspects' rights in litigation, or even intimidating lawyers for the defense in criminal cases, the future consequences of this will be serious. Employing illegal means to strike out against illegal elements leaves people with the unfortunate impression that might is right, that injustices can be used to deal with injustices.
>
> One important measure of rule of law in a country is the limiting of police power by the courts. Police must respect the courts, and they must accept the independent examination and supervision of prosecutors, and protect the independence of courts and judges.
>
> Actually, respect for judicial independence is just as important for those who hold major power in their hands. While he was still in favor, Wen Qiang no doubt had little idea of the value of this independence, but once he had fallen afoul of the authorities, he must have had a rude awakening, realizing only too well that without judicial independence, no one at all is safe.

Professor He's words proved to be prescient. Wang's own fall came eighteen months after Wen Qiang's.

As the police chief in Chongqing, Wang Lijun constantly had criminal suspects or political dissidents "disappear" for months without telling their relatives where they were imprisoned. During his investigation, he was afforded the same treatment. Wang's wife and his brother, Wang Lihui, who headed the security department at a mining company in Liaoning province, flew to Chongqing in February, requesting information about Wang's whereabouts from the Chongqing Municipal Public Security Bureau. Officials shunned them. The two traveled to Beijing and learned only that "we have nothing to share with you at the moment." Without any leads as to Wang's personal safety, Wang's father reportedly fell ill, refusing to believe that his son had taken refuge at the US Consulate. One of his relatives complained to an overseas media outlet, "This is an unfair system and I guess we just have to deal with it."

During Wang's incarceration, many analysts and Wang's victims had speculated and hoped that he would receive tougher sentencing. A journalist in Beijing stated her reasons: "Since the Communist takeover, Wang Lijun's defection was unprecedented. The leadership will have to punish Wang Lijun severely to stop future copycats within the Party. Moreover, when Wang served as the police chief in Tieling and Chongqing, more than eight hundred people were executed. While some deserved the death penalty, many were deprived of due process. Wang's hands are stained with blood. Third, as the head of law enforcement, he committed a serious offense by covering up Gu Kailai's [crime]. Lastly, while many senior leaders hate Bo, they feel equally threatened by Wang's betrayal. They wonder if their own subordinates are also secretly plotting against them."

Fortunately for Wang, he fared better in the end. His highly publicized defection at the US Consulate made it hard for his foes to execute him in secret and ignore proper legal procedures. In addition, investigators at the State Security Ministry, China's KGB, adopted a relatively humane approach to gain Wang's active cooperation—his testimony helped convict Gu Kailai and will be critical to the pending trial of Bo Xilai. Politically, Wang's defection and his revelations of Heywood's murder provided ample justification for the leadership to oust a formidable foe before the Party Congress.

In September 2012, Wang stood trial on charges of bending the law for selfish ends, defection, abuse of power, and bribe-taking in Chengdu, where the US Consulate is located. He received a sentence of fifteen years, but not the suspended death penalty for which many of his victims had hoped.

"Wang's lighter sentencing has offered us a valuable lesson," wrote Li Gang, a Chinese blogger. "For senior Communist Party officials, when you deliver your anti-American speeches during the day, don't forget to figure out the exact location of your nearest US Consulate after you get home at night. If you have offended your boss, the party won't be able to protect you. Run to the US Consulate, creating an international incident. In this way, you can effectively destroy your boss and save your life."

Even before his sentencing, the city where Wang ruled as police chief for three years launched a cleansing campaign, both physically and metaphorically. Starting in March 2012, many of the glowing media reports about Wang's heroic deeds were expunged, his portrait inside the Municipal Public Security Bureau complex was taken down, and the two eagle statues in front of the office building have been removed—Wang used to compare himself to an eagle flying over the Mongolian prairie. Two of Wang's handwritten quotes in large wooden frames used to hang inside the building for the bureau's investigative team. "We promote the interests of ordinary people through every small thing we do," said one, and the other, "Each single one of our actions is as critical as life." Now they are gone.

In May, as more scandals of illegal detention and the use of torture during Wang's rule surfaced, the new leaders of the Chongqing government announced the municipality was investigating each charge and any police involved in mistreating suspects should come forward and confess.

Wang's former friends and confidantes, who had been transferred from northeast China, have been either detained or convicted. Since his arrival in Chongqing, about 1,800 police officers were fired or sent to reeducation camps. Fear pervaded the police force. When news of Wang's "vocational style" treatment was announced in February, many police officers could not contain their excitement. The lit firecrackers and drank champagne at home to celebrate his departure, despite the new leadership in Chongqing specifically banning any form of celebration. As of now, about 80 percent of the officers who lost their jobs have been reinstalled.

Meanwhile, the Chongqing municipal court reversed its verdict against Fang Hong, who had served one year at a reeducation camp for calling Wang's lawsuits against a defense lawyer "a pile of shit" on a Weibo posting in April 2011. At present, many businesspeople who were convicted for or charged with colluding with organized crime are now petitioning the government to revisit their cases. The government has also returned previously seized assets and properties to some of Wang's victims, even though a large amount of the money originally taken by police has inexplicably disappeared.

Wang's supporters remained unswayed by these changes. Between February and September 2012, blogs were swamped with pro-Wang comments. A person from Huaihua city, Hunan province, wrote, "The state media are demonizing Wang, portraying him as a ruthless devil. Ordinary people are not easily deceived. Many still have sympathy for him. He might have problems, but he was one of the officials who truly sought justice for people." When my co-author visited Chongqing in November 2012, a resident at a petrol station in the city's Yubei district said, "Wang Lijun is a hero. He helped us wipe out corrupt officials and greedy businessmen. We need Wang Lijun . . . because we have too many corrupt officials in this country and we are short of people like Wang Lijun. The government propagates on TV and in newspapers every day about serving people's interest, but how many officials truly care about ordinary people? After Wang Lijun's downfall, the crime rates have gone up and bad guys are back with a vengeance."

Many political commentators also defended Wang's legacy: "Regardless of what Wang has done in the past and regardless how radical and reckless he was during the so-called anti–organized crime campaign, he has successfully used the Neil Heywood murder case to stop the radical Left from assuming a position at the Politburo Standing Committee and prevented the emergence of another Mao," Fang Yan, a Beijing-based journalist, wrote on *Mingjing News*. "In this sense, Wang Lijun's dramatic, three-year stint in Chongqing and his melodramatic exit changed the future of Chinese politics and contemporary Chinese history. This is something neither we nor Wang could have expected."

My favorite was a comment by a resident in Chengdu:

I advise the US Consulate to open a new window for senior government officials at the visa section to handle their walk-in political asylum requests. Wang Lijun was not the last one. More Wang Lijuns are waiting in line.

Even though Wang Lijun's supporters are still vigorously defending his legacy, they agree on one undisputable fact—their hero was a mere *kuli*, who, like many before him, was destined to become a pawn in a larger political intrigue. In an editorial I wrote on February 12, 2012, one week after Wang Lijun's flight to the US Consulate, I predicted:

At this moment, Wang Lijun is firmly under the control of the secret political machine in Beijing and we are awaiting the Party to cook up some convincing explanations for Wang Lijun's actions. At the same time, we shouldn't forget that the episode inside the US Consulate is only a prelude to a bigger political drama. The main characters have not yet revealed themselves. The senior leaders are frantically scripting and plotting the next episode, which, I am certain, will bring more political surprises. So, sit back and enjoy the show.

PART II

Tai

Zi

Dang

The Princelings

Princelings, or *tai zi dang,* refers to children of senior government officials and revolutionaries who fought in the early days of the revolution.

SITTING TIGHT ON THE FISHING BOAT

DIAN LAKE, the "Sparkling Pearl" in China's southwestern Yunnan-Guizhou Plateau, is a large inland body of freshwater reaching an elevation of more than 1,886 meters and covering 306 kilometers. With the misty mountain forest in the west, the lake looks idyllic in the warm winter sun. Every year, its rich aquatic resources and the perpetual spring weather attract large flocks of seagulls from Russia.

On February 8, tourists tossing bread crumbs at the Russian seagulls on the shores of Dian Lake spotted a familiar figure: Bo Xilai, the Communist Party secretary of Chongqing, whose name had become the most searched online after Wang Lijun's flight to the US Consulate only days earlier. Accompanied by two deputy party chiefs from Yunnan, Bo leisurely fed the seagulls fluttering around him. "It is amazing that there is such a huge lake on the plateau," said the tall, handsome, and photogenic Bo, dubbed by many reporters as the

John F. Kennedy of China, to a television reporter. The 63-year-old Bo behaved like a tourist who had stumbled on an unexpected piece of treasure. "It is a crown jewel for the nearby city of Kunming," he said.

Local TV reported that Bo had led a Chongqing delegation to neighboring Yunnan to "learn from each other and to promote regional economic cooperation." At an herbal medicinal shop, he praised the local leaders for commercializing the rich herbal resources in Yunnan and urged the company to set up stores in Chongqing. As Bo moved around Yunnan, political observers tried to decode everything he said or did to find clues as to what was happening. One online posting described Bo's trip as "Sitting tight in the fishing boat despite the rising wind and waves"—a well-known proverb that Mao Zedong constantly quoted in his articles to admonish Communist leaders to act confidently during times of trouble. To many, Bo's tour conveyed the impression that he was unaffected by the political storm swirling around him and he was invincible to attack.

One imaginative blogger even saw Bo's playful bird-feeding as a sign of defiance against those in Beijing who were said to have questioned his role in the US Consulate fiasco. In Chinese, the words for bird-feeding sound the same as "I'm not fucking afraid."

But beneath his seemingly jovial, even defiant appearance, Bo was afraid and concerned. After the attempted defection by his police chief was made public, there were many reports on Weibo and in the overseas Chinese-language media that Wang had told the Americans about how Bo had conspired with Zhou Yongkang, a member of the Politburo Standing Committee and planned to stage a coup to unseat Xi Jinping, the designated leader of the Party, before the upcoming Party Congress. One report stated that Bo's wife had taken bribes and moved 100 million yuan of assets abroad. Bo's playboy son, Guagua, had attended Oxford and then Harvard University with tuition paid from bribe money. At that time, the death of British businessman Neil Heywood had not yet been made public. Those media reports, mostly based on different sources inside the party, set in motion wild speculation about Bo's political future. Several political analysts, such as Gao Yu, a renowned journalist in Beijing, predicted that Bo's days as a Politburo member were numbered.

On February 9, the *Chongqing Daily,* the Communist Party paper in Bo's home city, carried a 2,000-word feature about Bo's activities in Yunnan. The article mentioned briefly that Bo had stopped by a military exhibit at the 14th Group Army, which is based near Kunming, the capital city of Yunnan. Interestingly, a national newspaper editor picked up on that detail and played up its possible significance. The 14th Group Army, with about 50,000 personnel, traces its lineage to China's resistance war against Japan in the late 1930s, when Bo's father was one of its founding commanders. The editor posted the *Chongqing Daily* story under a new headline: "Bo Xilai Visits Military History Exhibition at Kunming Military Unit to Commemorate Revolutionary Veterans." As expected, the headline stoked a new round of speculation. An unnamed military officer told the *Wall Street Journal* that Bo Xilai appeared to be flaunting his influence and courting support from his father's friends in the army.

An official in Chongqing said this was an unfair characterization of Bo's intentions. The trip to Kunming and the visit to the military museum had been on Bo's schedule for months. Because Bo was a Politburo member, he was accorded special treatment—the key leaders of Yunnan province accompanied him throughout the trip. The visit to the military museum was purely ceremonial, the official said, and Bo hardly knew the commander. Bo's father had retired in the 1990s and died in 2007. All of Bo's father's friends had long since left the military.

The insider also mentioned the embattled Bo had intended to cancel his Yunnan trip after the crisis broke out. He was to fly to Beijing instead to meet with the Central Party Committee and explain Wang's situation. But President Hu Jintao and other leaders turned down his request, saying his appearance in the capital could generate unnecessary attention and that he should come in March when the National People's Congress would be in session. Meanwhile, a friend of Bo's, who acted as a conduit between him and President Hu Jintao's office, told Bo to go to Yunnan as planned. The friend would fly in to brief Bo on Beijing's view relating to Wang's case and advise him on what to do next. The faraway province of Yunnan was a perfect venue for such secret discussions—we found out later that the meeting had been arranged by President Hu's chief of staff, Ling Jihua, also a Bo family friend.

At the meeting, Bo received a stern message from Beijing: He needed to control the situation in Chongqing, making sure that nothing jeopardized Vice President Xi Jinping's pending trip to the US or derailed the scheduled leadership transition later in the year. In return, President Hu Jintao and the Politburo Standing Committee might limit the scope of Wang's investigation.

An official at the Central Commission for Discipline Inspection told me that President Hu Jintao, known for his prudence and his uncanny ability to navigate political intrigue, reportedly expressed initial ambivalence about punishing Bo. His tenure as the Communist Party chief would extend only until the end of 2012 and he wanted a peaceful handover to his successor without triggering an implosion in the party due to pent-up internal conflicts. Besides, Hu was sympathetic with much of Bo's leftist ideology, and he too harbored a deep nostalgia for the Mao era. In addition, Hu felt the rise of Bo, regarded as something of a wild stallion, could check and challenge the powers of his successor, Xi Jinping, who belonged to a different faction within the party. Any challenge to Xi could benefit Hu's friends after his retirement.

The account by the Beijing official about President Hu's position proved to be accurate. Over the next week, the Chinese president said on several public occasions that Wang's defection was "an isolated incident," implying that Bo was not involved. When Huang Qifan, the Chongqing mayor, flew to Beijing in late February, President Hu met with him and reiterated his earlier promise.

At the same time, Bo was said to have reached out to his friends in Beijing, who vowed to help, including Ling Jihua and Zhou Yongkang, who had reportedly tapped Bo as his successor at the Politburo Standing Committee. Zhou had a hidden reason to back Bo—his son operated several business ventures in Chongqing and had benefited from Bo's generous patronage.

These reassurances restored Bo's confidence and allowed him to believe he would survive the crisis. A source in Chongqing said Bo became cocky. He even wrote a letter to President Hu Jintao, saying he welcomed an investigation by the Central Party Committee and if investigators found any wrongdoing, he would resign and take full responsibility.

But Bo had grossly underestimated the situation.

"HELLO, DEAR, IT'S YOUR WIFE CALLING"

FOR TWO WEEKS every March, more than 3,000 delegates and hundreds of media organizations converge on Beijing for the National People's Congress (NPC), and the capital enters a period of heightened security. Police round up petitioners who have come to Beijing with grievances, and Tiananmen Square is heavily patrolled to prevent any disruptions that might attract negative media coverage.

Under the Chinese constitution, the NPC is the top legislative body in China. Whereas Western legislators debate their laws in ornate ancient or contemporary parliamentary buildings, Chinese NPC delegates meet in the Great Hall of the People on the western edge of Tiananmen Square, a gigantic concrete auditorium built in the functional style architecture of the former Soviet Union and devoid of any aesthetic appeal. Delegates review the annual government report, pass legislation, and formalize appointments of government officials.

Several years ago, a Chinese website posted a series of pictures depicting the behaviors of legislators in different countries: in Turkey, a suited legislator is seen climbing onto the podium with a dozen others pulling his legs from behind; in Mexico, one legislator punches another in the face; in Japan, a female legislator rides on the shoulders of her supporters as others throw pens and paper at her; and in India, a female lawmaker slaps her colleague with a shoe. The site showed two pictures of China's NPC—in one, delegates are sound asleep in different poses, as one might see on a long-distance flight. In another picture, with a panoramic view, hundreds of delegates raise their hands in total conformity.

The two images of Chinese lawmakers mirror reality. Since the Communist takeover in 1949, the NPC has been considered a "rubber-stamp" parliament, passing virtually every measure, resolution, and law drafted and presented by government agencies and party organizations. Over the past decade, as the party has attempted to build and promote the "rule of law," the NPC has seen an increase in its legislative functions. Discussion is becoming more lively, and sometimes vigorous. The government media, which occasionally broadcasts NPC proceedings, may focus its cameras on some token "no" or abstention votes. But until China's one-party system is changed, conformity is the norm and everything that happens in the NPC is choreographed. One retired official who had served on the NPC for fifty-seven years recently told the media that she was proud to have never cast a single dissenting vote. "We were chosen by the party and we should support the party," she said.

There was a whiff of excitement and a hint of drama on March 3, 2012, at the opening ceremony of the Chinese People's Political Consultative Conference, a token political advisory body that holds its session simultaneously with the NPC. As the delegates came on stage, Bo was last in line, straightening to attention as the national anthem began playing. He was dressed in a black suit, white shirt, and blue tie with white dots. He sat in the second row, on the left side of the podium as viewed from the audience. Cameras started to flash, their white lights throwing a halo especially around Bo. He appeared poised, with a slight smile. After sitting, he did not bother to greet his neighbor, Xu Caihou, vice chairman of the Central Military Commission. Instead, Bo waved to people he recognized in the audience.

It was his first national appearance since the Wang scandal had broken a month before. The media and the public were looking for clues as to whether he was in trouble, whether he was about to fall, and if he fell, how far.

When the chairman of the People's Political Consultative Conference launched his opening speech, Bo fidgeted, looking bored and distracted. Occasionally he would gaze around,, shooting a glance or two at the media booths in the lower balcony, or tapping his fingers on his right thigh. Twenty minutes into the speech, Bo seemed to realize that he had some work to do. He took out his reading glasses from his coat pocket and began reviewing the written speech being read out in front of him and marking on it with a pencil. Moments before the ceremony adjourned, Bo stuffed stacks of documents into his bulky briefcase and left—some say "bolted from"—the stage while the other Politburo members stood and stretched, and lingered to chat with their colleagues. Reporters were outwitted and cross that they had let Bo slip away. A media manhunt ensued, during which several Hong Kong journalists discovered that, to avoid attention, members of the Chongqing delegation were not staying at any of the NPC-designated hotels.

On the afternoon of March 5, delegates from Chongqing gathered in small groups to review the government's annual work report. Bo led the discussions in his group and took the opportunity to propagate his views on a popular topic: achieving common prosperity. Thirty years after China's economic reforms, Bo said, income disparities between peasants and urban residents and between the wealthy and the poor had widened dramatically and needed government attention. Problems relating to the distribution of wealth had impeded consumption, stunted social development, and created anger among citizens. He urged the leadership to adopt different policies for different income levels to create a fair system. "Common prosperity, in my understanding, is a core value of socialism," he said. "While encouraging competition, we should also pay attention to social fairness and care about the lives of middle- and low-income families." Using his experience in Chongqing as an example, he said creating incentives for development should not be the government's sole target. "Shared prosperity can go hand in hand with China's rapid speed of development."

In his speech, widely reported by the government media, Bo defended his record in Chongqing, where he said the GDP in 2011 and the annual income for peasants and urban residents had doubled since 2007, when he had officially assumed the top leadership position there. The city had achieved an annual growth rate of 15.7 percent, and foreign investment increased 9.6 percent every year, to 10.6 billion yuan in 2011.

For a while, it seemed Bo had everything under control. However, on the morning of March 8, delegates from Chongqing who gathered after breakfast for the second plenary meeting noticed their party boss was missing. Delegates contacted Bo's security staff but could not reach anyone. Mayor Huang Qifan suspected something had gone awry. Could it be that the Central Party Committee had taken Bo away for questioning the night before? Had Bo escaped abroad? According to a Chongqing delegate, the mayor looked visibly disoriented and immediately contacted several senior leaders, inquiring in a round-about way whether Bo had been called to an urgent meeting. No, he had not, Huang Qifan was told. President Hu Jintao's office had ordered the Central Guard Bureau to check for Bo's name on all over-seas and domestic flights. Nothing turned up.

By late morning, the Beijing Capital International Airport had alerted the senior leadership that Bo Xilai and his bodyguards had flown to Chongqing on the private jet of Xu Ming, CEO of the Dalian-based Shide Group. Bo claimed he needed to take care of some "important matters." His conspicuous absence at the NPC plenary ses-sion was said to have infuriated Premier Wen Jiabao, who was presid-ing that morning, and sparked a renewed wave of speculation among reporters. One newspaper in Hong Kong said on its website that Bo had an emergency meeting with his close friends in Chongqing because he had received news that he would be under investigation.

In the afternoon, Bo jetted back to Beijing and appeared at a group meeting. On TV, he looked tired. His friend Zhou Yongkang, a Politburo Standing Committee member, surprised the media by showing up at the Chongqing meeting. In a brief speech, Zhou rec-ognized Chongqing's economic achievement and heaped praise on Bo's anticrime initiatives. Many Bo supporters were relieved. "Zhou's unwavering support showed that Bo could be spared the fall-out from the Wang incident," declared a commentator on the BBC's Chinese Service.

The next day, the Chongqing delegation had an open house. Bo and Mayor Huang Qifan held a press briefing in a conference room with 150 preregistered journalists. Those without tickets waited anxiously outside. It was Bo's first press conference since the Wang Lijun incident in February. A NPC delegate told me Bo had been asked explicitly to strictly follow the talking points and not to go into details about the former police chief or corruption allegations against his family. At the beginning, Bo did as he was told. When a reporter asked what would happen to Wang Lijun, Bo waved a piece of paper and read off from it several lines, urging journalists to report it verbatim:

> Wang Lijun is now being investigated by the Central Party Committee and the investigation has made progress. He has asked for a leave of absence and will not attend the NPC session. His issues are being handled carefully and we will publicize the results once the investigation concludes.

Reporters, especially those from Hong Kong, pursued the topic relentlessly. One asked if Mayor Huang Qifan had gone to the US Consulate with truckloads of armed police and attempted to abduct Wang Lijun.

Huang called the allegations pure fabrication, insisting that he had traveled to Chengdu by himself. But he acknowledged he had held an hourlong conversation with Wang Lijun inside the US Consulate. "I learned about his situation during our conversation and persuaded him to leave the consulate," Huang explained. "He was willing to come with us. The reports about his voluntary leave after staying in the US Consulate for thirty-three hours are true. Nobody forced him, and I was incapable of forcing him."

Bo continued to address the topic of Wang by recognizing his tremendous contribution to Chongqing's "Smashing Black" campaign. He lied to the reporters that taking away the police chief's position from Wang was part of a bigger plan to promote Wang to a more senior position. "His escape came as a total surprise," Bo said.

A reporter with *United Morning News*, a Singaporean newspaper that had numerous joint media projects with the city of Chongqing in the past, inquired if Wang Lijun was mentally ill. Bo evaded the question by admitting that he hadn't seen any warning signs. He blamed himself for hiring the wrong person. "It shows that we need to take precautions regardless of how well things are going. On the other hand, we should not be discouraged by these unexpected events. When it happens, we just need to reflect on our mistakes."

One Hong Kong reporter asked if Bo had submitted a resignation letter to the Politburo and whether his disappearance the previous day had anything to do with the Wang Lijun incident.

Bo vehemently characterized the resignation as pure fabrication, a rumor and a lie. He said his absence the previous day was due to a cough. "I didn't realize so many people were concerned about me and speculated over my whereabouts," he quipped. Bo's remarks contradicted the Chongqing government spokesperson, who had said the day before that Bo's absence had nothing to do with health issues.

When a Voice of America reporter asked whether Bo was under investigation, he responded emphatically, "No, no."

Two hours into the press conference, Bo and Mayor Huang Qifan had fielded more than twenty questions. Unlike other senior leaders who appeared stiff and packed their comments with meaningless jargon, Bo looked relaxed and confident even when he was telling lies about his "cough" and about Wang Lijun. Reporters occasionally laughed at his jokes and his straightforward answers.

In the middle of the press conference, the phone in Bo's pocket rang. He excused himself awkwardly and disappeared into an adjoining room, leaving the mayor alone at the podium. About fifteen minutes later, Bo rejoined Mayor Huang and switched topics. His mood changed and he launched a tirade against the media for what he called "throwing dirty water" onto him and his family:

> Some reports say that my son, who is studying abroad, lives a lavish lifestyle and drives a red Ferrari. It's pure nonsense. My wife and I do not own [many] personal assets. My wife used to be a lawyer [with] a very successful practice. Later, we worried that people might spread rumors, accusing us of making money through her law firm, so she closed all of her offices. That was twenty years ago. Now she stays home and takes care of house chores. I'm very touched by her sacrifice. Someone says that my son has attended prestigious Oxford and Harvard, and asks how we have the money to pay for tuition. He is supported by scholarships. I've clarified that many times.

Bo's remarks, most of which have subsequently proved to be lies, took many by surprise. No one had expected him to address the media reports about his wife and son. At the end of the press conference, a Japanese reporter, who noted that many senior leaders had visited Chongqing, except President Hu Jintao, wanted to know why the president had not done so. Bo responded, "We believe President Hu would be happy if he comes to see Chongqing for himself."

An official in Beijing later said the call Bo received during the press conference was from his wife, Gu Kailai, who urged him to dispel the rumors about their family. The official said the senior leadership, especially President Hu, was outraged that Bo had abandoned the agreed-upon script.

Wang Dan, the former leader of the 1989 student protest movement who now teaches a course of Chinese history in Taiwan, said that Bo put Hu in an awkward position by openly challenging his reluctance to visit Chongqing. In fact, at the urging of his chief of staff, a Bo supporter, Hu had intended to visit Chongqing but changed his plan after the Wang Lijun incident. "Bo's public invitation violated the party's unspoken rules," said Wang. "If Hu didn't go, the media would construe it as a sign of the party's internal division over Bo's Chongqing model. On the other hand, if he went, he would be forced to endorse Bo's policies. Issuing Hu a public invitation was a clever move, but it also carried a high risk."

Bo's "digressions" at the NPC press conference gave ammunition to his opponents within the powerful Politburo Standing Committee, such as Premier Wen Jiabao, who had always objected to Bo's leftist policies in Chongqing, and Jia Qinglin, chairman of the People's Political Consultative Conference, who was worried that Bo's rise could threaten Xi Jinping, the Party's designated successor. After the press conference, Bo's opponents convinced President Hu that Bo could wreck the leadership transition and that he needed to be taken down.

On March 14, the fifth plenary session of the 11th National People's Congress closed. At the end of the three-hour briefings, which mostly centered on China's housing, foreign trade, and local government debts, Premier Wen delivered a surprise.

The moderator gave the last question to Chris Buckley, the Reuters correspondent in Beijing. In fluent Mandarin, Buckley wanted to know Wen's personal view on the Wang Lijun incident and asked whether the incident would affect the central government's confidence in Chongqing.

Premier Wen did not look surprised. It was apparent that the session, which was broadcast live on China's state TV, was choreographed and Buckley's question had been submitted earlier for approval by the senior leadership.

Wen, who had talked freely without a script throughout the conference, took a cautious glance at a piece of paper and commented, "We will give the people an answer to the results of the investigation and the handling of the case, so that it can withstand the test of law and history."

This was the first time one of the top leaders had directly addressed the issue since February 6, when Wang Lijun entered the US Consulate. But Wen did not stop there. He went on to use the rare public opportunity to take aim at his real target, Bo Xilai. With unusual bluntness, he said,

> The present Chongqing municipal party committee and the municipal government must reflect seriously and learn from the Wang Lijun incident.

Asiaweek reported that Wen's tone and facial expression toughened and his hands rose to emphasize the point. For experienced China watchers, reading between the lines, Wen had hinted, without mentioning Bo's name, that Bo's leftist program, which aimed to revive Mao Zedong's much-discredited Cultural Revolution, went against the party's reform policies.

Wen's bombshell at the end of the press conference confirmed suspicion that Bo had been identified as the key culprit in the Wang Lijun scandal. Political analysts believed that the collective leadership had now made up its mind about Bo.

Professor Xueliang Ding, an expert in Chinese politics at Hong Kong University of Science and Technology, told the BBC's Chinese-language service, "Premier Wen warned Bo and other leftists who attempt to adopt far-left policies to resolve China's rising social conflicts that the path will meet a dead end and could lead China to disaster. Premier Wen's remarks mean Bo's political life is approaching its end."

Starting in mid-March, the media took a respite from Wang Lijun. With Neil Heywood's death still in the shadows, the spotlight quickly switched to Bo Xilai. Thus, the prelude ended and the real political drama officially began.

THE RED CONCENTRATION CAMP

SEVERAL YEARS AGO, at a press conference in Hong Kong, a reporter asked Bo Xilai, who was then China's commerce minister, if his father, former vice premier Bo Yibo, had used his influence and connections to advance Bo's political career. There was total silence. All eyes were on Bo, who was slightly taken aback by the reporter's frankness. He forced out a smile and responded calmly:

> I appreciate this straightforward question, which perhaps lingers on the minds of many of you here. I don't want to deny that I have benefited from my old man. I'm pleased to tell everyone that those benefits will last me a lifetime. When I entered high school and began to understand the world around me, I was locked up in a prison because of my father, who was labeled a traitor. I endured five years of imprisonment. The experience toughened my will and taught me how to think. I learned the importance of justice, democracy and law to a society. I learned the importance of food and shelter, freedom and dignity to a person. I see the five-year imprisonment as a gift. Not everyone can have this gift. Without the misfortunes of my father, I wouldn't have gotten the gift either. I guess you can say that I have taken advantage of my father's connections.

As expected, those touching remarks were often cited by Bo's supporters. Bo's description of his childhood was factual, if not entirely accurate.

Bo Xilai was born in July 1949, on the eve of the Communist takeover of China. The third of six children, he was known among his friends as "San Ge" or "Third Brother." He grew up at a time when his father was at the peak of his political career. At the age of seven, he attended the Beijing No. 2 Experiment Primary School, which enrolled a large number of children referred to as "descendants of the revolution." Because the school was also open to students from ordinary families, the principal insisted the children of senior leaders be treated the same. If any parents picked up or dropped off their children in government cars, they had to park their vehicles in side lanes away from the school. Because Bo's family lived on the other side of the city, friends remember that his father would drop him off in his car every morning and one of his bodyguards would fetch him after school. By any standards, Bo lived a sheltered and privileged life.

In 1962, he followed in the steps of his elder brother and was enrolled in the elite Beijing No. 4 Middle School—its alumni include many of today's influential business, political, and military figures from politically privileged families. Unlike his elder brother, who was a popular athlete and student leader, Bo Xilai was a quiet, bookish boy. In May 1966, Chairman Mao, claiming that bourgeois thinking was threatening the well-being of the Communist Party and the socialist society, launched a nationwide political campaign to purify the party of capitalists and remove traditional cultural elements from society. He encouraged young people to take the lead.

Inspired by his vision, a group of older students at Bo Xilai's school wrote a letter to Chairman Mao in June 1966, urging the party to abolish the national college entrance examination system, which they called "feudalistic shackles." Mao liked the idea and the State Council immediately reached a decision and suspended the college entrance exams, which were the basis for college recruitment.

In August 1966, children of the senior leaders at Beijing No. 4 Middle School formed an organization—"the Red Guard"—the first in the nation. Students toppled the school administration, kicked out the principal and teachers, and formed a "Revolutionary Committee," with Bo's elder brother, a firebrand, as the deputy director. Reuters recently interviewed ten alumni from the school who recalled students parading teachers around the sports ground to humiliate them. Some students looked down on schoolmates who lacked their "red" revolutionary pedigrees, contemptuously calling students of humble origins "bastards" and excluding them from the Red Guard organization. They built a jail, with a slogan written in blood on one of its walls: "Long Live Red Terror."

Other schools in Beijing, and throughout China, followed suit and Red Guards groups, consisting of twelve- to eighteen-year-olds, sprouted up all over the country. Young people carried Chairman Mao's portraits and the Little Red Book—a collection of Chairman Mao's quotations—and sang red songs: "The Revolutionary Rebels' Song" and "We Are Chairman Mao's Red Guards." Their initial targets were the "dark forces of society"—former landlords, capitalists, government, and military personnel under the Nationalist government and anti-party intellectuals. Soon they expanded their list to include lower-level Communist Party officials and teachers, who, the Red Guards felt, had failed to follow Chairman Mao's teachings. Song Yongyi, a US-based scholar and an expert on the Cultural Revolution, said Red Guards in Beijing killed more than 1,700 people between June and September 1966; more than 11,000 homes were raided and any valuables were destroyed or looted. About 77,000 children of those classified as bad elements of society were kicked out of Beijing.

As the Cultural Revolution escalated, the death toll from violence rose sharply. Many government agencies were paralyzed. Children of the senior leaders, who realized that the revolution could jeopardize the positions of their parents within the party, formed an alliance called the "Capital City Red Guards United Action Committee" in late 1966. United Action, as it was known, gained support from top leaders within the Central Party Committee and attempted to restore law and order by patrolling the streets every day. Members saw themselves as the true descendants of Communism and they were protecting the fruits of their parents' revolution. A popular slogan for the group read, "Heroes begat heroes and villains begat villains." Its members freely used violence to target nonmembers who dared to challenge them. In 1966 and 1967, members of United Action attacked several public security bureau stations which had detained their members, and stirred other Red Guard organizations to rally in support of their revolutionary parents. A year later, Chairman Mao recognized that United Action could jeopardize his plan to purge those who threatened his rule, and declared the organization illegal.

While Bo and two of his brothers, all of whom were part of United Action, were running around Beijing trying to rescue the revolution, Mao turned on their father, Bo Yibo. He was detained on charges of betraying the Communist Party in the 1930s. Bo Xilai and other children of disgraced senior leaders were urged to openly denounce their parents. At a public meeting against his father, Bo Xilai was said to have slapped his father's face and kicked the old man in the stomach.

Bo Xilai's cooperative attitude failed to shield him and his siblings from persecution. They were paraded around at school as "children of the traitor." After school, they wandered the streets, engaging in gang fights and stealing. In December 1967, Red Guards raided Bo Yibo's home. Bo Xilai was said to have collected a package of photos of his father with other senior leaders who had been purged, as well as some private documents. He gave them to a classmate, who later turned over the package to the Red Guards. Mao's wife, Jiang Qing, reportedly saw the photos and personally ordered the arrest of the Bo brothers.

Bo Xilai and his two brothers were incarcerated at a youth delinquency center in December 1967, and subsequently transferred to what was later known as Camp 789, a reeducation camp where more than sixty children of ousted party leaders were imprisoned. Initially, all the detainees studied Chairman Mao's works and were forced to report on their parents' crimes. In the next five years, they were allowed to attend regular classes and engaged in labor-intensive farmwork under the supervision of prison officials. Often the limited food ration could not satisfy the pubescent boys, and they would eat whatever bugs they could capture in the field. Gang fights were common.

Bo and his siblings were released in 1972. At the age of twenty-three, he was assigned a job at the Beijing Hardware Repair Factory. A former coworker remembered Bo Xilai as charming and handsome. He was well liked, even though people were aware of his questionable family background. Many older workers tried to fix him up with girls. It was through friends that he met a woman named Li Danyu, a military medical doctor. Their fathers used to be friends—both had joined the revolution in their home province of Shanxi. During the Cultural Revolution, while Bo Yibo had been brought down by Mao, Li's father had risen in the ranks and served as party secretary of Beijing. By the time the two young people met, Li Danyu's father had started to lose favor with Mao and was being investigated. Bo Xilai's former coworker said the plain-looking Li Danyu passionately pursued Bo as her boyfriend. They lived in different cities. Li Danyu told the *New York Times* in October 2012 that she and Bo used to write each other every three days. In one of the letters, Bo shared his views on romance, which shed light on his controversial lifestyle in later years:

> One should not be inflexible or old-fashioned. Besides studies and work, one should take time to soul-search and think about other things. Life is better with a little romance. . . . Many revolutionary leaps and achievements are accompanied by the colors of romance.

Bo and Li were married in 1976 and a son was born two years later.

In 1977, a year after Mao's death, China revived the national college entrance examination. Many of Bo's friends at Beijing No. 4 Middle School who had condemned the examination system during the Cultural Revolution jumped at the opportunity. At the age of twenty-nine, Bo Xilai took the exam and was enrolled as a history major at China's prestigious Beijing University. When his father was reinstated as vice premier a year later, Bo Xilai skipped his undergraduate studies and joined a master's degree program in international journalism at the Chinese Academy of Social Sciences.

Upon graduation in 1982, Bo Xilai joined the Party Central Committee Secretariat as a researcher, but he aspired to higher things. In the 1980s, the Communist Party found itself in a leadership crisis. The revolutionary veterans were in their seventies and eighties and ready to retire. A new generation of leaders was badly needed to fill the power vacuum. The Central Party Committee proposed the concept of building a "third echelon"—placing a large number of well-educated and politically reliable candidates in positions within the Communist

Youth League or at grassroots levels, and preparing them for senior positions.

Bo Xilai was energized by the news. In the name of conducting social research, he requested a transfer in 1984 to a poverty-stricken area in China's northwestern province of Gansu so he could gain first-hand knowledge of people at the bottom rung of society. He ended up in a region closer to Beijing—Jin County in northeastern China—where he was appointed deputy party secretary. Bo Xilai's marriage to Li Danyu had disintegrated and he filed for divorce in 1982, but his wife rejected his request. The transfer provided a perfect respite, a friend said.

Bo Xilai followed the examples of two of his childhood playmates who had taken similar steps two years before to enhance their political careers. Xi Jinping, who is now the general secretary of the Communist Party, took up a post in a small county outside Beijing. And Liu Yuan, the son of former president Liu Shaoqi and currently deputy director of the Army's General Logistics Department, settled in the impoverished province of Henan. Driven by idealism and raw political ambition, the trio began accumulating political capital at the ground level.

A contemporary profile in a government newspaper indicates Bo initially had a hard time in Jin County. Local officials treated him with caution and, knowing he was using the experience merely as a launching pad for his political career, nobody took his policy initiatives seriously. Bo Xilai was said to be so frustrated that he thought of quitting, but his father scolded him: "If you can't even handle such trivial setbacks, how do you expect to be a competent official in the future?" So Bo persisted and by the time he left, the county had won several regional awards for innovative township enterprise development, education, and family planning programs. It is doubtful that Bo personally deserved credit for the accomplishments, but he did achieve his purpose: the grassroots experience gilded his credentials. Coincidentally, the name of Jin County means "gold."

In Jin County, Bo's personal life also got a boost. Gu Kailai, a young woman he met when he was a student at Beijing University, came to Jin County in 1984 for an art project. Gu was the daughter of a military general and had majored in law at Beijing University.

Bo Xilai hosted Gu and her traveling companion at his small apartment. Gu described their meeting to a Chinese newspaper:

> I didn't expect to meet my Beijing University alumnus. When I saw him, this talented young man was squatting on a deserted beach, engaging in an enthusiastic discussion with local leaders about rural development. He was idealistic like my father. I went with him to his apartment. He lived in a tiny room, which seemed perpetually dusty and dirty, no matter how hard you clean it. He took out a few small local-grown apples from a cardboard box underneath his desk and offered them to me and my professor. Then, he began to talk about his plan for the county. . . . He looked like someone from a novel I have read—well-educated and with a strong sense of responsibility. He was a born workaholic and he was not a family man, but he is a trustworthy and reliable man.

Although both Gu and Bo claimed that they first met in Jin County in 1984, Bo's ex-wife, Li Danyu, insisted that all three of their families had known one another for years before that—Li Danyu's brother had married Gu's sister. In an interview with the *New York Times,* Li claimed that she and Bo Xilai helped Gu get into Beijing University through their connections. Bo became Gu's dance partner at school and might have had an affair then.

Following their encounter or re-encounter in Jin County in 1984, Bo began to openly pursue Gu, who was nine years younger and known for her head-turning beauty. Still married, he pressed Li Danyu for a divorce, but to no avail. Instead, the obstinate Li wrote letters to Bo Xilai's employer and friends, depicting him as a treacherous husband who had used her in his downtrodden years and dumped her for a young woman when his situation took a turn for the better. In the 1980s, Chinese courts seldom granted a divorce involving a third party. In addition, Li Danyu worked for the army and any man or woman who caused the marriage of military personnel to dissolve would be prosecuted. It was a nasty divorce and dragged on for four years, with many court mediations. In the end, Li consented and gained sole custody of their son, changing the child's last name from Bo to Li.

In 1986, Gu Kailai had the rare opportunity to study in the US, but the now-single Bo Xilai proposed to her. They were married the same year and a son, Bo Guagua, was born in 1987. A year later, the family moved to the city of Dalian, where Bo Xilai was named a district party chief.

THE PRINCELINGS

IN APRIL 1989, thousands of college students in Beijing gathered in Tiananmen Square to mourn the death of former party secretary Hu Yaobang, who had been purged for his liberal views. At first the group was relatively small, compared with the enormity of the square itself, which was designed to comfortably hold a million people when Chairman Mao wanted to address "the revolutionary masses." Soon, a crowd gathered around the mourning students, some to share the grief over Hu Yaobang's death, others with broader grievances about the way China was being run, and before long the square became the center of a protest movement. Emboldened student demonstrators called for an end to government corruption and political liberalization. The widespread corruption within the party was a unifying element. The movement quickly spread to cities around the country. In the southern city of Shenzhen, where I was a journalist and protest organizer, angry residents took to the street, in part because of rumors that children of senior leaders had purchased popular consumer goods, such as color TV sets, from manufacturers at below-wholesale prices and made a huge killing in the market.

At the height of the movement, student leaders, whose command of English made them the focal point of Western correspondents, led a hunger strike. Government officials agreed to engage in a dialogue with them. Despite a virtual news blackout in China, the international media freely reported the hunger strike and within a week, the overseas news galvanized sympathy and support from all sectors of Chinese society. Fearing that the Communist Party would lose its power—military units based in Beijing and local police refused to intervene—Deng Xiaoping and other party elders, including Bo Xilai's father, decided to use force to stop the protests. Military units based on the Mongolian border, who were effectively isolated from news about what was happening in Beijing, were mobilized.

Troops and tanks rolled into Beijing on the night of June 3, and the order was given to open fire on unarmed students and residents, and the so-called prodemocracy movement was crushed. It has been reported that the troops were told by their commanders that the right-wingers within the party were attempting to overthrow the government. Many of the casualties were reportedly trying to flee Tiananmen Square when they were killed on side streets. The official death toll was never publicized, but student organizers now claim more than 1,000 people were killed.

Following the crackdown, officials who opposed the use of force, including party general secretary Zhao Ziyang, were ousted. Party veterans, who gathered to discuss leadership succession in the fall of 1989, expressed disappointment that Zhao, the designated successor to Deng Xiaoping, would betray them by supporting the protestors. General Wang Zhen, who was then vice president of China, was quoted as saying, "Nobody is more reliable than our own children. We need our children to protect the red China that we have established." His views were widely shared by Bo Xilai's father and other veterans. At that gathering, the veterans agreed in a secret deal that the government should pick one child from the family of each veteran leader who had fought with Mao during the revolution in the 1940s and gradually elevate him or her to the equivalent of a vice minister's position or higher in the government and the military.

This special group of senior leaders' children were the original princelings. Over the next two decades, the princeling definition was expanded to include children of all senior leaders, national and regional, and the princelings have emerged as a formidable political faction. At the recently concluded Party Congress in November 2011, three have made it to the seven-member Politburo Standing Committee, the highest decision-making body.

Rising political clout has also given many princelings access to wealth. According to a widely-circulated report, supposedly conducted by the Chinese Academy of Social Sciences, there were 3,200 billionaires (in yuan terms) in China by the end of 2006. Of those, 2,932 were princelings, controlling assets of 2,450 billion yuan (US $395 billion). It is inconceivable that a Chinese official institution would prepare such a report, but based on my knowledge, the figures cited reflect the reality.

In the Bo family, the youngest son, Bo Xicheng, was initially chosen to inherit his father's political fortune. In the 1980s, Bo Xicheng had bigger name recognition than Bo Xilai, serving first as party secretary of a state-run artifact company, and then as director at the Beijing Municipal Tourism Bureau. However, in the early 1990s, Bo Xicheng suffered a series of setbacks. He failed to garner support for a spot on the standing committee of the Beijing Municipal Party Committee despite his father's active maneuvering. Official records show that the local government removed him as director of the Beijing Municipal Tourism Bureau in 1992. The youngest son's apparent political demise prompted the family patriarch to shift his attention to Bo Xilai, who willingly accepted the newly-available role. He moved up steadily from a district party chief in Dalian to become the city's acting mayor and subsequently mayor in 1993.

Bo's vision for Dalian might have been shaped by his visit to New York City a decade earlier. Liang Anren is a retired engineer from Long Island, New York. Liang's father had saved Bo Yibo's life in the 1930s and the two families were close friends. In 1983, Bo Xilai made a personal trip to New York City and stayed at Liang's home. Liang remembers Bo Xilai as a smart young man filled with curiosity. He bought a metro pass and toured the city himself on the subway. Liang said Bo Xilai took a keen interest in Harlem and visited the borough twice to study the cultures and living conditions of African Americans. He marveled at the pristine beaches of Long Island and the clean air.

Liang says Bo's personal interests in New York probably inspired many of his public projects in Dalian, a seaport city in northeast China, wedged between the Yellow Sea to the east and the Bohai Sea to the west.

Built and founded by Russians who defeated Chinese imperial troops and occupied what was then Manchuria in 1900, Dalian—or Dalny, as it was known—became the southern tip of the Trans-Siberian

Railway and a gateway to the East. Following the Russian defeat in the Russo-Japanese war of 1904–1905, the city was transferred to Japanese control and renamed Dairen.

China regained control of the city after the Second World War. A friend, Dong Ayi, who grew up in Dalian in the 1950s and 1960s, recalled the city as a heavy industrial port of shipbuilding, chemical processing, and industrial equipment manufacturing. When Bo Xilai took over the mayor's position in 1993, the city was going through a tough financial time. The majority of state-run enterprises had gone bankrupt after losing government subsidies, and thousands of workers had lost their jobs, previously seen as cradle-to-grave iron rice bowls. The city's unemployment rate was higher than the national average, and its air and water quality was poor due to pollution from heavy industry plants.

Among many of Bo Xilai's policy initiatives to rejuvenate the city and improve the city's image, two are worthy of mention: beautification and soccer.

During his first five years in office, Bo Xilai stirred up a "green" storm, aiming to build Dalian into China's northern Hong Kong. He made ambitious plans to move nearly one hundred pollution-causing factories out of the city proper. The government tore down old factories and barracks to build different styles of public squares, plant trees along streets, and create thousands of square kilometers of lawn in public places. In 1995, the city created 2 million square meters of lawn, with grass covering 37 percent of the city. Bo Xilai's vision was a challenge for many who still saw idle land as a Western luxury and waste of space. In the Mao era, Chinese were urged to cut trees and burn grass to make space for crops. For a while, some people in Dalian joked that their mayor "paid more attention to grass than crops."

Bo Xilai was also credited with increasing the number of sewage treatment facilities as part of a campaign to clean up the city's forty foul rivers and converting old fishing villages into commercial beach resorts and tourist sites.

Dalian soon became a model for the rest of country's mayors to emulate. It became known as China's Singapore, a city built around parks. In 2001, the United Nations Environment Programme recognized the Dalian Municipal Government for its outstanding contributions to the protection of the environment. In 1993, the *Wall Street Journal* named Bo Xilai as one of the top twenty most promising officials in China.

But Bo's experiments in Dalian were criticized by many as public relations exercises to attract attention from Beijing. For example, Dalian, located in China's dry north, suffers severe water shortages. Critics say the city wastes its scarce freshwater resources on useless plants and grass, while public squares rob Dalian of precious land that could be put to profitable commercial use.

To counter his critics, Bo claimed that beautifying Dalian had helped attract more foreign and domestic investors. His environmental initiative led to a rise in property values. And of the 2 million residents in Dalian, more than half lived in new housing complexes and 450,000 moved to new buildings with government subsidies. Rising property values provided the city with more taxes, enabling the government to underwrite the relocation of pollution-causing factories to the suburbs.

In addition to his environmental projects, Bo Xilai was also known as the soccer mayor, who saw a competitive soccer team as "an attractive business card" for the city. His pro-soccer stance captured the mood of the city, which is passionate about the sport. In the early 1980s, the Dalian Football Club was a national top-tier team. In 1993, the club was reorganized into a professional team. The city offered Wanda Group, a Dalian-based real estate and entertainment conglomerate, subsidies and tax benefits, making it a model enterprise for sponsoring the club, which won the first fully professional Chinese Jia-A League title in 1994. Subsequently, the team achieved a total of eight league titles, becoming the most successful club in Chinese soccer history.

"Soccer is not just sport and entertainment, but also a spirit," said Bo Xilai on numerous occasions. In an effort to make soccer the city's official sport, the government established a soccer development zone, and allocated funds to train new players and popularize the sport among children. Under Bo, Dalian had a well-funded and prolific soccer academy that produced numerous prominent players. Facilities were constructed to host international matches. In the early 2000s, its overall strength in the sport was unmatched in the country. Children in Dalian idolized their soccer players like movie stars.

Before Bo's rise as mayor, officials in Dalian were notoriously lazy, and corruption was rampant. Many spent their evenings eating, drinking, and playing mah-jongg at expensive restaurants, all paid for with taxpayers' money. Work started late in government offices. Bo initiated tough rules to improve government efficiency. Leaders at key government agencies were equipped with beepers so they could be on call anytime he needed them. A reporter with the *China Enterprise Newspaper* recalled that Bo Xilai would deliberately make random phone calls to certain officials to check if they were out entertaining. As a consequence, many chose to stay home for fear they would be caught. One night Bo called a director at a government agency but received no response. The next morning, the director claimed that he had gone to bed early. "Sounds like you don't have too much to do," Bo said. "We should probably assign you more projects."

Restaurants and businesses asked Bo to write comments about them to be displayed to customers. For poorly run businesses, he would embarrass the managers by writing things like "Mismanagement leads to bankruptcy."

Bo Xilai was a hands-on mayor. There is a story about Bo leaving his office late one night and noticing water leaks in the bathroom. He immediately called the building manager and ordered him to attend to the matter right away. At a year-end party for foreign businesses in Dalian, one foreign businessman complained about being mistreated at a government agency. Upon hearing the complaint, Bo Xilai banged on his desk and ordered the head of the agency to look into the issue immediately.

Bo was keen to make Dalian a showpiece. In 1994, in anticipation of Hong Kong's return to Chinese sovereignty in 1997, he built Xinghai Square on the site of an old salt mine. It is the largest public square in Asia, covering 1.1 million square meters. Its name, which means a "sea of stars," is reflected in the shape and design of the center of the square, which looks like a gigantic star. As an illustration of Bo's pro-people style, the square boasts 1,000 pairs of footprints left by Dalian residents.

The square raised many eyebrows—in the middle of the square stands a pair of *huaibiao,* or white marbled ornamental pillars, 19.97 meters (66 feet) high and 1.997 meters (6.6 feet) around, with dragons carved on them. The ornamental columns, which once would have represented the power of the emperor, were copied from a pair erected in Beijing's Tiananmen Square, near the Forbidden City. The ornamental columns in Dalian are taller and bigger, and Bo's critics claim they symbolize his secret desire to overpower the emperor, or in modern terminology, the general party secretary. When former president Jiang Zemin visited Dalian, he was said to be shocked by the imperial symbols. It is unlikely he missed their significance.

After Bo Xilai's downfall, Chinese state media said his vaunting political ambitions left many imprints in Dalian. Whereas the US president supposedly carried a suitcase that contained "the football"— giving him the power to launch nuclear weapons at a moment's notice—Bo Xilai installed a switch on his desk that could turn on or off all the city's water fountains so he could feel that he was in control.

Like emperors of the past, Bo was said to be a notorious womanizer. Bo had multiple mistresses, one of whom was Zhang Weijie, an anchor at the local TV station in Dalian. It is widely reported on the Internet that Zhang used to openly brag about her cozy relations with Bo Xilai in front of her colleagues. Her favorite line was, "I'm going to see the mayor tonight. If you need anything from him, let me know." An official familiar with Bo's investigation at the Central Commission for Discipline Inspection said Bo fathered a little girl with Zhang in 1998. When his wife, Gu Kailai, learned of the affair, she was outraged at Bo and urged leaders at the TV station to fire Zhang. As a result, the anchor lost her job and vanished from the public eye. For years, people in Dalian believed that Gu Kailai had the anchor "evaporated"—a euphemism for death. In September 2012, I learned from a reporter in Beijing that Zhang is alive. She allegedly received 10 million yuan in 1998 from Xu Ming, Bo's billionaire business friend, on the condition that she and her baby girl leave the city for good and never bother Bo again. When Bo was under investigation, authorities in Beijing located Zhang to collect evidence against Bo. The update that I posted on my website about Zhang prompted one Weibo user in China to congratulate Bo's son, in a typical sarcastic manner, on finding a young sister.

An official who worked for Bo in Dalian said Bo's insatiable lust for women gained him a nickname, "Bo Qilai," which means "Erections Bo" in Chinese. He flaunted his propensity for young, pretty women through a "face" program for the city. Under his order, the Dalian police department formed a squad of female officers on horseback, a first for China. Bo instructed the first recruits to "become the beautiful calling cards for Dalian." The average age of the first fifty female officers chosen was twenty-three. There were unsubstantiated reports that Bo had chosen his favorite officers to entertain other senior leaders who were in town.

In addition to his womanizing, Bo's former colleagues said he was ruthless toward his political enemies. In China, the central and provincial governments are operated on a dual hierarchy system. The Communist Party chief, being the de facto political head, takes charge of policy and personnel issues, while the leader of the executive branch implements party policy and is responsible for day-to-day matters. The premier of China reports to the general secretary of the Communist Party, and a governor or mayor of a certain province or city reports to the provincial or city party secretary.

When Bo Xilai first arrived, he was appointed mayor of Dalian, and his party boss was a technocrat who grew up in the region. They enjoyed a brief honeymoon before Bo saw his party chief as a political obstacle. A person familiar with the situation said that Bo never treated the party boss seriously and constantly challenged him at internal and public meetings. Eventually the party boss lost the battle and was forced out in 1999. Bo assumed his position and became both party chief and mayor. An online report said the former party chief in Dalian harbored grudges against Bo and started to ally himself with other victims of Bo's bullying. Over the next two years, the former party chief had a thick file of incriminating information against Bo and submitted it to Li Yanfeng, an official at the State Security Ministry, for investigation.

In May 2002, China Northern Airlines Flight 6136 from Beijing to Dalian crashed, killing all 103 passengers and nine crew. Li Yanfeng was among the dead. Government investigators ruled the accident was arson, blaming a former member of the secret police for setting fire to the plane in a suicide attack. Still, a former journalist in Dalian told a British newspaper that Bo Xilai and his wife had orchestrated the accident to destroy Li Yanfeng. This claim has never been verified, and the case is said to have been reviewed and investigated by the Central Inspection and Discipline Commission.

Bo's high-profile successes in Dalian, and his father's relentless lobbying, earned him a promotion in January 2001: he was appointed deputy party secretary and interim governor of Liaoning province. When he stepped out of the municipal government building on the morning of January 17, 2001, he was greeted by enthusiastic residents who lined the streets to see him off. Some well-wishers rushed up to touch his hands and the police had to form a human wall around him. In the city's Marine Square, more residents were waiting for him. The next day, all the major newspapers and TV stations carried articles and video of residents mobbing the popular mayor. The headline in *Dalian Daily* read, "Touching Scene on the Streets of Dalian—Tens of Thousands Send Off Their Mayor." Just how spontaneous the scenes were has been questioned by many people, since it was a common criticism that Bo Xilai was intent on creating his own cult of personality. Residents later disclosed the so-called spontaneous farewell scene was organized by various street committees. In some areas, local officials promised to buy residents a bag of Kentucky Fried Chicken, a popular but relatively expensive American "import," if they showed up on the street.

Liaoning was not an easy posting. It was a notoriously depressing industrial junkyard, an example, if one was needed, of what happened after the government withdrew support for state enterprises. Bo was nothing if not bold, and he teamed up with nearby provinces and, working with the State Council, formulated a regional economic cooperation pact dubbed Northeast Area Revitalization. The program aimed to solve the soaring unemployment by courting investment from geographically close South Korea and Japan.

In 2002, the Central Commission for Discipline Inspection, with the cooperation of Bo Xilai, uncovered a corruption scandal that involved 120 officials, including the mayor and deputy mayor of Shenyang, both of whom had been hailed by Bo Xilai as savvy reformers line Liaoning's largest city. The key figures in the scandal were sentenced to death on corruption charges—illegal gambling, having connections with the triad, and embezzling public funds. The experience probably gave rise to Bo Xilai's later headline-grabbing anti–organized crime campaign in the city of Chongqing.

Bo's tenure in Liaoning was not without controversy, largely the result of his arrogance. Yang Rong, who went by Benjamin Yeung in the West, was a Chinese financier who founded China Brilliance Automotive, the first Chinese company to be listed on the New York Stock Exchange. In 2001, *Fortune* magazine listed Yang Rong as China's third-richest businessperson. But in 2002, Yang offended Bo by setting up a new manufacturing facility outside Liaoning, which Bo Xilai had wanted as he lobbied for badly needed investment. Bo retaliated by accusing Yang of embezzling public funds and claimed Yang Rong was not a private entrepreneur, but an agent and operator of state assets. He went so far as to threaten to take over Yang's company, and instructed the Liaoning provincial procurator to issue an arrest warrant against him. Yang Rong was tipped off and fled to the US.

From a safe distance, Yang fought back. He countered that the Liaoning provincial government had not invested a single penny in his company, that it was a "state enterprise" in name only, and that he had owned the company outright from the very beginning. He filed a lawsuit in federal court in Washington, DC, alleging the Liaoning provincial government had illegally seized his private assets. Several prominent US lawyers, including a former counsel for President Ronald Reagan, were hired to serve on his legal team.

The Chinese found it hard to accept that a federal court in the US could allow a lawsuit against a local government in China. But after receiving a summons through diplomatic channels, the Bo Xilai administration in Liaoning urged the US court to dismiss Yang Rong's lawsuit. In the end, upon careful deliberation, the court ruled in favor of the Liaoning government. Yang Rong's subsequent appeal was rejected by the appellate court in Washington, DC, in 2006.

As the governor of Liaoning, Bo reported to Wen Shizhen, then provincial party secretary, who disliked Bo's superficiality. He reportedly criticized Bo's work in Dalian, calling it public-relations stunts, and coined the famous phrase "Developing China's cities like Europe and its countryside like Africa." In response, Bo insisted that Wen Shizhen was personally responsible for several corruption scandals. Beijing was well aware of the cankerous relationship between the two.

When Commerce Minister Lu Fuyuan retired early for health reasons in February 2004, President Hu Jintao considered Bo Xilai as his replacement—some reports say that former president Jiang Zemin, a friend of Bo's father, also played a role. Bringing Bo to Beijing would eliminate the tension among the leaders in Liaoning. Besides, the Ministry of Commerce involved many foreign trade missions and Hu's administration needed a charming, charismatic, and articulate leader to represent China. So, Bo returned to the capital city, where he had grown up, and took over the high-profile position. He kept his head down for the first three months, declining media interviews and limiting his public appearances. When reporters mobbed him during the annual National People's Congress in March 2002, his words were unusually cautious.

General gossip had it that a fortuneteller advised him to lie low and quietly prepare himself for better opportunities ahead. His father's friends inside the State Council also encouraged Bo Xilai to be modest and low-key, an important quality for a new official inside the central government.

Media interest in the tall, good-looking celebrity politician remained high. When Bo Xilai took a quick tour of an international trade show in Guangzhou on April 15, 2002, reporters crowded around him with questions. And although Bo spoke little in public, he allowed *Esquire* magazine to include him at the top of China's "Fashionable Men" list. Calling him "the most fashion-conscious Chinese official," the magazine credited Bo for making Dalian one of the most fashionable cities in China by creating an international fashion festival there and described him as "suave and competent, with public charm."

Such hagiography in the Chinese press was hard to come by, but as the media attention grew, Bo's initial restraint failed him. Soon he was back courting the spotlight—confident, straightforward, and eloquent.

Bo took over the Ministry of Commerce at an inauspicious time. In 2004, the ministry faced many challenges: foreign direct investment was stalling and trade friction with the US and Europe had reached new levels. In response to US textile makers' claims that 16,000 domestic jobs had been lost due to cheap Chinese goods, the George W. Bush administration followed up on its campaign promises to save American jobs by imposing textile quotas. The European Union soon followed suit. Restricting access to key foreign markets was not good for Chinese manufacturers and Bo knew it was essential for textile makers that he break the impasse.

Bo Xilai participated in several of the tough trade fights. He and Chinese vice premier Wu Yi flew to Washington, DC, in 2004 for intense negotiations. Bo's colleagues told the Chinese media that the new minister of commerce maintained a conciliatory but assertive attitude. The *International Financial News,* a magazine affiliated with the official Communist Party paper, the *People's Daily,* reported that Bo spoke relatively fluent English and that during a meeting with American officials, he told a struggling American interpreter to stop translating and save time because he and his assistants could all understand English.

Ten days after he came back from the US, Bo accompanied Premier Wen Jiabao on a five-country trip to Europe in May 2004. Hong Kong reporters raved about his charisma, which they said was a drastic departure from other dogmatic and conservative leaders in Beijing. One Chinese newspaper even referred to him as China's John F. Kennedy.

In Brussels, Belgium, he impressed everyone with his wit. In one speech, he compared the European Union and China to a married couple who needed to get over their squabbles and move closer because both relied on each other. When an Italian reporter asked his views on the flood of cheap Chinese textile products in the Italian markets and their devastating impact on the well-being of traditional Italian textile manufacturers, Bo answered:

It's true that we have exported many cheap textile products to Italy. You shouldn't forget that we have also imported a lot of expensive textile machinery and fabrics from your country. There was a person called Marco Polo. Even though he was born in the thirteenth century, he set his sights on the faraway China and traveled all the way there to do business. If Marco Polo suddenly woke up from his grave and learned that the Italian government is imposing quotas on high-quality and low-price Chinese goods, he would be shocked and feel regretful.

On the same trip, Bo Xilai imitated a TV commercial at a China–EU foreign investment seminar. "The Commerce Ministry is always at the service of EU investors. If you have any questions, remember to call our hotline at 0636308534." His words generated laughter and applause.

Just as he had been as mayor, Bo was a demanding boss to his colleagues at the Ministry of Commerce. Staff members had to be on call twenty-four hours a day and many called Bo "Mao Zedong Jr." behind his back. Meanwhile, Bo started to display a pattern of behavior—his bullish style clashed with that of his own boss, Vice Premier Wu Yi, who oversaw the Commerce Ministry and provided enthusiastic support during Bo's transition to the ministry. Bo initiated a series of moves to restructure the ministry and eliminated officials favored by Wu Yi. A US-based Chinese-American businessman who met with Bo Xilai and Wu Yi to discuss a joint venture outside Beijing in 2006 recalled Bo Xilai speaking contemptuously of Wu Yi barely before she walked out of the conference room.

"THE CITY OF DOUBLE HAPPINESS"

// MUSICAL CHAIRS" is a common political game in China that ensures no one minister or governor builds up too strong a power base within the party or in a certain region. In September 2007, an official at the Ministry of Commerce said in an e-mail to me that Bo Xilai might be leaving the ministry to take up a post in Chongqing, as the city's party secretary. President Hu Jintao intended to move the then-Chongqing party chief to Guangdong province and the Guangdong party chief to Beijing.

Soon after *Mingjing* published the news of Bo Xilai's new appointment, a pro–Chinese government newspaper in Hong Kong reported that Bo Xilai was scheduled to arrive in Chongqing the next day. But Bo never showed up. *Mingjing* learned later that he was reluctant to accept the new assignment and kept postponing his start date. Bo and his friends saw the job as a demotion that effectively banished him from the political center. In those days, he was eyeing the vice premier's position, which would be vacated by Wu Yi, who had announced that she would retire in the spring of 2008. Premier Wen Jiabao was said to be considering Bo Xilai as her replacement. However, Wu Yi, who intensely disliked Bo, opposed the move. The vice premier's position eventually went to Wang Qishan, an expert in finance and the son-in-law of former vice premier Yao Yilin. Wang currently serves on the Politburo Standing Committee.

As Bo Xilai was deliberating on his next move, the 17th Communist Party Congress convened in October 2007 and he was elected to the then twenty-five-member Politburo, a top policy-making body that meets about once a month to address important issues facing the party and the government. Joining the Politburo was considered a political milestone for Bo because membership is tightly controlled by a few senior leaders and each candidate is appointed only after extensive investigation, and with near unanimous agreement among the sitting Politburo members. The elevation moved Bo Xilai one step closer to the Politburo Standing Committee, the highest and most powerful body in China. With the media once more calling him "a rising political star," Bo needed to make a decision about his new post.

A friend of Bo's disclosed later that he followed his most trusted advisers, who believed that Chongqing was the ideal launchpad for his political future. Chongqing, with a population of 32 million people and thirty-eight subdivisions, covers about the same land area as Austria. The city, situated next to the Yangtze River, is responsible for the Three Gorges dam project. As China attempted to address the uneven economic development between the coastal cities and inland regions, Chongqing had emerged as strategically important in the government's grand plan to develop the backward southwestern region. Since 1997, when the city was elevated to the same status as Beijing, Shanghai, and Tianjin, and became a municipality under the direct control of the central government, the Central Party Committee had switched party secretaries four times and none had made any visible impact on the city. If Bo could turn the city around, joining the Politburo Standing Committee was inevitable.

For someone with unchecked political ambition, Bo Xilai must have been aware of the story relating to the city's auspicious name. Legend had it that during China's Song Dynasty, a prince was sent to rule and tame what was then called Gongzhou, a city famous for its rebellious streak against the central government. In January 1189, the prince was made duke of the region. A month later, when the emperor died, he ascended to the throne. In honor of his double good fortune, Zhao named the city Chongqing, or "double happiness."

Chongqing's distance from the political center meant Bo would have more autonomy and less constraint, allowing him to freely test his political ideas.

Bo arrived in Chongqing on November 29, accompanied by another princeling and rising star, Li Yuanchao, who was in charge of the party's personnel matters. At the changeover ceremony, Li introduced Bo Xilai as an official who was "politically mature" and a man with strong principles. "Having started at the grassroots level and gradually moved up, Comrade Xilai has accumulated rich leadership experience. He is sharp-minded, open to new ideas and has a strong pioneering spirit. He is honest, upright and dedicated to his career," said Li.

A reporter who saw Bo for the first time at the changeover ceremony described her feelings in a blog: "I'm so excited. I didn't realize he is better looking and more charming than his photo conveys. He donned a dark suit and walked up to the stage politely. The microphone seemed to be too short for him. Throughout its history, Chongqing has not encountered a leader who is this tall and handsome. He seldom reads off his script and his speech is very stirring. He's so sexy. I love it!"

There is an old Chinese saying that goes, "All newly appointed officials have three bundles of fire to make an impression." Bo Xilai's three "bundles of fire" took the form of what later became known as the "Singing Red and Smashing Black" campaign—singing revolutionary songs, and attacking corruption and organized crime. At that time, Bo's campaign was considered a safe bet. "If an official became overly enthusiastic about capitalistic practices or democratic reforms, he could easily be accused of being too Westernized and straying away from Communism," commented Xiaoping Chen, a US-based analyst. "But if you turned left and held up Mao's banner, nobody dared blame you for going back to the party's Communist roots."

At his inaugural ceremony in 2007, Bo lectured several hundred senior municipal leaders: "As party officials, we should be clean and honest, and gain public trust and confidence. My wife and I have already decided not to allow any of our relatives or friends to come to Chongqing in search of opportunities and privileges. If you know or hear about anyone who does business in our name, please stop the person and call us right away."

Bo took over at a time when the city was plagued with serious social and economic problems, such as poverty and pollution. Among the thirty-eight subdivisions that make up Chongqing, seventeen were on the government's poverty list. About half of the 32 million people in Chongqing lived below the poverty line, which is measured as 2,300 yuan per capita income (about $360). The city was shrouded year-round in a yellow smog—a combination of industrial pollutants, smoke, coal, dust, and fog from the heavily polluted Yangtze River. In the summertime, acid rain was common. In addition, organized crime and government corruption ran deep, with deals struck at relatively high levels for control of many of the city's enterprises, from taxis and hotels to restaurants and nightclubs.

Moreover, every day, hundreds of people gathered in front of the municipal building, rain or shine, protesting unpaid wages, forced relocation, and corrupt government officials. Though demonstrations never again reached the peak established at Tiananmen Square in 1989, discontent bubbled just below the surface.

In the face of these challenges, Bo Xilai, following the steps of senior leaders in Beijing, declared himself a Maoist and carried out a series of radical policies in the pursuit of a viable social and political solution for Chongqing.

As part of his "common prosperity" program, the Chongqing government had spent 15 billion yuan (US $2.4 billion) building 800,000 apartments for low-income families and new college graduates, with rents at 40 percent below market rates. The units are built in the center of the city, near higher-income housing to prevent the creation of slums. The government in Chongqing also spent nearly 50 billion yuan (US $8 billion) on rural education, health care, and housing.

Bo was one of the first in the country to grant urban residential permits to migrant workers from the rural areas so they could enjoy the better health care, education, and social security available to urban residents. To improve public security, the Bo administration established five hundred kiosks in the city staffed with police, making it easier for residents to report crimes and access police. The city planted trees and set up government funds to rebuild infrastructure to attract more foreign investment.

During the financial crisis in 2009, when the rest of the country's economy slowed, GDP in Chongqing reached 16.4 percent, and 17.1 percent in 2010. Some 87 percent of its growth was in the state sector. Under his regime, half of the budget of Chongqing was spent on health care, housing, pensions, education, and other public services. Bo used large state subsidies to woo flagship foreign firms, such as Apple, Foxconn, and BASF. Direct foreign investment increased 50 percent annually during his reign. Bo also launched a giant social housing program predicated on rural migrants trading their land for development by the city.

Chongqing is home to two notorious Nationalist concentration camps that imprisoned, tortured, and killed more than three hundred young, underground Communists and social activists before the Communist takeover in 1949. The city has long been known as a "red city." A revolutionary martyr's museum built near the sites of the concentration camps at the foot of Gele Mountain attracts thousands of visitors from around the country. Bo Xilai played up this revolutionary heritage and launched his "Singing Red and Smashing Black" campaign at a ceremony in front of the museum in 2008. As part of the campaign, Bo, known for belting out Mao-era songs at conferences or private parties, made singing revolutionary songs obligatory in Chongqing. In 2008, his office issued a circular that required all government and party organizations to sing classic "red" songs to strengthen people's trust in the Communist Party and "lift the spirits of the heroic mountain city of Chongqing." He personally picked one hundred popular Mao-era songs, which were sold on CDs and aired repeatedly on radio and TV. Within a short time, the whole city was mobilized—children and adults waved red flags and sang their hearts out. During major holidays, such as National Day and Labor Day, the city organized red-song competitions. Over a three-year period, the city organized more than 100,000 public performances. Bo Xilai even sent his red song–singing troupes to Beijing, Shanghai, and Hong Kong. A mental asylum in Chongqing incorporated this into its treatment regimen, urging patients to sing red songs every day after taking their meds. "The red 'supplement' can inspire patients, improve their mood, and enhance their confidence in the treatment," claimed a doctor.

The red singing has continued after Bo's fall. During a recent trip to Chongqing, my coauthor witnessed a band consisting of sixteen retirees performing old Communist songs in a public square near his hotel. On a weeknight, the singing lasted until one o'clock in the morning and residents nearby did not seem to mind.

Bo's "red culture" revival campaign also included a series of little books of ancient and modern classics, from the teachings of Confucius and Mao Zedong's poems to Martin Luther King's "I have a dream" speech. Every official was asked to carry the pocket-size books, reminding one of the Little Red Book, a collection of Mao's quotations that people carried during the Cultural Revolution. In the preface of the little-book series, Bo wrote, "Reading the classics is like taking a multiple vitamin pill. If you take one a day, it could boost your spiritual health."

When Bo Xilai was in power, the omnipresent outdoor advertising billboards were removed. No commercial was allowed to be aired on TV channels controlled by the local government. A brand new TV program was created with the sole purpose of airing old Communist propaganda movies and featuring Communist storytelling.

To improve the image of public officials, Bo initiated the "connecting with your poor relatives" campaign, encouraging officials to visit poverty-stricken regions, stay with peasants for a period of time, adopt a poor family, and help them solve problems. In the spring of 2008, he caused a political earthquake by changing leadership in seven districts and counties, and sent hundreds of officials to training sessions where he was a lecturer, teaching them about Communist theories on modern economic management.

Bo's tenure in Chongqing was dominated by a protracted war ostensibly directed at the mobsters and powerful officials who colluded with the gangs, enabling them to flourish. Wang Lijun was the campaign's architect and handler. From 2009 to 2012, an estimated 5,000 people were arrested in the sweeping campaign that ensnared criminals, businessmen, members of the police force, judges, government officials, and political adversaries who were accused of corruption or criminal collaboration. The campaign generated a groundswell of support from the public, which was fed up with corruption and rising crime. Under Bo, the city claimed to have reopened 27,000 unsolved criminal and civil cases, and reduced the number of petitioners appealing for help against corruption by 90 percent.

Bo's popular social and economic development model, which was enthusiastically endorsed by many senior leaders and scholars as a refreshing approach to China's problems, also caused controversy. Government statistics show that Chongqing's 2011 fiscal deficit exceeded 100 billion yuan (US $16 billion), or about 30 percent of the city's GDP, of which half was caused by Bo's spending on social welfare and environmental programs. In 2010 alone, Bo spent 10 billion yuan (US $160 million), to plant expensive imported gingko trees and plants that are not suited for the local climate.

Critics say Bo suppressed the growth of private enterprise through discriminatory lending and taxation policies and practices. Businesspeople complain that private enterprises in Chongqing lost their status guaranteed in the Chinese constitution. A 2012 survey conducted by the Chinese Academy of Social Sciences, the Communist Party's think tank, revealed that Bo's radical policy instilled fear in many Chinese entrepreneurs, who opted to leave China and move their assets abroad. About 86 percent of those surveyed expressed their willingness to emigrate to the West.

Despite Chongqing's success in attracting such investors as Ford Motor Company and Foxconn Technology Group, foreign businessmen worried that government-backed businesses could squeeze them out. A crackdown by city officials in 2010 on Walmart stores over mislabeled pork forced the world's biggest retailer temporarily to close thirteen of its stores, spooking foreign investors. Christian Murck, president of the American Chamber of Commerce in China, said, "If the Chongqing model is one that favors a greater role for the government, with state enterprises managing the economy, that is a negative for foreign businesses."

Once hailed as a pioneering effort to wipe out corruption, Bo's anticrime initiative revealed a security apparatus run amok. It was said to have framed victims, extracted confessions through torture, extorted business empires, and visited retribution on the political rivals of Bo Xilai and his friends while protecting those with better connections.

In April 2010, a Beijing court, assisted by the Central Commission for Discipline Inspection, handed out a suspended death sentence to fifty-four-year-old Wang Yi for taking bribes totaling 12 million yuan (US $1.9 million). Wang, who served as vice president of the China Development Bank, was a loyal associate of the Bo family. When Wang attended Beijing University, he was in the same class as Bo Xilai's sister, who was impressed with Wang's literary talents and recommended him to be the secretary of Bo Xilai's father. Following Wang's arrest, the Bo family was said to have lobbied He Guoqiang, the head of the Central Commission for Discipline Inspection, for lighter sentencing, but to no avail.

Three months later, Bo Xilai initiated a tit-for-tat retaliation. He ordered the arrest of Chongqing's former deputy police chief Wen Qiang, who was supposedly a friend and protégé of He Guoqiang when he was Chongqing's party secretary a decade earlier. Based on information provided by a Chongqing-based Hong Kong businessman who was well connected with local officials, Bo ordered Wang Lijun to extract negative information about He Guoqiang. Initially, Wen refused to cooperate, but when Wang Lijun tortured Wen and had his only son arrested, Wen complied and made some false accusations about He Guoqiang, depicting him as a corrupt official who had mob connections. Bo showed Wen's confession to President Hu Jintao's chief of staff, trying to destroy his credibility as the country's anti-corruption czar. The businessman acknowleged that he had not read Wen's confession.

Based on the evidence collected against Wen, Wang Lijun was said to have recommended a suspended death penalty, but Bo insisted on immediate execution. After his death in July 2010, Wen's relatives hinted on numerous occasions that Wen had not deserved the death penalty and that he was a hapless victim of a political feud.

In 2011, Tong Zhiwei, a professor of constitutional law at the Eastern China University of Political Science and Law, completed an internal study of Bo Xilai's anticrime program. In his report, Tong pointed out that institutions and party officials in Chongqing had forcefully interfered with legal procedures during the "Smashing Black" campaign and some of the measures clearly exceeded constitutional and legal powers. "Arrest without criminal evidence, secret detention, and extracting confession through torture are very common," he said.

Often, trials were conducted in secret. Even for the so-called public trials, Professor Tong stated, the courts would set aside most of the seats for government officials and court staff. Reporters and ordinary citizens who covered or intended to observe the process were denied access. Sometimes the defendants' relatives were kept outside the courtroom.

In the name of combating crime, Bo Xilai launched a major electronic surveillance operation in the city, turning Chongqing into an Orwellian state. Tong said Bo Xilai's anticrime measures intimidated the public and silenced his critics: "Millions of citizens can only cheer for public initiatives that concern their everyday life and are forbidden to air their views in public forums. This is a scary social phenomenon."

Bo's intimidation tactics were not empty. A reporter, Gao Yingpu, used his blog to criticize Bo's anticrime initiatives and the invasive surveillance program. He "disappeared" in July 2010. Later, his wife was told that Gao had been secretly sentenced to three years in jail for endangering state security. His family was pressured to sign an agreement not to discuss the case with the media, or anyone else, in exchange for lenient treatment. When neighbors asked about Gao's whereabouts, his wife said he was doing business in Iraq. Jiang Wanyuan, a policeman who posted three comments criticizing Bo Xilai on an online forum called Tianya, was fired and sent to a labor camp for six months.

When a Hong Kong magazine published an article in January 2010 that quoted a retired official saying that Bo Xilai was not premier or president material, police managed to track down the retired official. During the lunar New Year holiday, Bo personally sent him a postcard containing veiled threats.

An article in the Beijing-based *Caijing* magazine highlighted another problem associated with Bo's "Smashing Black" campaign. Each time a criminal was sentenced or executed, the law enforcement agencies confiscated all of his or her assets; there were no guidelines on whether the assets were acquired legally or illegally, so they took everything. The assets were simply transferred to the government or designated state enterprise, with the result that certain individuals or the state acquired considerable property and money in the name of fighting organized crime.

In a typical case, in February 2010, the Chongqing No. 3 Intermediate People's Court sentenced Chen Mingliang to death for gambling, bribery, and running a prostitution ring as part of a group of thirty-four people who stood trial in a crackdown on the city's violent underworld. After Chen's execution, all of his assets were confiscated. There is no record of where the 200 million yuan's worth of assets went.

Bo Xilai's critics also asserted that many of those targeted in the campaign were not criminals, but private businessmen. Their assets were reportedly used to help pay for Bo's popular social housing programs. In June 2010, Bo ordered the arrest of Peng Zhimin, a top shareholder of the Hilton Hotel in Chongqing and a former municipal legislator. Peng was later sentenced to life imprisonment for his connections to organized crime. The government seized more than

1 billion yuan (US $162,000) worth of assets from him. In an internal article, former police chief Wang Lijun admitted that Peng was crushed because he had openly attacked Bo's anti-crime campaign.

With a master's degree in international journalism, Bo displayed a degree of ease with the media unusual for Chinese politicians, and deftly used local outlets at his disposal to push his image and agenda. Before his arrival in Chongqing, editors at the *Chongqing Daily,* the city's Communist Party paper, specifically organized a team to visit Bo in Beijing and become familiar with his style and approach. Between 2007 and 2012, the *Chongqing Daily* editors were required to obtain approval for every article and photo relating to Bo's activities. Bo would stay up late and spend a couple of hours reviewing and rewriting the articles before they were published. All other media outlets in the city were ordered to adopt the standard *Chongqing Daily* version. Unlike Bo's predecessor, who specifically instructed the media to put ordinary people's stories on the front page, Bo insisted that any articles about him be prominently placed. He demanded that reporters covering his office read *Selected Works of Mao Zedong* and he was never shy about imposing his preferred writing style on journalists. One reporter, who had worked with Bo for three years, said he became so afraid of making a mistake he suffered a nervous breakdown.

Bo's propensity for showmanship prompted his critics to label him as an egomaniac trying to build a personality cult in Chongqing. In 2010, Bo gave tacit approval for two banners to be displayed in the city center, which read, "Party Secretary Bo Is a People's Hero and the Whole Nation Salutes Your Team. President Hu Is Wise, Premier Wen Is Remarkable, and Bo Xilai Is Incredible." A pro-Bo scholar compared Bo and his mayor Huang Qifan to Chairman Mao and Premier Zhou Enlai.

When such criticism and allegations of impropriety leaked out to the overseas media, Bo shrugged them off. He told Glen Kuo—a US businessman who met Bo in Chongqing in the summer of 2011, when Kuo planned to build a resort there—that "Each time you do something, people will always criticize and judge you unfairly. I'm not concerned at all. My motto is, Go your own way and let others talk. It is up to the future generation to make the judgment."

THE FINAL PUSH

A POPULAR GREETING during the 2012 New Year's celebration was "Hope your career soars like the dragon." More than anyone else, Bo Xilai wanted his political career to take off. He would be sixty-three on July 3. The 18th Party Congress later in the fall would be his last chance. During the congress, which is held every five years, the majority of the powerful Politburo Standing Committee would be replaced and he had to get in before he reached the mandatory retirement age of sixty-eight. Time was not on his side.

His "Singing Red and Smashing Black" campaign, despite its controversies, was earning him widespread popularity in China. At a time when the legitimacy of the Communist Party was being challenged by the masses, and when the leadership was seeking solutions to the country's rising social problems, Bo's program stood out. The national and international media showered attention on the so-called Chongqing model. Seymour Topping, a former *New York Times* reporter, was invited to tour and lecture in Chongqing and wrote an enthusiastic report about Bo. Henry Kissinger traveled to Chongqing three times in 2011 and even attended a red-song performance, even though an online report claimed that Kissinger wrote a scathing memo upon his return saying the Chongqing model could harm Western interest.

Between 2010 and 2011, six Politburo Standing Committee members either personally visited Chongqing or were generous with their praise of what had been achieved there. Wu Bangguo, who was ranked high on the list of the Politburo Standing Committee, said Bo's low-cost housing program embodied the central government's pro-people policy and that the anticrime initiatives strengthened people's trust in the party and the government. "I'm very encouraged by what I have seen," Wu told the media.

Meanwhile, many princelings, including the grandchild of Mao Zedong and the children of revolutionary veterans such as Chen Yun and Zhu De, publicly voiced their support for the Chongqing experiment. General Liu Yuan, the son of former president Liu Shaoqi and political commissar of the General Logistics Department, launched a similar anticorruption campaign inside the military. In February, General Liu Yuan ordered the investigation of the deputy head of the General Logistics Department, which oversees much of the military's real estate holdings and commercial enterprises. General Liu told fellow officers at a meeting that corruption in the military had reached a "dangerous level" and that he would fight it "even if it costs me my job." Liu's anticorruption campaign, and similarly high-profile steps such as a belligerent editorial he wrote for a friend's political book in 2011, mirrored Bo Xilai's strategy in Chongqing.

Bo's spirit was probably buoyed by another piece of good news. A group of princelings, with the encouragement of former president Jiang Zemin, secretly speculated on China's new leadership makeup and put together a list that had Bo Xilai as head of the Political and Legal Commission inside the Politburo Standing Committee. The list was said to have gained wide support among the princelings.

Another propitious sign was the misfortune of Wang Yang, Bo's predecessor in Chongqing and now the party chief of Guangdong province. Wang was a rival contender for the Politburo Standing Committee. Four months earlier, in September 2011, thousands of peasants in Guangdong's Wukan village staged a protest after local party officials sold land to real estate developers without properly compensating the villagers. They attacked a government building, a police station, and an industrial park. The local government arrested five protest leaders, and one died while in police custody. The villagers turned on the police and drove them from the village. The police blockaded the village, preventing food and goods from getting through. Newspapers around the world picked up the story of what they called "the Wukan Riot," highlighting once again what Bo had warned about: inequality in wages and government corruption would lead to instability. In December 2011, Wang Yang—Guangdong's party chief (and now the vice premier of China)—intervened. Village representatives and provincial officials were able to reach a peaceful agreement, satisfying the villagers' immediate requests.

Barely a month later, roughly 1,000 people from another nearby village held a rally in front of government headquarters in Guangdong's capital city of Guangzhou against land seizures and corruption.

The villagers threatened to stage a riot similar to Wukan's if their grievances were not resolved.

These group incidents, as they are called in China, made Bo Xilai believe that his rival's conciliatory approach showed weakness in the face of protesters and could encourage more such mass demonstrations. In January 2012, a week before the Lunar New Year, Bo Xilai gathered several confidantes, including his police chief, Wang Lijun, for a small party at a restaurant. An official who attended the gathering recalled discussing the Wukan riot over dinner.

"If it had happened in Chongqing, we would have crushed it with force way before foreign journalists got wind of it," Bo bragged. He believed that the Wukan incident could be his rival's Waterloo and the Politburo Standing Committee could use the incident to purge liberals like Wang Yang from the senior leadership ranks. He urged his people to get ready for his ascension.

Optimistic though he was, Bo also sensed a strong headwind. Premier Wen Jiabao and his designated successor, Li Keqiang, had ignored his doings in Chongqing, neither commenting on his programs nor expressing any desire to visit Chongqing. President Hu Jintao's chief of staff secretly promised that he would get Hu to visit Chongqing but Bo never received any specific details. When Bo took a 1,000-strong red singing troupe to Beijing for a four-day, seven-performance tour in June 2011, not a single senior leader came to watch the performance. He had also reportedly contacted former president Jiang Zemin, who still possessed considerable political clout over personnel arrangements, but no meeting came of it.

An official at the Chongqing municipal government recalled that Bo Xilai became so obsessed with the upcoming leadership transition in late 2011 that he was intent on clearing every possible hurdle and did not want to take any chances.

One of the obstacles was Li Wangzhi, his son from the previous marriage. (I mentioned earlier that Li was raised by his mother, Li Danyu, who made him take her family name.) After graduating from Columbia University in 2001, Li Wangzhi went back to China and became a business consultant and investment banker. In early 2007, when Bo Xilai was still at the Ministry of Commerce, Li allegedly obtained a business license for his father-in-law through Bo's connections. At the end of 2011, Bo found out that Li's father-in-law had used the license to run a pyramid scheme in northeastern China. Victims had filed petitions with the Central Commission for Discipline Inspection. Fearing that his son could become a political liability, Bo reportedly had his son detained. A friend of Li's disclosed to the overseas media that Bo's real intent was to hold his son hostage so his first wife, Li Danyu, would not bad-mouth him before the Party Congress. However, during Li's subsequent interviews, she never confirmed the story about her son's detention.

Around the same time, the murder of Neil Heywood must have weighed heavily on Bo's mind. Although official transcripts from Wang Lijun's trial indicated that Bo was first made aware of his wife's connection with Heywood's death by Wang in January 2012, a senior official in Chongqing surmised that Bo knew about his wife's involvement not long after Heywood's death. He said Bo became very paranoid and had two of his bodyguards arrested, accusing them of sneaking into his office and reading his work-related notes and personal diary on his desk. In China, a senior leader's bodyguards are supplied by the Central Guard Bureau in Beijing with the dual purposes of protecting the leader's safety and monitoring his or her activities. The two guards were eventually set free after President Hu Jintao's chief of staff intervened.

On the morning of January 28, as was previously noted, Wang briefed Bo on Heywood's death, implicated Bo's wife, Gu Kailai, and then promised to keep things under wraps. Bo questioned his wife after the meeting and her denial of Wang's accusations, coupled with Bo's anger over Wang's apparent greed for power, caused him to call another meeting with Wang the next day that ended with Bo slapping him. The incident opened a rift in the Bo–Wang relationship and the damage soon grew past the point of repair.

In the following two days, Bo interrogated Wang's personal assistants and found out that Wang Lijun had been monitoring his private conversations and had even installed a pinhole video camera to record him in hotel rooms with his mistresses. Worse still, Bo Xilai suspected that Wang might have conspired with senior leaders in Beijing. Otherwise, the police chief wouldn't be so bold.

Meanwhile, Bo detained the four police investigators, who admitted writing fake resignation letters and agreed to sign investigation reports stating that Neil Heywood had died of natural causes, and that Wang Lijun attempted to frame Gu Kailai for murder.

On February 2, against the advice of his colleagues, Bo sacked Wang as police chief. The next day, Bo received a letter of apology from Wang, who pledged his loyalty to Bo. But Bo's friends inside the police department reported that Wang had smashed a water glass and threatened to expose Bo's family secrets if he was not reinstated. The news exasperated Bo, who was determined to get rid of Wang before he became even more of a liability.

Bo tried to figure out what to do about Wang while he continued to use the media both to attack his opponents and unabashedly champion his ruling philosophy. Bo was a polarizing figure, and he knew that he probably would not win if he relied solely on the goodwill of several senior members of the Politburo. He needed to generate a groundswell of public support to pressure the leadership from the outside, as Mao had to do when he strengthened his power through mass campaigns during the Cultural Revolution.

At a municipal Party Congress on February 3, Bo Xilai lashed out at his critics:

> There are some really strange people. Each time we talk about singing red songs, they pour cold water, calling us "leftist" or "restoring the past." . . . Some people are not concerned at all about the rampancy of pornography, but become really sensitive to the "singing red campaign." They never speak up on vulgar and pessimistic materials or programs, but when someone tries to start something uplifting or patriotic, they begin to feel uneasy and spread rumors. I have to ask these people, "Isn't red good for our country?" Our national flag is red. The Gate of Heavenly Peace is red. Do we really want to change their colors? We sing about our people, our Party, our motherland. We will take a firm, clear-cut stand.

Analysts construed Bo's remarks as a manifesto of defiance. He was sending a belligerent message to those who opposed him in the Politburo, especially Premier Wen Jiabao.

"He acted as if he were general secretary of the party and randomly scolded other leaders," said an insider. "That didn't go very well."

As Bo went about his public campaign, he did not expect Wang Lijun to outsmart him and slip away. On February 6, 2012, Wang walked into the US Consulate in Chengdu, elevating their personal conflicts into an international incident, the consequences of which were beyond Bo's grasp. Thus, by making a series of reckless decisions against Wang, Bo violated a cardinal rule, which Confucius summarized succinctly for politicians: "Lack of tolerance for small slights will bring destruction to big plans."

THE DISMISSAL

B O'S GONE! Yes, it's true, a senior official told me after I rang to confirm a cell phone call from a Beijing-based journalist I had known for twenty years. It was morning in Beijing, March 15. She had revealed, "Bo Xilai has been removed from his party secretary's post. My contacts have already verified the news. It's safe to post it on your website."

In fact, half an hour earlier, Yang Haipeng, a former journalist with *Southern Metropolis,* whose blog in China attracts 200,000 followers, had already revealed similar information. "I'm willing to shut down my blog as self-punishment if it's proven otherwise," he wrote.

The official Chinese government news agency, Xinhua, tried to catch up and issued a fifty-four-word statement ten minutes after my posting that Bo Xilai no longer held the Chongqing party secretary's position. The Xinhua news quickly appeared prominently on all Chinese news websites. Bo's downfall elicited strong reactions among the Chinese public. Within an hour, some 62,000 comments appeared on Tencent, one of China's largest Internet portals. Leftist websites such as Utopia, Red China, and Maoflag were filled with angry rants over

Bo's dismissal. A large number of residents in Dalian and Chongqing expressed their sympathy and support for Bo on Weibo.

Worrying that the news could trigger chaos, the government immediately ordered all government-run news sites to downplay the story. By the afternoon, all the eye-catching headlines had disappeared and the story blended in with other news of the day. Portal sites such as Sina and Netease shut down their feedback section.

Kong Qingdong, a professor at Beijing University, openly opposed the party's decision to remove Bo Xilai, calling it a "counterrevolutionary coup" during a TV appearance. Kong was detained for five days. Subsequently, he admitted in his blog, under apparent pressure from the government, that he had accepted 1 million yuan from Bo Xilai in exchange for his services to promote Chongqing's political and economic accomplishments.

Worried that Bo supporters might stage demonstrations against his dismissal, the senior leadership allegedly ordered public security departments to deploy armed police in public areas in Chongqing and key major cities. The Hong Kong–based *Oriental Daily* featured pictures posted online by residents in Chongqing, showing armored personnel carriers on the streets and a heavy police presence.

When I was growing up in China, there was a popular saying, "The government policies are as changeable as the summer storm weather." People in Chongqing waited to see which way the storms would blow.

A few hours after Bo Xilai was deposed, a notice went up on a bulletin board near the People's Square in the center of Chongqing, where a large group used to gather to sing red songs. The notice read:

> We have received complaints from residents living nearby that the nightly singing and dancing are too loud and disrupt their normal lives. We will take measures to regulate the activities.

An official with the police department disclosed that they had been notified of Bo Xilai's departure a few hours before the official announcement. The city government banned "celebrations, open discussions, and gatherings." Many police were relieved that the "red terror" was over.

On the evening of March 15, Chongqing Star TV broadcast the news about Bo during its prime-time news program. At the end of the newscast, a liquor commercial appeared, followed by an announcement from Chongqing Star TV to recruit sales representatives for its advertising department. Under Bo's order, the TV station had banned such commercials a year earlier. Ironically, Bo had just reiterated his promise to continue with the commercial-free TV programming at the just-concluded National People's Congress.

The liquor commercial prompted many bloggers to marvel at how fast politics changed directions. A blogger using the alias "Journalist Yang Wanguo" posted a mini-essay called "Chongqing Is Opening Up Again," which said:

I saw several people giving out business cards for "massage services." I got a card and called the number on it. A woman who picked up the phone said she was actually a "sex service provider." The woman said she and two of her friends had just resumed their business. For a quickie, she charged 300 yuan and an all-night service, 600 yuan.

"Aren't you worried about getting arrested by our police chief Wang Lijun?" I asked.

"Didn't he just get sacked?"

"But what if the public security bureau comes to check up on the hotel?"

"Don't worry. Chongqing is open for business again."

Several political dissidents told overseas Chinese media that online references to the 1989 Tiananmen Square student protests, the Falun Gong movement, and the deposed Chinese premier, Zhao Ziyang, were accessible after being blocked for several years. On Baidu, another popular Internet search engine, historic photos of the 1989 protesters, including one showing tanks on the streets of Beijing, were available. In addition, the ban was lifted on an article written by a former professor at Beijing University to condemn the Communist Party's Propaganda Department. The thaw was ephemeral. By the time overseas Chinese media began to report on the phenomenon and decipher whether the change heralded another political spring, the ban had been reinstated. The interpretation with the most traction was that anti-Bo factions within the senior leadership were hoping to convey to the international community that political reforms would be possible if Bo Xilai and his supporters were eliminated.

In the era of the Internet, the usual secret style of the Central Party Committee and its tendency toward cautious investigation did not hold with the public's craving for fast news. For more than two decades China's political environment had been relatively stable. The sudden removal of Bo Xilai came as a surprise for most Chinese. The absence of clear and timely government reports on Bo Xilai's situation generated more speculation and rumors about Bo Xilai's future. Many wondered if the government would press charges against him or simply force him to retire quietly.

Gu Kailai posted two lines on her Weibo on March 16, in which she thanked everyone for their concern. "I want to clarify some facts—I'm doing very well and none of us is under investigation. We will share the truth with the media soon." She said Bo's departure had nothing to do with Wang Lijun's attempted defection. Bo's other family members also talked to the media. His sister-in-law Gu Dan told a reporter that "Bo is at peace with himself at home," adding that for someone who had gone through the turbulence of the Cultural Revolution, "the current setback is nothing."

The government's continued silence on Bo Xilai's fate served only to stoke further interest. A Chinese reporter falsely disclosed in his blog that Bo Xilai and thirty-eight members of his family had been rounded up by the Central Guard Bureau and were imprisoned in a small town outside Beijing. He claimed at least fifty people, including some current and retired senior officials, would be implicated. On the night of March 19, a resident in Beijing posted a message on Weibo saying that a large group of foreign reporters had gathered in front of the Diaoyutai State Guest House and were anticipating some major breaking news related to Bo Xilai. Soon after, someone claimed that the Capital International Airport and the main thoroughfares in Beijing were blocked by fully armed policemen and soldiers. An editor with *Stock Market Weekly* wondered on his blog why there were many military trucks on the streets. He said he had seen plainclothes policemen guarding every crossroad. A well-known poet in China wrote, "Intrigues are in the air tonight. Rumors are flying all over and it looks like a major storm is on its way." One person reported hearing "incessant gunshots" in Beijing, without mentioning where or when. No shooting that night could be verified.

These postings prompted an overseas Chinese site to post a story saying troops loyal to Bo Xilai had teamed up with armed police in Beijing, staged a coup, and "put President Hu Jintao and Premier Wen Jiabao under arrest." A reporter in China told me that several of his friends in the US called him at midnight to ask if there was a coup. The next day, the Weibo postings and the stories proved to be false. It turned out that the foreign reporters who had waited outside the Diaoyutai State Guest House were there to interview the deputy foreign minister of North Korea, who was visiting Beijing with a delegation. There were some armed policemen on Chang-an Boulevard, but they were there to guard the motorcades of several foreign dignitaries.

The government used the excuses of quashing rumors to launch coordinated cyber-attacks against legitimate and reputable news sites both in and outside China. In late March and early April, my *Mingjing News* site was under constant siege from hackers. Readers accessing *Mingjing News* would get an automatic fake virus warning message. Following those attacks, we worked with the FBI and determined that the hacker or hackers had struck from a site in Mexico. Boxun, a user-generated Chinese-language news site that featured many inside stories about the political intrigues surrounding the Bo Xilai scandal, had to shut down for weeks and switch servers, such was the severity of the hacker attacks on its site.

In March, the government temporarily shut down sixteen microblog sites in China, especially those run by two of China's largest portals, Sina and Tencent, for allegedly "spreading harmful information and causing negative social impact." A dozen websites, some of which supported Bo Xilai's overall policies in Chongqing, were closed for "viciously attacking the party leadership and engaging in irresponsible speculation on the upcoming Party Congress." Several bloggers wrote that they had been contacted by police, who invited them out to tea and urged them to impose "self-discipline" and restrain from making trouble for the party and the government.

Interestingly, while the government was trying to block "hostile" websites, party insiders from both sides continued to feed information to domestic bloggers and overseas media.

On March 24, an important piece of news caught public attention. Yang Haipeng, who first disclosed Bo's dismissal on his blog inside China, revealed that the "British nanny" of Bo's son had died in Chongqing the previous year. "The body was cremated without any autopsy. Wang Lijun handled the case. It looked like Bo Xilai was connected with the death."

The "British nanny" Yang erroneously referred to was Neil Heywood. It was as if Heywood's body had floated to the surface of the river into which it had been thrown at a most inconvenient time for Bo Xilai.

In fact, Yang was not the first to reveal the Neil Heywood connection. Back on February 15, a reporter with *Southern Weekend* received a text message from Wang Lijun, claiming that Bo Xilai's wife was connected with the murder of a British businessman named Heywood. The reporter posted the news on Weibo, but the government quickly deleted it.

News that Bo Xilai's family might be linked with Neil Heywood's death failed to make any waves in the Chinese media, which continued to focus on the political aspect of the Bo Xilai scandal in March and early April. Without much information about Neil Heywood, many simply believed the link to be too farfetched. It seemed an ultimate oxymoron that the wife of a Communist Party chief, who thrived on his anticorruption and anticrime platform, would kill a foreigner over a business transaction. Several online postings called the news preposterous, something cooked up by members of the anti–Bo Xilai faction.

But the British and US media jumped at the new development. The mysterious death of Neil Heywood, along with Wang Lijun's flight to the US Consulate, injected new international twists to what had originally been a mere domestic power struggle. In a matter of two weeks, the *Wall Street Journal,* the *New York Times,* the *Daily Telegraph,* the BBC, and the *Guardian* pieced together a profile of Neil Heywood and added to the drama more salacious and intriguing details, some of which proved to be speculative.

Born in 1970 in Kensington, London, Heywood attended the prestigious English public school Harrow, and after graduating from the University of Warwick in 1992, he received a scholarship to study Chinese at the Beijing Language and Culture University. London's *Daily Telegraph* worked out that Heywood went back to the UK after graduation and, among other business schemes, launched a venture with his father, "attempting to produce a 'blind date auction' television show" but was unsuccessful.

In the late 1990s, Heywood traveled to China again and attempted to try his luck there. The timing couldn't have been better. At a televised Chinese New Year celebration a few years before, a Canadian, whose given Chinese name was Da Shan, or Big Mountain, wowed the audience with a stand-up skit in impeccable Chinese. Overnight, he became a household name and people started to look at foreigners differently, especially those who spoke broken or fluent Chinese. Young Westerners who majored in the Chinese language suddenly found themselves in great demand. Local TV stations put a Westerner on the show as a fun prop and Caucasian faces became a common feature in Chinese commercials. Western companies generally hired one of their own who knew the culture and language to help them navigate the still-murky business world, and, similarly, Chinese companies employed a Westerner to show off their strength as international companies and to help them set up operations overseas.

Henry David Hwang's Broadway show, *Chinglish,* describes a young Mandarin-speaking Australian man named Peter Timms who came to China to teach English and insinuated his way into the family of a senior official by helping the official's son get into an elite school in Australia. With his political connections and language talents, he gave up his teaching job and became a "consultant." While trying to school an American businessman in the niceties of building relationships in China, he found himself duped and inadvertently linked in a political power struggle. The character might as well have been based on Neil Heywood, for that is the path he chose in China.

In 1998, Heywood obtained a job in Dalian, teaching English to the children of affluent families, many of whom eyed the West as the destination for their children's education. A Chinese businessman who met Heywood remembers him as a suave English gentleman who boasted about his aristocratic lineage—his great-grandfather had served in the House of Lords and was the consul general of the British mission in Tianjin in 1929–1935. Heywood claimed to have arranged for the granddaughter of the wartime British prime minister, Winston Churchill, to visit China. When asked how he befriended the Bo family, Heywood would tell his friends that Gu Kailai hired him to be Bo Guagua's English tutor in the late 1990s, and that he had used his connections to get Bo Guagua admitted into his alma mater, Harrow, an elite preparatory school in the UK.

However, a Bo family friend disputed Heywood's claim, saying the Briton did not know Gu Kailai until 2003, when he heard that Bo Guagua was attending Harrow. He wrote Gu a letter in which he introduced himself as an alumnus of Harrow living in China, and asked if he could meet her while he was in London. She agreed, and at their meeting, Gu Kailai—who had already spent three years in the UK in order to accompany her son—expressed her intention to return to China soon. Heywood volunteered to be Guagua's caretaker during her absence. Over the next month, as they became acquainted, Gu Kailai accepted Heywood's offer, allowing him to be Bo Guagua's family contact for Harrow. Heywood was supposed to pick up Bo Guagua during weekends and spend time with him at the Bo family apartment in London's West End. Heywood's service paid off. Upon his return to China, Heywood became a frequent guest at the Bo home.

As Bo Xilai's political career took off—governor of Liaoning and then commerce minister—Heywood jettisoned his low-salaried job and launched a consultancy business to help British manufacturers gain a foothold in China.

An official at the Central Commission for Discipline Inspection disclosed that Gu Kailai, over a period of three years, had asked

Heywood to transfer several million dollars of her family assets—presumably bribe money—to the UK, and that Heywood's death might have been caused by a dispute over such transactions.

The revelation of Bo's connection with Neil Heywood's death offered his opponents inside the Politburo an unassailable reason to oust him.

An official who had access to the record of a high-level debate over possible charges against Bo said the leadership had argued over the following allegations, but failed to reach consensus:

- That Bo harbored unbridled political ambitions and turned Chongqing into an independent kingdom. He intended to take over the Central Law and Legal Commission so he could control armed police, and force Xi Jinping, the new party general secretary, to step down.

- That Bo and his wife had accumulated millions of yuan through illegal means and transferred the funds overseas.

For the first charge, the source said it was hard to prosecute Bo on account of his aspiration to join the Politburo Standing Committee. In the Mao era, several senior leaders who were seen as a challenge to Mao's absolute power were persecuted on charges they harbored political ambitions and tried to split the party. But Mao's practices had long been discredited and so could not be deployed to go after Bo. Nowadays, ambition and aspiration are considered key motivating factors for politicians. Besides, there was no substantial proof to show that Bo was planning to seize power and be the head of the country. Furthermore, Premier Wen stated during the National People's Congress that Bo had strayed from the party's platform of reforms and was attempting to restore the Cultural Revolution. His remarks indicated that the nature of Bo's case was ideological rather than criminal—even though differences in opinion had been construed as criminal in the past.

The corruption allegation against Bo could also be politically risky, said the source. No government official is immune to corruption, or in a popular vernacular, "Nobody's butt is clean." Extensive investigation into Bo's case could implicate more senior leaders and trigger a backlash among the public.

As details about Gu Kailai's possible involvement in the Heywood murder emerged, senior officials agreed that they had found a powerful weapon that could fatally destroy Bo. The murder allegation weakened the defense of Bo's supporters and a consensus was quickly forged within the Politburo. In his book, *The Mysteries of Bo Xilai Incident,* Dong Peidong said President Hu Jintao personally consulted with former president Jiang Zemin, who fully supported the Politburo's decision to investigate Bo. "Jiang urged the leadership to handle the case according to the law and make it a solid legal case, which can stand the test of history," wrote the author. Based on Jiang's idea, Hu should put politics aside and focus on hard criminal evidence. "Bo's problem has exceeded the bottom line of human civilization," Jiang added.

On March 19, four days after Bo's dismissal, Japan's *Sankei Shimbun* quoted an inside source as saying that Bo had been detained by the Central Commission for Discipline Inspection, the party's anticorruption body, for investigation. The article said Bo would be transferred to a small town outside Beijing to undergo interrogation and that he could face criminal charges.

A high school teacher, who claimed to be a Bo family friend, spoke out online, declaring the Japanese report to be a rumor and saying that Bo Xilai was staying in the comfort of his home in Beijing. But everyone knew that Bo's detention was merely a matter of time.

On April 10, the website of the *People's Daily,* the official party newspaper, posted a message on its Weibo site that the Central Party Committee was preparing to make a major announcement. Nothing further was reported that day, nor was there any announcement on the evening television news. People began posting complaints online, castigating the *People's Daily* for fueling rumors. At eleven o'clock that night, when most people had already gone to bed, China Central Television interrupted its regular programming and broadcast the following announcement:

As Comrade Bo Xilai is suspected of being involved in serious discipline violations, the Central Committee of the Communist Party of China has decided to suspend his membership of the Politburo and the Party Central Committee, in line with the Party Constitution and relevant rules.

The Central Commission for Discipline Inspection will file the case for investigation.

Chinese police have set up a team to reinvestigate the case that British citizen Neil Heywood was found dead in Chongqing on November 15, 2011, which was alleged by former Chongqing police chief Wang Lijun, who entered, without authorization, the US general consulate in Chengdu on February 6 and stayed there, Xinhua learned from authorities.

Police authorities paid close attention to the case, and set up the team to reinvestigate the case according to law with an attitude to seek truth from facts.

According to investigation results, Gu Kailai, wife of Comrade Bo Xilai, and their son were on good terms with Heywood. However, they had conflict over economic interests, which had been intensified.

According to reinvestigation results, the existing evidence indicates that Heywood died of homicide, of which Gu Kailai and Zhang Xiaojun, a personal assistant at Bo's home, are suspected.

Gu Kailai and Zhang Xiaojun have been transferred to judicial authorities on suspicion of the crime of intentional homicide.

To those who had followed the scandal via Weibo and overseas Chinese media coverage, the short announcement barely confirmed what they had heard and speculated. The next day, a Hong Kong newspaper quoted an official who described in vivid details the final scene before Bo was taken away:

At two o'clock on the afternoon of April 9, two senior officials appeared at Bo's home in Beijing with four military officers. They notified Bo of a meeting at the Great Hall of the People. "As a veteran politician," says the report, "Bo knew that his career [had come] to an end." The sixty-two-year-old Bo asked to make a phone call to inform his relatives, but his request was denied. Bo said calmly, "Even though I've long prepared for this moment, I'm still surprised when it comes."

Before he was led away, he told his household staff, "I need to go. Please take care of yourself. You have to believe in history and believe in the Central Party Committee."

At the Great Hall of the People, Bo met Li Yuanchao, the head of the party's organization department, who presented Bo to Chongqing five years before. Li informed him of the party's decision to remove him from the twenty-five-member Politburo and investigate his wife's involvement in the Neil Heywood murder case. Before he was led away, Bo was quoted as saying that "he only believed in truth."

The version offered by a source of mine in Beijing was more dramatic:

At the Great Hall of the People, Bo yelled at the three Politburo Standing Committee members, who were there to get him. They simply ignored him. Bo was then taken away by members of the Central Commission for Discipline Inspection and confined at a secret location near Beijing.

The source said that at the beginning of the investigation, Bo requested a private meeting with President Hu. After his request was denied, he refused to cooperate with his interrogators, insisting they had no right to question him. One time, he even slapped one official in the face. For a week, he remained silent. To pressure him, officials in charge of his case told him his wife had also been detained. The news further depressed Bo.

Meanwhile, the Chinese official news agency Xinhua published an editorial on April 18 to dispute claims by overseas media, including *Mingjing News,* that the Bo Xilai case was politically motivated. "From our investigations and reviews, it is in no doubt a criminal case," said the editorial. "If these types of criminal activities happen in any modern country with developed laws, the government will handle it like a criminal case. For those who look at China with 'tainted glasses,' they should wait and see. Truth will prevail."

LIKE FATHER, LIKE SON

WHEN BO XILAI was designated as heir to the family's political fortune in 1990, he could never have imagined that his father's history of misfortunes had also rubbed off on him. Father and son would share an eerily similar fate.

Bo Xilai's father, Bo Yibo, was imprisoned four times in his life, the first three in the 1930s by the Nationalists for his Communist beliefs and activities, and the fourth in the 1960s by his fellow Communists who accused him of supporting the Nationalists. Bo Xilai, having once been imprisoned by Maoist radicals who had brought down his father during the Cultural Revolution, now faced incarceration at the hands of his fellow Politburo members who felt threatened by his own radical attempts to restore the Maoist Cultural Revolution.

Both father and the son were accused of abandoning the wives who had supported them when they were at the low points of their lives in favor of younger and more attractive women as their careers and lives turned the corner. Both second wives were fatally compromised by their husbands.

Bo Yibo was born in 1908 in an impoverished region of China's central province of Shanxi at the beginning of the twentieth century. Bo Yibo's biographer said that when Bo Yibo was a young boy, his family was too poor to feed four children. After one of his younger brothers was born, Bo Yibo's parents tossed the infant into a local river. Poverty most surely shaped Bo Yibo's worldview on life. As a high school student, he organized several protests against the local government's unreasonable land taxes. After he was enrolled in the prestigious Beijing University, which was a hotbed of liberal ideas in

China in 1924, he met a group of similar-minded rebels and joined the Chinese Communist Party a year later.

In subsequent years, Bo became an underground Communist Party organizer, first in his hometown of Shanxi and then in the port city of Tianjin. After Nationalist leader Chiang Kai-shek started to suppress Communists across China, Bo was in and out of jail. In 1931, he was sentenced to eight years and sent to a prison for military personnel in Beijing.

In 1936, before Japan launched its full-scale invasion of China, the Communist Party leadership was concerned that Bo and his comrades would be executed if the Japanese troops occupied Beijing. The local party branch, with approval of the senior Communist Party leadership, urged Bo and other imprisoned Communist Party members, more than sixty of them, to falsely confess their crimes and sign an anti-Communist declaration, which was later published in a local newspaper. Bo followed party orders and was released.

At the invitation of a close friend, Bo returned to his hometown and worked as a Communist under a sympathetic warlord, who had rallied troops to fight the Japanese. When the warlord later turned against the Communists in his army, Bo Yibo collected his supporters and joined Mao Zedong's army, conducting fierce guerrilla operations against the Japanese in southern Shanxi. After Japan's defeat in 1945 by largely American-led Allied forces in the Pacific, China collapsed into civil war between the Nationalists and the Communists. Bo Yibo became an influential military and political figure in the Communist ranks. Mao claimed victory in 1949 and Bo served as China's first finance minister, deputy chairman of the State Planning Commission, and vice premier. To the public, he was Mao's close friend and the two were constantly seen swimming together.

Bo Yibo's political career came to an abrupt end during the Cultural Revolution, which started in 1966. Kang Sheng, head of China's version of the KGB, dug out a newspaper that featured the "anti-Communist" declaration that Bo Yibo had signed in order to gain release from prison in 1936. Kang brought up the issue to Mao, condemning Bo as a Communist traitor. At a Central Party Committee meeting, Mao, who was well aware of Bo's false confession back in 1936, did not approve the traitor charges, but a month later, at the urging of other radicals in the party, he switched position.

Mao openly criticized Bo Yibo at a meeting in February 1967, in front of a delegation from China's Communist ally, Albania:

> Some of the Communist Party members had been arrested by the Nationalists, betrayed the cause and published anti-Communist declarations in a newspaper. At that time, we didn't know they were anti-Communists and did not know the details of their release. Now we have discovered that they actually supported the Nationalists and opposed Communism.

Mao's remarks sealed Bo Yibo's fate, just as thirty-five years later, Premier Wen Jiabao's statement about the Chongqing model at a press conference would lead to the downfall of his son.

In March 1967, Bo Yibo and sixty-one other senior leaders who had languished in a Nationalist prison in the 1930s for their unwavering faith in Communism found themselves prisoners of the Communist state that they had fought to establish. Bo Yibo was dragged before "struggle sessions" at stadiums in Beijing and paraded around with a big iron plaque around his neck, but he remained defiant and demanded to speak in his own defense.

To justify Bo Yibo's jail sentence, the government launched a nationwide propaganda campaign to "expose his decadent bourgeois lifestyle," the same tactic that was used thirty-five years later against his son.

Back in the 1960s, as the Cultural Revolution swept the country, it was almost impossible to determine what constituted a crime. Corruption charges against Bo Yibo included watching foreign movies and owning fourteen winter coats for a family of eight.

A party pamphlet titled "The Dirty Mind and Decadent Lifestyle of Bo Yibo" said that Bo Yibo loved "decadent British, American and Hong Kong movies that display women's thighs" and that he enjoyed banned classical Chinese novels and traditional operas that were vulgar and pornographic:

For many years, Bo Yibo led a decadent bourgeois lifestyle. His eight-member family occupied three courtyard houses. Before an overseas trip, Bo's wife spent 600 yuan [US $100] on high-end luxury pajamas. Both Bo and his wife frequently drank ginseng soup. When the house was raided, we found a wooden box full of ginseng roots. In the 1960s, when our country was experiencing economic difficulties, Bo and his wife abused power. Each time they took a business trip, they would always purchase bolts of cloth, watches, vegetable oil, candy, fruits, watermelon, peanuts and some stinky tofu. They even bought chopsticks and brooms. Oftentimes they asked the government for subsidies, claiming that they had financial difficulties. At a conference in Guangzhou in 1962, Bo secretly bought a bolt of cloth. Many people saw him carry the cloth from his car to his room. He left a bad impression among the public.

Every one of Bo's children had their own room, with carpets and sofas. Each child owned a watch, a transistor radio and an imported bicycle. Bo's second daughter never read Chairman Mao's books and refused to participate in political campaigns. She used all sorts of excuses to avoid physical labor. She asked her father's staff members to do her homework and constantly yelled at them if they did not perform to her satisfaction. . . . When she was feeling slightly sick, she would refuse to attend school and stayed home, wandering around in her slippers. She would carry a wooden back massager and patted her back while walking. It was disgusting. She never cooked and did not know how to sew. She even asked her nanny to wash her handkerchief and her menstrual belt. She was a typical stinky bourgeois princess.

When Bo's eldest son once said contemptuously, "Who cares about serving the people. I want to do a good job at school. I will attend Qinghua University in the future and become an expert on science. It doesn't matter if I join the Communist Party or not." When staff members heard about it, they told Bo, who simply laughed and did nothing to correct his son. When Bo's eldest daughter graduated from college, he used his connections at the Foreign Ministry and had his daughter and son-in-law assigned to the British government office in Beijing. His third daughter was able to transfer to a different college through his connections at the Education Ministry.

In comparison with the corruption allegations against Bo Xilai and his wife—transferring millions of dollars overseas—the charges against Bo Yibo in the 1960s seem trivial, even laughable. But they were enough to keep Bo Yibo in prison for twelve years.

Following Mao's death in 1976, Hu Yaobang, who was in charge of personnel matters at the Party Central Committee and was to become the general secretary of the Communist Party, received a letter from Bo Yibo requesting a review of his case. Hu Yaobang organized a special team to quietly investigate the charges against Bo Yibo. In those days, even though Mao's widow and other radicals had been arrested, many supporters of the Cultural Revolution were still in power and resisted any attempts to reverse political decisions made by Mao. Fortunately, Hu Yaobang obtained support from senior leader Deng Xiaoping, who had just emerged as an important figure in Chinese history after years of political persecution.

In 1977, the special team presented a report to the Central Party Committee, which included hundreds of interviews and testimonials to illustrate that Bo Yibo and his fellow Communists were wrongly convicted and that they never betrayed the Communist Party during their incarceration in the 1930s. The Central Party Committee adopted the recommendations and Bo Yibo's conviction was officially overturned on December 16, 1978. He was reinstated as vice premier of China and joined the Politburo. Despite his imprisonment and harsh treatment, Bo Yibo remained loyal to Mao's Communist ideology. In the post–Mao era, Bo supported China's economic reforms but resisted any political liberalization espoused by reformists.

Throughout his life, critics say, Bo Yibo had the habit of biting the hand that fed him. In May 1927, when he was pursued by the Nationalists for his underground Communist activities, Bo Yibo sought shelter at the house of a wealthy friend, who risked his life to save Bo. While in hiding at this friend's house, the young Bo Yibo fell in love with the friend's daughter. The two were married and had one daughter, who later became an official at the Chinese Foreign Ministry.

Once his situation turned for the better, Bo Yibo had an affair with his secretary, a Guangdong-born Communist activist, in the early 1940s. He requested a divorce from his wife, but she declined. Bo Yibo continued the affair and three times got his secretary pregnant. For a young woman, premarital pregnancies were considered a disgrace. The secretary had to undergo three abortions. This eventually moved—or appalled—Bo Yibo's wife so much that she agreed to the divorce, probably saving the young woman's life. Many years later, his ex-wife was quoted as saying:

> His divorce request really hurt my father's feelings. My father had risked his life to rescue him. . . . But I had to grant the divorce. I had no choice. The secretary already had three abortions. As a woman, I can't see her going through these abortions again and again. Her life could be endangered.

The secretary's name was Hu Ming. Known for her beauty and intelligence, the idealistic Hu Ming had joined the Communist revolution at the age of sixteen and specialized in youth, publicity, and woman-related work. She married Bo Yibo in 1945, and after they moved to Beijing in 1949, Hu Ming held various midlevel jobs at government ministries and bureaus. She gave birth to four boys and two girls. Bo Xilai was her second child.

When Bo Yibo was purged in the Cultural Revolution, Hu Ming, who was then in Guangzhou, was escorted back to Beijing on January 5, 1967, to expose her husband's crimes. On the Beijing–Guangzhou express train, Hu Ming died mysteriously. The Red Guards accompanying her claimed that she committed suicide, but later reports hold that she was beaten to death by her handlers. She would have been forty-eight that year.

In the 1980s, when Bo Yibo's son Bo Xilai requested a divorce from his wife so he could marry Gu Kailai, some people brought up Bo Yibo's two marriages, calling Bo Xilai "a replica of his father." Before his death, Bo Yibo's reputation was tainted by his treatment of Hu Yaobang, the reform-minded party general secretary who was instrumental in ending his ten-year imprisonment. In November 1986, when university students around the country started to hold small-scale demonstrations—in hindsight this was a warning of the much bigger movement that would come three years later—demanding transparency in government and action against the corruption of officials, Bo Yibo sided with hardliners and blamed Hu Yaobang's liberal policies for creating the chaos. Hu Yaobang resigned in January 1987, under the pressure of Bo Yibo and other veteran revolutionaries. When Hu Yaobang suffered a heart attack in 1989 and a nationwide student prodemocracy movement broke out, Bo Yibo supported Deng Xiaoping's decision to suppress the movement with force.

In a final twist of the overlapping lives of Bo father and son, twenty-two years later, President Hu Jintao and Premier Wen Jiabao, both considered Hu Yaobang's protégés, ended the political career of the son.

SECRET INVESTIGATION

BEFORE THEIR TAKEOVER of China in 1949, the Communists spent years fighting a guerrilla war against the better armed ruling Nationalists and operating an extensive network of underground Communist agents in China's key cities. Spies were a popular theme in propaganda movies, depicting heroic underground Communist agents who eavesdropped on enemy conversations, left important notes for other Communists in secret locations, sent secret telegraphic messages to the party from their bedrooms at midnight, and assassinated traitors and enemies with silent handguns. I and millions of others grew up watching such films, long before James Bond movies were allowed into China. For years, being a Communist was almost synonymous with being a secret agent. When my father joined the Communist Party, I was disappointed that he was nothing like the mysterious Communist spies I saw in movies.

In hindsight, our childhood impressions of the Communist Party are probably fairly close to truth. Sixty years after the Chinese Communist Party took power, it still conducts business like an underground organization in enemy-occupied territories. All the key Communist Party organs, such as the Central Organization Department, the Central Propaganda Department, and the Central International Liaison Department, operate in office buildings without signs, without street numbers or listed phone numbers. Major decisions are made in closed-door meetings. Senior leaders act like members of the mafia, mysterious and secretive. Any personal information about them is considered a state secret. In September 2012, the then vice president Xi Jinping reportedly hurt his back and disappeared from public view for two weeks without explanation. The Party Central Committee refused to divulge any details, triggering wild speculations that there might have been a coup.

In the case of Bo Xilai, any information relating to his investigation is considered top secret. The public has no idea where he is being detained or how he is being interrogated. In April 2012, the government announced only that he is being investigated by the Central Commission for Discipline Inspection, which is headquartered inside a nameless office complex at 41 Pinganli Avenue in Beijing. What kind of organization is the Central Commission for Discipline Inspection? Many Chinese have heard it mentioned frequently in the state media, but few understand how it works.

The Chinese leadership, in its desperate effort to maintain the monopoly of the Communist Party, relies on an internal anticorruption organization—specifically the Central Commission for Discipline Inspection, with a network of branches extending to the township level—to monitor the conduct of some 80 million party members, or 16 percent of China's 1.3 billion people. The commission has eight divisions, the first four of which handle corruption offenses among party members above the vice-ministerial level within the central government or party organizations; the rest handle graft among those of vice-governor level or higher in different regions.

Without a regular open channel for the media and the public to supervise the party, the commission depends heavily on tips and clues provided by petitioners and anonymous whistle-blowers. A recent state media report said nearly half of the cases under investigation were based on tips or anonymous reports. Other important sources come from instructions by the top leaders or petitions or complaints sent to high-level party organizations, and legislative and judicial bodies.

Since the late 1980s, as corruption within the party has become more rampant, the party has actively promoted the role of the commission, giving it more power to discipline corrupt leaders and rank-and-file members. Thus, the commission has established an unassailable position. The judiciary and law enforcement agencies have given up some of their legal responsibilities to the commission. Criminal investigation used to be a key job for the prosecution organ, but the commission has taken over the initial investigation and prosecutors simply coordinate cleaning up the postmortem work.

During an investigation, the Central Commission for Discipline Inspection employs a practice known as *shuanggui,* or "double regulations." The accused will be taken to a secret place for a specific period of time for harsh interrogation. This practice allows the commission to intervene before a judicial investigation begins. Sometimes investigators detain a suspect at a place away from his or her home or workplace to avoid the suspect's access to his or her own network of power, influence, and connections in a particular area. Analysts say the secrecy is intended to shield the public from details that might harm the party's image and to limit collateral damage to those higher up the chain of command. Investigations of officials above vice-ministerial levels are approved by the Politburo, which deliberates on the allegations first. This means that by the time the official is pulled into the system, he or she is already considered guilty by the Politburo. Therefore, few emerge unscathed, if they emerge at all. The state media said that between 1999 and 2009, the court convicted more than 100 senior officials due to the commission's investigations. Among them, eight were executed and twenty received a suspended death penalty or life imprisonment. There is a popular phrase among senior officials, "I am not afraid of God, neither am I afraid of ghosts, but I am afraid of being summoned to talk to the Central Commission for Discipline Inspection." Some, including the former deputy mayor of Beijing, had committed suicide or died under mysterious circumstances before they were detained.

During detention, the accused are subject to harsh interrogations. Once investigators obtain a satisfactory confession, detainees are often stripped of their leadership positions and party membership, and their cases are handed over to government prosecutors for summary trials, which are closed to the public. Since 1992, the commission's investigations have led to the fall of several senior leaders, including the deputy party chief of Sichuan province, the vice president of the Supreme People's Court, the railway minister, the deputy party secretary of Shandong province, and the assistant director at the Ministry of Public Security.

But in the eyes of ordinary Chinese who have been victimized by rampant government corruption, the commission stands as their only hope for justice.

Even though the party produces impressive statistics on the commission's work, few observers believe corruption is being systemically addressed. Corruption occurs because of the lack of transparency in the system. Ironically, anticorruption works the same way. In the past few years, the commission has emerged as a monster that is growing in size, placing itself above the judiciary and obstructing China's efforts to build the rule of law. Mo Shaoping, a well-known human rights lawyer in Beijing, said the commission's double regulation practice violates the Chinese constitution:

> The law stipulates that no organization has the right to restrict a citizen's freedom without the approval of the court, but the Commission places itself above the law. Communist Party members or government officials are citizens and the law should apply here.

When a major case involving a senior leader is assigned, the commission, with permission from the Politburo, organizes a special team of several hundred people to conduct investigations, turning itself into the most authoritative law enforcement and judicial organ. In Bo's case, the commission reportedly dispatched two big teams, one to

Dalian and the other to Chongqing. In addition, smaller groups traveled to Hong Kong and Guangzhou to collect evidence relating to Bo's family finances. The commission's investigation is not part of the judicial process, but takes precedence over any other legal proceedings. During the double regulations process, members of the commission can enlist the help of public security agents and armed or traffic police. Nobody dares disobey. The commission has access to stacks of court subpoenas, detention permits from the Public Security Ministry, arrest warrants from the prosecutor's office, and auditing permits from the taxation department. It has the authority to detain, collect evidence, and dictate how a target will be punished. The judicial system is a mere prop in its activities. Upon the completion of the investigation, the commission denies the court any independence by imposing its own sentencing recommendation.

On May 29, 2007, Zheng Xiaoyu, director of the National Food and Drug Administration, was tried for dereliction of duty after he allowed counterfeit drugs to enter the market. Dereliction of duty carries a maximum sentence of seven years, but the committee, which investigated Zheng first, recommended the death penalty to appease public anger. The court acquiesced and found him guilty of corruption—because he accepted bribes—and dereliction of duty, and duly sentenced him to death.

Often, it appears the commission has more power than the Supreme People's Court, which reviews all death sentences imposed by the lower courts to ensure that the punishment fits the crime. In the name of anti-corruption and in the rigorous pursuit of "truth," Chinese legal experts say, the commission detains the accused for long periods of time and denies the person access to a lawyer or due process. Even though Chinese law explicitly prohibits the use of torture during interrogation, it does not recognize the right to remain silent. Forced confessions and torture are common.

Li Heping, another Beijing-based lawyer, said the commission resorts to torture more than other judicial organizations do. Moreover, it ignores the presumption of innocence, the most important symbol of human rights protection in modern criminal law. Thus, a person under investigation has no right to hire a lawyer and yet the confessions obtained by any means during the investigation can be used as evidence in court.

The regional version of the commission has now become a very important tool used by local leaders to eliminate their opponents. There are incidents where a new provincial leader has taken over a new assignment, but had problems controlling subordinates who resist his leadership. Under such circumstances, the new leader can fabricate petitions to the commission's local branch, requiring investigation. Sometimes, when multiple people are competing for a spot in a midlevel government agency, the candidates backstab each other by writing petition letters, thereby eliminating their competition.

At the central level, the commission enforces the law selectively. An anticorruption investigation is a tool to protect the interests of a handful of senior leaders. One of the commission's most important tasks is to filter out and if necessary remove any suggestion of impropriety that might be harmful to the senior leadership, or attack opponents, or protect certain privileged persons by warning and offering a way out of a potential political scandal. Those who are punished lack connections or are deemed to be of no political significance. Experts say this two-tiered approach, where some are favored over others, explains why corruption is endemic in China. It has been embedded in the political system. As mentioned before, under normal circumstances, any investigation relating to officials at the vice minister levels and above must be signed off by the Politburo. Members of the Politburo Standing Committee enjoy absolute immunity, because the threat of purges at the highest level would be too destabilizing.

In Mao's time, political purges were conducted randomly and largely at the behest of Mao himself. Any member of the party's hierarchy, regardless of his position, could be labeled a "traitor" or "capitalist" overnight if he was perceived to be a threat. There were no rules or laws to protect the victims. Mao acted like an emperor and his words were law. Often the persecution extended to the families of the disgraced official. Bo Yibo was a typical example.

After Mao died in 1976, party elders such as Deng Xiaoping, who had been victims of Mao's persecution, tried to avoid the arbitrariness and brutality in the party's power struggles and protect the basic rights of the members of the ruling elites by installing certain procedures and introducing an orderly system of leadership transition. However, revolutionary veterans violated their own procedures when they used the Central Commission for Discipline Inspection to purge officials known as "rebels"—they were promoted by Mao supporters during the Cultural Revolution and had participated in the persecution of senior leaders.

In the post-Deng era, when the country was trying to promote the rule of law, if only to placate foreign governments with which China traded, and foreign investors it wished to attract, Deng's successors employed the Central Commission for Discipline Inspection as a tool to criminalize political opponents in the name of anticorruption. Former president Jiang Zemin successfully brought down Chen Xitong, the former party secretary of Beijing and a Politburo member, because Chen and his supporters in the Beijing area, collectively known as the "Beijing Clique," were undermining his authority.

In Bo's case, the party once again resorted to the powerful Central Commission for Discipline Inspection to oust him. A source at the commission said that the initial focus of the investigation was related to Bo Xilai's role in Neil Heywood's murder. Soon investigators ran into challenges: Bo Xilai might have attempted to cover up his wife's act of murder, but there was no concrete evidence to prove that he had participated in the killing. The cover-up charge alone was not a strong enough excuse to destroy Bo Xilai for good. The senior leadership reportedly instructed the commission to turn to areas of corruption and subversion. Starting in May 2012, the party's propaganda machine launched a massive campaign, depicting Bo as a corrupt official who used illegal means to attain political and economic gains. Meanwhile, insiders in Beijing were feeding what they called preliminary results of Bo's investigation to media outlets overseas.

For example, in May, "nearly a dozen people with party ties" confirmed to the *New York Times* that Bo Xilai had installed a widespread program of electronic bugging across Chongqing and he had recorded the conversations of senior party officials, including President Hu Jintao. A similar report came out in early March, portraying Wang Lijun as the chief architect of this program.

Mr. Bo's eavesdropping operations began several years ago as part of a state-financed surveillance build-up, ostensibly for the purposes of fighting crime and maintaining local political stability. . . .

But party insiders say the wiretapping was seen as a direct challenge to central authorities. It revealed to them just how far Mr. Bo, who is now being investigated for serious disciplinary violations, was prepared to go in his efforts to grasp greater power in China. That compounded suspicions that Mr. Bo could not be trusted with a top slot in the party, which is due to reshuffle its senior leadership positions this fall.

In the same month, a Hong Kong–based newspaper quoted an insider as saying Bo Xilai had used surveillance devices to collect negative information about senior leaders' families and their mistresses. Bo had planned to unleash the information before the Party Congress as part of his scheme to seize power and, if necessary, arrest Xi Jinping, the heir apparent.

Qi Hong, a Chongqing-based technician who has been hired by local officials to detect and debug surveillance devices in their offices, cars, and bedrooms, told *Chongqing Evening News* that wiretapping became prevalent in Bo's Chongqing. In 2011, he deactivated more than three hundred audio and video monitoring devices secretly planted by officials' wives, lovers, supervisors, and competitors. *Chongqing Evening News* revealed that bugging is now being used as a common tool in power struggles at all levels of the government— officials spy on each other and collect needed audio and video evidence to get rid of a competitor. Qi Hong's story has proven to be true, as Lei Zhengfu, a former district party chief in Chongqing, was recently fired from his position after a video of him having sex with a young woman was posted online by a former journalist. The whistle-blower, who was planning to release similar tapes of more city officials, told *Chongqing Evening News* that 90 percent of the tapes came from party insiders. In addition, according to Feng Qingyang, a blogger, some local officials in China are said to be so paranoid about bugging devices that they will pretend to hug their colleagues "intimately" before conducting a sensitive conversation, to make sure nobody is carrying a mini tape or video recorder. Some even choose to discuss businesses naked in noisy bath-houses. A former police officer in Chongqing blamed Bo and Wang for the widespread abuse of wiretapping. "The two egomaniacs not only snooped on political opponents, dissidents, and criminals, but also on each other," said the official. "In the end, others began to follow suit. If you didn't conspire against others, others would plot to get rid of you. You have to do it. It's a survival technique."

In addition, from March to July 2012, I received regular e-mails or phone calls from "insiders" who claimed to have "exclusive information" relating to Bo's subversion attempts. One e-mail said that Bo had ordered his police chief to purchase 5,000 guns and 500,000 rounds of ammunition from the government's munitions factory in Chongqing for a possible coup.

The *Wall Street Journal* received similar information. A party official at an influential government think tank told the paper that Bo had cultivated his military contacts and "at least two prominent army generals have been questioned about their connections to Mr. Bo."

At issue now is whether Mr. Bo went too far by cultivating support among senior military figures—especially his fellow princelings—for his controversial policies and for his elevation to the Politburo Standing Committee, which he coveted.

Mr. Bo lived in a military area, which he rarely left while in Chongqing, according to a city official who worked under him. In 2011, he poured about $500 million of public funds into developing a helicopter industry in Chongqing to meet the army needs.

Last November, he hosted military exercises in Chongqing, attended by Defense Minister Gen. Liang Guanglie, after which Mr. Bo staged one of his "red singing" performances for his guests, according to state media reports.

After the *Wall Street Journal* article was published, several Chinese-language newspapers in the US also reported that one of Bo's friends in the military had supplied Bo with weapons and secretly helped him establish a private army. But the weapons that Bo had supposedly acquired were nowhere to be found.

I contacted two military experts who castigated the overseas media for trusting those insider stories and exaggerating Bo Xilai's influence in the military and his military ambitions. Over the past three decades, the two experts said the Chinese Communist Party has gradually tightened its grip over the military through the rotation of senior military leaders, making it impossible for one military commander to cultivate support. And the military's access to modern weaponry is limited by the tight control exercised over the General Equipment Department. Even if Bo enjoyed close ties with two princeling generals, his ability as the Chongqing party secretary to stage a coup would be very limited.

According to the experts, Chongqing is home to a big army garrison and a military engineering university where weapons are designed. Bo Xilai's contacts with local and national military figures were nothing unusual. The experts did acknowledge that many in the military were pressured to pledge an oath of loyalty to the party and President Hu Jintao in May to ensure that army leaders fully supported the decision to oust Bo. A vice chairman of the Central Military Commission visited the Chengdu Military Region in April. He urged soldiers "not to listen to, believe, or spread any kind of political rumors, and to strictly guard against political liberalism" in an apparent attempt to prevent military personnel from reading the various corruption scandals relating to Bo and other senior leaders, and boost the army's confidence in the party.

In addition to the subversion rumors, the state media and party insider leaks depicted Bo Xilai as a hypocrite. In a February speech, Bo was quoted as admonishing other officials with the following words:

What is a person's true wealth? Is it money? Money ruined so many people. The true value is to do good things for the country and for ordinary people; your life will be noble and fulfilling.

Yet, he never practiced what he had preached, said an insider. Bo and his wife were greedy money grabbers. Over the past decade, his wife was involved in more than thirty commercial property development projects and received more than 1 billion yuan in commissions or "legal consultation fees"; in Dalian and Chongqing, Bo Xilai abused power by granting several government projects to his friends, including billionaire businessman Xu Ming. In addition, Bo encouraged the whole city to study Chairman Mao's works and love the country by singing patriotic songs, but he sent his son to study political science at elite schools in the UK and US, with the majority of expenses paid for by Xu Ming.

It was interesting to notice that in March 2012, insiders disclosed that the amount of money the Bo family was said to have acquired was 100 million yuan. Barely a month later, it increased to 1 billion yuan. Some online reports even claimed 5 billion yuan (US $806 million).

On April 11, the US-based Bloomberg publicized the results of an investigation into the finances of Bo Xilai's family members. The report indicated that his son from his first marriage and his elder brother helped manage companies with offshore registrations, from Mauritius in the Indian Ocean to the British Virgin Islands in the Caribbean, amassing a fortune of at least US $136 million. Bo Xilai's relatives used multiple names, making it more difficult to track their titles and business dealings. Bloomberg said companies in Dalian and Chongqing, where Bo Xilai held office, were among the beneficiaries of their investments.

The Bloomberg article, which was widely quoted in China's Weibo, gave the anti-Bo camp plenty of ammunition. However, they did not expect the article to spawn a series of reports in the Western media about how the families of other senior leaders, including Premier Wen Jiabao and former Politburo Standing Committee member Zeng Qing-hong, are wealthy businesspeople and have profited handsomely from their family status.

These exposés made China's top leaders, who all have family members and relatives engaging in questionable or illegal business deals, realize that no one would be absolutely safe if the Bo Xilai investigation was allowed to expand. Because Bo had been successfully barred from the Politburo Standing Committee, sources said his foes started to cool off with their attacks. In July and August, the party called for political stability within the party. The true intention was to protect its leaders' vested interests.

Of all the Bo corruption-related gossip, the item that received the most attention was related to his womanizing. Boxun and a Hong Kong newspaper quoted an inside source as saying that actress Zhang Ziyi, the star of *Crouching Tiger, Hidden Dragon*, allegedly had been investigated for a sex scandal linked with Bo. The source said the actress had agreed to sleep with Bo Xilai for 10 million yuan and they had at least ten encounters between 2004 and 2007. The report went on to say that Zhang was barred from leaving the country to participate in the Cannes Film Festival in May 2012, when her movie *Dangerous Liaisons* was competing. In response to such reports, Zhang, who claimed to have never met Bo Xilai, filed a lawsuit at the High Court of Hong Kong against Boxun and two publications in Hong Kong that carried the allegations. At the time of writing, no verdict has been reached and there has been no ban on Zhang's travel.

As insiders were busy feeding the overseas media with their usual mixture of truth and lies about Bo Xilai, his legacy in Chongqing was being quietly washed away. The big banners bearing Communist slogans in public places were quickly replaced with Gucci and Radar watch ads. Police removed gigantic poster boards that advocated Bo's signature "Five Chongqing" program—building a livable Chongqing through low-cost public housing, a traffic-friendly Chongqing through more infrastructure investment, a forested green Chongqing through environmental programs, a safe Chongqing by aggressive anticrime initiatives, and a healthy Chongqing through better delivery of health care. The Five Chongqing program, initiated a year after Bo Xilai came to the city, became a model for other cities to emulate. Bo's replacement, who has ascended to the Politburo Standing Committee, overhauled the government finances and suspended many of Bo's large-scale public projects.

By mid-May 2012, government officials who were detained, demoted, or resigned during Bo's reign had submitted applications to the Central Commission for Discipline Inspection, seeking review of their cases, and many have gotten their jobs back. Currently, more than a dozen senior municipal officials favored by Bo have been placed under investigation or fired.

But the steady reversal of the Bo Xilai policies upset several Chongqing residents, especially after they heard rumors that the government was planning to pull out the expensive gingko trees that Bo had planted as part of his high-profile environmental programs. "Secretary Bo has done a lot for the city and his program has truly benefited ordinary folks," said a volunteer staffing a traffic control booth on a busy street downtown in November 2012—he still referred to Bo by his former title of party secretary. "Everyone knows that the streets were safer when Bo Xilai and Wang Lijun were in power and the environment improved. We had more trees and the air was cleaner. We shouldn't reverse everything he did, simply because he made some mistakes," the volunteer added. And Bo Xilai's followers in Dalian and Chongqing have remained persistent. On his birthday in July 2012, many anonymous "Happy Birthday, Secretary Bo" posters popped up in public places in the two cities.

The memory of Bo was not easy to erase.

huo

shui

Poisonous Water

The Chinese version of femme fatale is *huo shui*, which means "poisonous water." *Huo shui* specifically refers to a beautiful woman who ruins the lives and careers of powerful men.

THE GIRL BUTCHER

FOR SIX WEEKS in October and November 1952, on a forested ridge near what would become the demilitarized zone dividing North and South Korea, Chinese soldiers repelled repeated attacks by US-led UN and South Korean forces in what became known as the Battle of Shangganling, or the Battle of Triangle Hill to the US. General Gu Jingsheng, who had helped Mao Zedong found the People's Republic of China, knew the position was strategically important and he led the tough defense that inflicted heavy casualties on American forces despite their superior artillery and aircraft. The battle was made into a movie, now regarded as a Communist propaganda classic. After the war, General Gu held various leadership positions in China's air force and the defense department. He worked with Qian Xuesen, the father of rocketry, to develop China's space and rocket programs and subsequently the country's first atomic bomb.

Fan Chengxiu was the direct descendent of an illustrious eleventh-century writer, politician, and militarist, whose writings are still part of the Chinese high school curriculum. Fan joined Mao's troops at the age of fourteen; she fought in the Resistance War against Japan in the late 1930s and the Chinese Civil War in the 1940s. When the revolution succeeded, Fan was appointed a leader of the Central Party School.

The revolutionary Fan married General Gu in the 1940s and gave birth to five daughters. The youngest was Gu Kailai, who would marry Bo Xilai.

Neighbors called the five Gu girls "Five Golden Flowers," the title of a popular 1950s musical featuring the love stories of five beautiful, strong-willed young Chinese women. The Gu sisters possessed not only good looks but also business acumen. Three of them operate business ventures worth a cumulative US $1 billion.

Despite her parents' extraordinary past, Gu Kailai grew up in a family rocked by political upheavals. The year she was born, her mother was labeled a rightist and a counterrevolutionary for defending a young staff member who had dared criticize the party's policies. Following her mother's detention, the local party organization demanded she file for divorce to protect the political career of General Gu, who was a crucial figure in developing the country's national defense industry. Forced to choose between his career and his family, General Gu picked the latter and asked his wife to ignore the party's demand. "I understand Fan Chengxiu very well," General Gu wrote. "She joined the party at the age of fifteen and studied Marxism at the party school. She repeatedly risked her life for the party during the war years. She has been loyal and given her whole life to the party. Calling her a counterrevolutionary is the biggest injustice under heaven. Divorcing her would ruin her life. I will not do it. The party can do whatever they want with me."

General Gu paid dearly for his defiance. He was sidelined and barred from participating in important defense projects. In 1966, when the Cultural Revolution started, General Gu and his wife were separated and imprisoned for twelve years, during which time they had no contact with their children. Gu Kailai and her sisters lived like orphans. In a letter to his daughters, General Gu offered a glimpse of their lives in that period:

> You should not have second thoughts about the party, just because your mother and I are being paraded around for public denunciation every day and our homes are being raided every couple of days. I know that Zheng Xie [the second daughter] has been disqualified from joining the Red Guard organization. Don't be angry. If you are a true revolutionary, you should carve out your own path. The younger girls should manage to finish school. Practice your calligraphy at home and learn to protect each other. Don't be scared of knocks on the door and raids at midnight. Stay away from the bullies among other children in the neighborhood.

At the age of thirteen, Gu Kailai graduated from junior high school. Although her four siblings had been sent to remote rural areas for what was then called reeducation, she was spared the harsh treatment. The local government assigned her a job in the city with a construction firm. Gu Kailai became a bricklayer first and was subsequently transferred to a state-run meat store, where she became a model female butcher. One of Gu Kailai's friends told the Chinese media she looked tiny for her age, but she was tough and dedicated. She established a reputation as the woman with a "single cleaver cut"—with one strike of the cleaver, she could give customers the exact amount of pork they requested.

In her spare time, Gu Kailai picked up the *pipa,* a traditional pear-shaped Chinese musical instrument, hoping that she could improve her career and become a professional musician. She was a fast and diligent learner. Within a short time, she could play like a professional. Indeed, in 1976, she joined the orchestra at the Beijing Film Studio as a *pipa* soloist and was selected to play the theme music for the documentary *The Passing of Chairman Mao.*

After Mao's death, her parents were released from jail and the family became whole again. With the return of the national college entrance examination system, Gu Kailai set her sights on college, but having quit school in her early teens, she had never received training in mathematics and scored a near zero in that examination. Fortunately, she performed well in her social science subjects, especially her Chinese calligraphy, and in the fall of 1978, Gu, then age twenty, was enrolled at Beijing University, one of the oldest and most prestigious academic institutions in China. She pursued a bachelor's degree in law and a master's degree in political science. Bo's first wife, Li Danyu, told the *New York Times* in October 2012 that Gu's admission to Beijing University was rejected initially and that the Bo family helped her get in through their connections at the request of Gu's mother.

At the university, Gu Kailai found herself a member of the much-admired princelings group on campus. Her talent, good looks, and family background soon made her popular among boys. In the late 1970s, dance parties were held every weekend at Beijing University and Gu Kailai was said to be a regular. She met a tall and handsome but quiet young man at one of the parties and fell deeply in love. The young man's father was a military commander and a friend of General Gu's. In her second year, Gu Kailai and her boyfriend became inseparable, and soon she became pregnant. In the late 1970s, premarital sex was considered a serious moral and political offense. If found out, Gu Kailai and her boyfriend would face expulsion. The boy became scared and disappeared for several weeks. His cowardice and indifference devastated Gu Kailai. With the help of his sisters, she reportedly procured an abortion and dumped her boyfriend. A classmate remembered her as a tough, unconventional woman.

In 1984, during a field trip with a professor at the Central Academy of Fine Arts, Gu Kailai told the state media that she had become acquainted with Bo Xilai and was starstruck. Li Danyu, Bo's first wife, claimed that Bo and Gu were good friends while they were at Beijing University—both were regulars at student dance parties. In a profile in the Singapore-based *United Morning News,* Gu compared the young party chief to her father—"educated, idealistic, and reliable," like "those heroes in movies." Bo and Gu also bonded over their shared experiences: both their parents had come from Shanxi province where they joined Mao's revolution, and were later persecuted during the Cultural Revolution. While Gu Kailai and her sisters had grown up in prison with her mother, Bo Xilai and his siblings were left to wander the streets when their father was detained and their mother died in the hands of the Red Guards.

The relationship soon blossomed, even though Bo Xilai had to maneuver through his messy divorce. In 1986, Gu Kailai gave up an opportunity to study in the US and married Bo Xilai, who was nine years older. The next year, their son, Bo Guagua, was born.

At the end of 1987, she passed the newly installed National Lawyer's Examination, an equivalent to the American bar examination, and became one of the earliest licensed attorneys in China. In 1988, after Bo Xilai moved to Dalian to take up a district party secretary's job, she followed him and set up the Kailai Law Firm in the city. She was one of the first lawyers in China to start a private practice under her own name. As her husband rose through the ranks, Gu Kailai's practice flourished. In 1995, she established a branch office in Beijing.

In her short career as a lawyer, two high-profile cases boosted her reputation. In 1997, she represented a Chinese manufacturer of laundry detergent, which had purchased a computerized assembly line from a machinery company in the US in 1987. The US company filed for bankruptcy before it transferred any of the main software or operating instructions. The equipment that had arrived was useless and the Chinese manufacturer lost US $5 million. When it attempted to retrieve the relevant technology needed to run the equipment, a court-appointed bankruptcy trustee sued the Chinese for stealing trade secrets and for intellectual property infringement. The court entered a default judgment, ordering the Chinese company to pay US $1.4 million in damages. Because the Chinese company was a state-owned enterprise, the federal court in Alabama notified the Chinese Foreign Ministry in 1996, threatening to freeze the assets of Chinese state companies operating in the US if the government refused to pay. The latter part of the court order triggered a strong response from the Chinese government. According to an official Chinese media report, Gu Kailai agreed to take on the case pro bono. She flew to Alabama and hired a legal team to argue the case. In March 1997, a federal appeals court in Alabama overturned the verdict.

In the mid-1990s, Sino–US business disputes were relatively rare and there was little by way of precedent. The case made Gu famous.

The Chinese public saw her as a hero who had dared to stand up to American bullying to protect the interests of Chinese enterprises. Based on the experience, Gu Kailai wrote a book, *Winning a Lawsuit in America,* which became a best seller. However, some critics later accused Gu Kailai of exaggerating her role in the case. On August 14, 2012, the Hong Kong–based *New Century Magazine* released an article that pointed out Gu Kailai had no license to represent clients in court and that her role was limited to advising American counsel and monitoring the court proceedings. Besides, China did not really win the lawsuit, because the Chinese company never recouped the US $5 million loss from the US equipment manufacturer.

Gu Kailai seemed to thrive on controversy. In 1998, she projected herself into another contentious case involving Ma Junren, a track coach in Dalian. Ma had captured worldwide attention when his team broke national and world records sixty-six times in middle- and long-distance women's track events. Amid the praises came an unexpected article in the *Chinese Writers* magazine, which alleged Ma had engaged in "illegal activities," such as physical and sexual abuse of athletes, confiscation of athletes' prize money, and more important, doping. The exposé shocked the nation and dented the reputation of the once seemingly invincible coach. Supported by her mayor husband, Gu Kailai threatened to launch a lawsuit against the magazine to defend the iconic figure, who was closely associated with Dalian. While preparing for the legal battle, she wrote a book, *My Defense of Ma Junren,* which listed one hundred alleged errors and inaccuracies in the magazine article. The release of her book pitted her against the magazine writer, making them the center of the controversy.

The lawsuit never materialized. During an interview with state media, Gu Kailai said that she had decided not to sue the magazine because the lawsuit had the potential to turn into a farce and could damage the reputation of her city and the coach. That proved to be a smart political move, which probably spared her national embarrassment. Two years later, many of the allegations in the magazine article were proved to be true: during random drug testing, investigators suspected that Ma had used performance-enhancing drugs as part of his training regime. Despite his strong denial, six of his athletes were barred from China's team at the Sydney Olympics in 2000 after they failed blood tests. Ma Junren quit the Chinese Olympic team and is now breeding mastiffs in Liaoning province.

It was also in 1998 that Gu Kailai decided to leave her practice and devote more time to her son's education. Her decision was uncontroversial; many senior leaders' spouses took similar paths—relinquishing their careers and keeping a low profile to support their husbands' political futures. The wife of Li Keqing, China's new premier and former party chief, used to teach American literature at a university but switched to research that did not require much presence in the public. President Hu Jintao's wife was a hydroelectric engineer at a government agency before she quit.

Gu Kailai's sacrifice did not go unappreciated. In October 2011, Bo Xilai talked about his wife to a group of visiting Hong Kong media representatives in Chongqing, saying he was "grateful and guilty":

> Kailai has made tremendous sacrifices for me. She gave up her law practice and instead focused on research. She quietly accompanied me when I later moved to Shenyang and Chongqing. Each time I encountered a challenge, she supported and helped me wholeheartedly. I'm very grateful for that. . . . To tell you the truth, I'm over sixty now and as you get older, you like to think about the past. Each time I think of what she has done, I feel guilty. Twenty years have flown by fast. I think she's a very capable person and did well in so many things, but she is willing to make tremendous sacrifices for me.

The adoration seemed to be mutual. One of the illustrations of her love was the adoption of her husband's family name, an unusual practice in Chinese culture, in which women generally keep their maiden names after marriage. In April, when the government announced Gu Kailai's detention and the official media identified her as "Bogu Kailai," many were taken by surprise, assuming that the government might have deliberately associated her with Bo Xilai. In June, a source in Beijing unveiled the mystery. It all started with Gu Kailai's mother. When she married General Gu in the war years, she adopted her husband's name as a vow that whatever happened, she would always be part of the Gu family. Gu Kailai was touched by her mother's devotion and did the same with Bo Xilai.

In the public eye, Bo Xilai and Gu Kailai were seen as a loving, compatible power couple. Some of his staff members unabashedly called them the "John and Jackie Kennedy" of China. The Singapore-based *United Morning News* published an anecdote now widely circulated online:

> In the 1990s, when a Korean friend gifted Gu Kailai a jewelry box, she said to Bo Xilai, "I'm giving your beautiful wife this beautiful jewelry box. You need to buy some beautiful jewelry to fill the box." Without thinking, Bo Xilai answered, "I will put my heart in there."

Gu Kailai's friends say she also was dedicated to her only child. While she and her husband were busy with their careers, Bo Guagua was raised by his maternal grandparents and Gu's fourth sister in Beijing. By the time Gu Kailai quit her law practice, Bo Guagua was eleven. Gu Kailai intended to send him abroad for his education. Many affluent one-child families in China send their children to boarding schools in the UK, Australia, New Zealand, the US, or Singapore for their high school education so they can more easily attend elite universities and graduate schools in those countries. Official statistics show that the number of Chinese students studying abroad has doubled every three years since 2000 to nearly 340,000 in 2011. A young person with bilingual skills and an advanced degree from the West is considered "*dujin,*" or gilded with gold.

Around 2000, the Singapore government launched an aggressive recruitment campaign in China for the country's universities, which were considered to have an excellent combination of Western and Eastern traditions. The universities became a big draw because Singapore is closer to China and many students found the cultural environment easier to adjust to than that of Western countries. Gu Kailai tried Singapore first and stayed there for several months before she decided to move with her son, Bo Guagua, to the UK so he could study "authentic" English. According to a British documentary, Bo Guagua first attended an English language school at Bournemouth and then, through

Fido Vivien-May, a Royal British Legion volunteer, he was admitted to Harrow.

Though her husband said in many speeches she had retired from work to spend more time with family, reports say that Gu Kailai never stopped working even when she was accompanying her son in the UK. The *Wall Street Journal* and the *Guardian* reported Gu Kailai changed the name of her law firm to Angdao and remained on its books as a registered lawyer. An April 2012 article in China's *Southern Weekend* newspaper indicated that Angdao's biggest investor was the Bo family friend Xu Ming, a billionaire businessman in Dalian, and the firm handled mergers and bankruptcies for many large state-run enterprises in the northeastern province of Liaoning, where Bo Xilai was governor in the early 2000s. Gu Kailai was said to bring in the clients and take millions of yuan in commissions. She also entered into partnerships with several foreigners and founded Horus Consultancy and Investment, which advised clients wishing to do business in China. Horus, which is the name of an Egyptian deity, was Gu Kailai's English name.

While in the UK, the *Guardian* reported that Gu Kailai had taken a keen interest in hot air balloons she saw when she lived in a penthouse flat with Bo Guagua in central Bournemouth, a seaside resort. It was a minor piece of business, but illustrates how she operated. Gu Kailai contacted a balloon manufacturer there and inquired about the possibilities of bringing them to Dalian. The deal was struck and the billionaire Xu Ming agreed to sponsor a gigantic balloon that would offer grand views over the city. However, the transaction soon hit a snag, according to the *Guardian*:

> As the deal progressed, however, Mr. Hall [Giles Hall was the coordinator for the deal] became suspicious. Money was coming from more than one account—including Mrs. Gu's personal account, which he recalls as being at Coutts [a large, London-based wealth management and private banking institution]—and then an extraordinary suggestion was made.

The cost of a secondhand winch was about £100,000 but Gu offered to pay £200,000, half of which she wanted Giles Hall to use to pay for her son's school fees. When Hall refused, Gu "changed from someone very friendly and gentle to someone who clearly didn't like not getting her own way."

The balloon flew over Dalian for two years until it was destroyed by a hurricane. A replacement balloon was purchased, only to be burned after getting hit by fireworks during a celebration in the city.

In 2002, Gu Kailai became restless in the UK and wanted to spend some time in China. Heywood, a Harrow alumnus, had specifically come to the UK to build connections with Gu and offered to take care of Bo Guagua during her absence. The Briton's affability and sincerity eventually won Gu Kailai over—she allowed Heywood to spend time with Bo Guagua during school breaks and bought a used Mercedes for Heywood to pick up her son and run errands. Wang Kang, a Chongqing scholar, told the British media that Heywood and Gu might have had an affair while they were in London, but his claims have never been substantiated.

Gu Kailai was grateful to Heywood for his help with Bo Guagua upon her return to the UK. In 2005, after Heywood moved his family from Dalian to Beijing, Gu Kailai introduced him to Xu Ming, a billionaire businessman and princeling who managed a large state-run enterprise. The four of them agreed to work on land development deals in China. Heywood's job was to connect Chinese developers with British investors. If any project succeeded, he would be awarded 15 percent in commission.

Gu Kailai stayed in the UK four years, and a person close to the couple said their marriage further deteriorated. "Many outsiders might still see them as a perfect family, but their marriage began to fizzle out in the late 1990s, especially with leaked stories of Bo Xilai's many infidelities," the source said. "Gu Kailai became suspicious and moody."

One of Bo Xilai's infidelities allegedly involved a well-known actress named Ma Xiaoqing. The affair started after Bo moved to Beijing and became minister of commerce in 2004. Several colleagues at the ministry claimed to have seen the two together. There were reports that Bo and Gu had separated around that time. At one point, Bo even pressured the actress to quit acting and marry him. The affair supposedly ended after Bo decided that reconciling with his wife could gain him a wholesome image and benefit his political career.

Following the breakup, the distraught actress never revealed her lover's name, but numerous stories identified the "secret boyfriend" as Bo Xilai. In 2008, the actress talked about her former boyfriend in a media interview and said, "It's all over now. I don't want to mention that person's name. He was in a field different from mine. If I publicize our past, it's not good for me and for him. It's meaningless to sacrifice for love."

One could only imagine the devastating impact of Bo's womanizing on Gu Kailai. She was said to have suffered from severe depression after she returned from the UK in 2003. A Beijing-based businessman with intimate knowledge of the Bo family disclosed in April 2012 that Gu Kailai also had skin cancer in 2006 on the left side of her face. The surgery was successful but she needed to undertake hormone therapy. "She was very self-conscious and she begged her friends to keep her illness a secret," said the friend. "For months, she seldom stepped out of her house."

In January 2007, Gu Kailai passed out at her father-in-law's funeral. After she was taken to a hospital, the doctor found that her nervous system had suffered irreversible damage because she had been ingesting a mix of lead and mercury someone had slipped into the capsule of her daily herbal medicine. Gu Kailai suspected that there was a plot to assassinate her. She allegedly filed a report with the Ministry of Public Security. The *New York Times* also reported that Gu Kailai had suspected that Li Wangzhi, Bo's son from his previous marriage, was masterminding a scheme to kill her. People around him, including her husband, dismissed her claims, believing she was simply paranoid.

In December 2007, Xu Ming, the billionaire businessman in Dalian, asked Wang Lijun, the nationally-known police chief of Jinzhou, to look into the matter. Wang did not disappoint and solved the mystery in a short time. He concluded that the Bo family driver and a domestic helper were responsible for the poisoning. Gu Kailai insisted that Bo's ex-wife and first son were behind the scheme.

The Beijing businessman said the lead and mercury poisoning was very serious and Gu Kailai then became socially withdrawn:

I know that doctors from the Third Medical University used to come see her at home. One of the effects of the poison was that it caused

Gu's hands to shake. The doctor advised that she practice all kinds of games to reduce the shaking in her hands by making all sorts of artifacts from used papers and plastics. When her son, Bo Guagua, heard about his mother's illness, he volunteered to take a one-year leave of absence from school and came back to China to take care of her. Gu didn't give permission. When Bo Guagua was home in the summer, the boy allowed his mother to cut his hair as part of the exercise to balance and stop her shaking hands. Gu Kailai was a strong-willed woman and she was desperate to reverse the situation.

Despite her poor health, Gu Kailai moved from Beijing to Chongqing after Bo Xilai was appointed the city's party chief in late 2007. The Beijing businessman said Gu Kailai had high hopes for her husband and their marriage. They decided to get over the bad feelings they had around them and start afresh.

When they first arrived, Gu Kailai lived in a secluded apartment nestled on the side of a mountain on the south side of the Yangtze River. She seldom stepped out of the house to socialize with locals. However, at the height of her husband's "Singing Red and Smashing Black" campaign, Gu consulted with Bo's staff on many legal issues during the investigation of several anticorruption cases.

When Bo Xilai needed a police chief for Chongqing, Gu Kailai strongly recommended Wang Lijun. In June 2008, after Wang was relocated to Chongqing, he became a frequent guest at Bo's house. In his court statement, Wang Lijun said Gu Kailai "treated him very well" during his daily visits to her home, known among officials as "No. 3." In the midst of his anticrime campaign, Wang received many death threats from a triad organization against his wife and daughter. In October 2009, a widely distributed vicious rumor stated that Wang's wife and daughter had allegedly been skinned alive as a tit-for-tat move against Wang's execution of a triad leader. To protect the safety of his wife and daughter, Wang decided to move them to Beijing. Gu Kailai used her connections and found a school for Wang's daughter and a job for his wife. Xu Ming, Bo's friend who was president of Shide Group in Dalian, bought two apartments for Wang in Beijing for 2.85 million yuan (about US $460,000).

Wang Lijun paid back Gu Kailai's generosity with utter obedience. According to an official in Chongqing, Gu Kailai once hosted a dinner for a group of friends at a five-star hotel. At the end of the meal, she had severe stomach upset. The news reached Wang Lijun and he immediately ordered the hotel to shut down and launch a full investigation. Wang even visited the hotel personally to check the food toxicity reports. There was a popular saying among Chongqing police: "Wang Lijun is not afraid of heaven, nor is he of earth, but he is in awe of Gu Kailai." According to a feature in *Nandu Weekly* on December 16, 2012, Gu Kailai used to call Wang intimately by his nickname, "Devil," and Wang addressed her as "Gua Ma," short for Bo Guagua's mom.

When Wang Lijun first started an anti-crime exhibition inside the building of the Chongqing Public Security Bureau, Gu Kailai, dressed in a red raincoat, black skirt, and tall black boots, showed up at the exhibits with her mother, who was visiting from Beijing. In the summer of 2010, when Wang Lijun took the lead and encouraged his subordinates to leave their offices and help direct traffic on the street, Gu was concerned that Wang could suffer a heat stroke and personally delivered water to him.

"Wang Lijun and I were close friends," Gu Kailai told the court. "After the December 6 incident [when Gu Kailai claimed to be poisoned by lead and mercury and Wang Lijun helped capture the perpetrator], Wang Lijun personally headed a medical team to treat my illness. He was so dedicated to me and I became very dependent on him. In addition, when Guagua studied at Harvard, [Wang] was in charge of his security in the US." Therefore, in July 2011, when Gu Kailai learned that Neil Heywood had made a threat against her son while he was in London, she immediately went to Wang for help.

A DEATH AT THE LUCKY HOLIDAY HOTEL

ON A CHILLY November night, the Lucky Holiday Hotel looks like a desolate castle perched alone on top of the forested South Mountain, deemed as Chongqing's crown jewel. Most travelers choose to stay, or dine, elsewhere—at the convenient and bustling downtown establishments—despite the Lucky Holiday Hotel's attractively-discounted room rates and the enticing Mongolian barbecued lamb at its restaurant, which boasts a full view of the city's spectacular lights.

At first glance, the hotel is deceptively dingy and small. The main building, with its fading yellow exterior, brings to mind a roadside motel in the US, where budget-conscious tourists can pay US $50 for a sparsely-furnished room. But out of sight is the hotel's main attraction—ten European-style villas with rooftop balconies are clustered discreetly in the wooded areas around the main building. Along a narrow, winding path leading to the villas, menorah-shaped street lamps cast a faint glow on the polished brick surface, elongating the flickering human shadows. The luxury suites feature queen-size beds and European or Chinese-style faux antique furniture. They pander to wealthy entrepreneurs and senior officials with big expense accounts who want a quiet getaway or privacy for a secret liaison.

It was inside one such villa, at the end of the pathway, that the hotel staff found the body of Neil Heywood. Gu Kailai later confessed to the court that she had put Heywood up in Room 1605 and then poisoned him on the chilly night of November 13 because Heywood was black-mailing her family and had threatened to kill her son.

The "threat" arose from a land development deal in Chongqing. According to Gu Kailai's confession, she introduced Heywood to Xu Ming and another princeling, a man who managed a state-owned enterprise. Xu and the princeling were planning a big construction project in Chongqing's Jiangbei District. Upon completion of the project, Heywood was promised £140 million in commission. Unfortunately, the deal fell through for political reasons. A source in Beijing claimed Bo Xilai had personally killed the projects for fear that they could turn into a scandal and jeopardize his political future. According to a British documentary, which offered a differ-ent version of the deal, Gu Kailai introduced Heywood to Xu Ming, who had purchased a plot of land in Chongqing and planned to build English-style luxury townhouses. Heywood was hired in 2005 to lure wealthy British investors for the project. In 2008, Heywood was sacked because he had not been able to get a single investor involved.

Having put so much time and effort into the deal, Heywood was upset about the outcome. Subsequent court documents showed that Heywood, in 2008, demanded one-tenth of what he had earlier been promised as commission via e-mail exchanges with Bo Xilai's son, twenty-five-year-old Bo Guagua—who appeared to be in control of the family assets overseas. Heywood also cited the help he had given to Bo Guagua in the past to justify his demand. Bo Guagua refused to pay but agreed to meet Heywood for further discussions. Bo Guagua had arranged a meeting between Heywood and Gu Kailai in Beijing during the Beijing Olympics in 2008. The two sides reconciled and Heywood apologized for his inappropriate request.

In July 2011, Neil Heywood went back to the UK and was pressed for money. Out of desperation, he met Bo Guagua, who was staying at the Bo family apartment in London, and brought up the compensation issue again. When Bo Guagua rejected his request, Gu Kailai said their conversation turned ugly. Heywood held Bo Guagua against his will inside the apartment for several hours. When Gu Kailai learned about the incident, she reportedly called Heywood a lunatic and looked to Wang Lijun for help. Noting that Heywood's alleged threats against her son happened in the UK, Wang could not come up with a plausible solution. In August 2011, while both Heywood and Bo Guagua were in Beijing, they had a drink together but failed to resolve the compensation issue.

Based on an investigative report in the Guangzhou-based *Nandu Weekly*, Heywood contacted Bo Guagua again via e-mail in early November, saying that "if you don't keep your promise, you'll have to face the consequences. I haven't given up on you yet." In his reply, Bo Guagua said he would take legal action if Heywood continued to threaten him. Heywood backed down. "If it is not the time to resolve it now, let's wait for another time then," replied Heywood. Guo Weiguo, the former deputy police chief in Chongqing, had examined all the e-mail exchanges between Heywood and Bo Guagua and told the court that he did not detect in them anything that could be construed as serious threats on Bo Guagua's life.

However, Gu Kailai told a different story. She said in her confession that Heywood had written to her son "I will destroy you" in early

November. She also said that in July 2011, prior to the threatening e-mail, Bo Guagua had telephoned Gu Kailai to tell her he had been "kidnapped"—that Heywood detained him for several hours at the Bo's London apartment. Upon hearing the news, Gu said in her testimony that she became worried and severely distressed. "To me, that was more than a threat. It was real action that was taking place. I must fight to my death to stop the craziness of Neil Heywood."

Several of Heywood's friends disputed Gu's claim. "I find the idea of Neil threatening the safety of Bo Guagua to be extraordinary," one person close to Heywood's family told the *Wall Street Journal*. "He was a good and loyal friend to Guagua over the years, and was a mentor to him while he was studying in Britain. Whatever difference on business matters there might have been, he remained throughout as a kind uncle figure."

Meanwhile, a source familiar with the Bo Xilai investigation at the Central Commission for Discipline Inspection said Heywood told his friends that he had kept records of all the transactions he had completed for the Bo family. He said Gu Kailai moved millions of dollars to overseas banks via Heywood and he would not hesitate to show them to the international media. Such a disclosure could damage Bo Xilai's political career as he maneuvered for a seat on the Politburo Standing Committee. In the words of a Chinese analyst, "Heywood knows too much about the Bo family, and too much knowledge could be a dangerous thing."

After Heywood sent an e-mail to Bo Guagua in early November, Gu admitted in court that she wanted to get rid of the Briton. Meanwhile, she was unhappy with the police chief's reluctance to help and complained to Xu Ming, who traveled to Chongqing and visited Wang Lijun on November 11, urging Wang to do something about Heywood. When Wang Lijun failed to come up with a feasible solution, Xu suggested that the police frame Heywood with charges of taking and selling drugs—China has some of the toughest laws against drug traffickers and sixteen foreigners have been executed for drug trafficking since 1997. Wang embraced the idea and instructed Xu Ming to send an anonymous message to the Chongqing Public Security Bureau,

"alerting" police that Heywood was the ringleader of a large drug trafficking network in Sichuan and its neighboring provinces.

After Xu left, Wang Lijun contacted Gu Kailai, advising her to lure
Heywood from Beijing to Chongqing. "It's not easy to arrest him in
the capital city," the prosecutor quoted Wang as saying. "You should
get him to Chongqing, and I can ambush him." Over the course of discussions, Wang proposed killing Heywood in a shootout and planting
drugs on him, but he quickly abandoned the idea for fear that a shooting could cause a diplomatic nightmare and stain Chongqing's reputation. Gu eventually settled on a plot to poison Heywood first and with
Wang's help, make Heywood's death look like it was from a drug overdose or natural causes.

Because highly toxic materials are under strict government control
in China, court documents showed that Gu obtained a type of rat poison, called "Drop Dead After Three Steps," from an organized-crime
syndicate in the name of "conducting a scientific experiment." The rat
poison provided to Gu was supposed to contain cyanide. However, a
police officer in Chongqing told an overseas Chinese media outlet that
Xia Zeliang, a district party chief in Chongqing who was angling for
the Chongqing deputy mayor's position, had allegedly obtained the
poison for Gu.

Nandu Weekly reported that Xu texted the drug allegations against
Heywood to the Chongqing Public Security Bureau via his mobile
phone on the morning of November 12. That afternoon, Wang Lijun
came to Bo's house. 3 and helped Gu Kailai unwrap the rat poison
sealed inside a lump of red wax. During the process, she accidentally
hurt her hands and Wang went around the house to get medicine for
them. Gu's helpers witnessed Wang's presence.

Gu enlisted a former military man, Zhang Xiaojun, to invite Heywood to Chongqing. Zhang served as the bodyguard and personal
assistant to Gu's father and was employed by the Bo family following
General Gu's death in 2004.

"On November 12, 2011, Gu Kailai asked me to contact Neil Heywood, saying that she wanted to see him and I shall pick him up and
bring him to Chongqing," Zhang, who was put on trial along with

Gu Kailai, told the court. "She instructed me repeatedly that I should accompany Heywood to Chongqing. Heywood replied that he also wished to see her, but had to check his schedule. Within half an hour, Heywood called me back, telling me he would be available the next day and asking me to book a flight for him."

On November 13, Heywood flew first class on China Southern Airlines, Flight 8129, which departed Beijing at 11:35 A.M. After he landed and left the airport, Wang Lijun notified Gu Kailai that Heywood was under police surveillance and everything would be under his control now. Heywood's hotel registration form showed that he checked into Room 1605 in the secluded villas of the Lucky Holiday Hotel, which was operated by the Chongqing government. The hotel was almost empty in November and provided a discreet venue. Besides, Gu Kailai had hosted guests there before and was familiar with the hotel management. In case anything went wrong, her friends at the hotel could help cover up.

On that evening, Gu offered to meet Heywood in his room and discuss future business plans. On her way to the hotel, she instructed her driver to buy a bottle of Royal Salute whiskey. At nine o'clock, Gu and Heywood sat down for a drink inside the split-level villa. She had prepared two bottles: a glass bottle of poison and a medicine bottle of capsulated crystal methamphetamine and herbal ecstasy pills. Gu later bragged to Xu Ming that she wore a nylon top and a pair of baggy pants with multiple pockets, where she stuffed her tea bags, poison bottles, and a small soy sauce container. Gu asked her family assistant, Zhang, and the driver to wait in the spacious living room on the first floor while she entertained Heywood in the upstairs bedroom.

Heywood ended up having half a 350-milliliter bottle of 80-proof (40 percent alcohol) whiskey. Due to his low tolerance for alcohol, Heywood became intoxicated quickly. According to Gu's confession, after Heywood ran to the bathroom to vomit (a large amount of vomit was also found near the toilet bowl), Gu brought out the tea bags and the poison bottle from her pockets to get herself ready. She then called Zhang into Heywood's room and the two of them dragged Heywood to the bed. When Heywood gasped for air and asked for water, Gu Kailai poured the poison into the small soy sauce container filled with tea and dripped the toxic mixture into Heywood's mouth. Gu and her family assistant then pinned him down until they discovered Heywood's pulse had stopped. (Gu admitted they were not sure if he was dead.) Before she walked out, Gu scattered some capsuled drugs on the hotel floor, making it easier for the Chongqing police to claim that Heywood died of an overdose of drugs if the heart attack scenario did not pan out. Before stepping out of the room, Gu switched on the "Do not disturb" indicator on the door and told hotel staff Heywood was drunk and needed to sleep it off. At 11:38 P.M., Gu Kailai, her family assistant, and the driver left the scene.

At noon on November 14, Wang went to Gu's residence and asked about the killing. "When I met Wang Lijun that day, I told him in detail about how I met and poisoned Neil on the night of November 13," Gu said in her testimony. "Wang Lijun advised me not to be bothered by the case, which would have nothing to do with me in the future. He also told me to erase my memories about the case. I said I was a bit worried; he told me it would be fine within a week or two." What Gu didn't know was that Wang had secretly recorded her conversation with him. Wang defended his decision to tape the conversation by claiming that he feared being set up in the future. Later, he also used that tape to blackmail Gu's husband, Bo Xilai. After he was detained in February 2012, Wang Lijun turned the tape over to investigators in Beijing.

On the morning of November 15, hotel staff discovered Heywood's body and contacted Wang, who assigned the Chongqing police to inspect the crime scene. According to court documents, police took a blood sample from an area near the victim's heart and conducted a CT scan of his body. Before leaving the hotel, Wang quietly drew another blood sample and took it home. Through subsequent interviews and on-the-scene investigations—checking the hotel security tapes and examining the fingerprints on mugs in Heywood's room—police investigators identified Gu Kailai as a possible suspect in Heywood's death. Instead of continuing with a full investigation, the prosecution stated, the four officers "fabricated interview records and hid material evidence and other measures" to cover up for the wife of the city's party chief. They hastily concluded the investigation, and in consultation with Wang Lijun, listed the cause of Heywood's death as a heart attack triggered by heavy alcohol intake. Investigators did not file Heywood's death as a criminal case.

On November 16, Heywood's widow, Wang Lulu, arrived in Chongqing. Gu met Wang Lulu in an empty coffeehouse near the Chongqing police headquarters and persuaded her to accept the investigators' conclusion and agree to have the body cremated without performing an autopsy.

On November 17, Wang Lijun gave Gu Kailai the hotel security tape that showed she was with Heywood before his death and that no one visited after she left. Wang lied to Gu, telling her it was the only copy.

Heywood was cremated on November 19. That evening, Wang phoned Gu Kailai, telling her that Heywood had become "smoke and ashes, gone to the west."

As noted earlier, a week after Heywood's death, Wang Lijun revealed his true intentions and allegedly pressured Gu to talk with Bo Xilai and persuade him to help with Wang's friends in Tieling. And after Gu tried lobbying her husband without success, Wang turned hostile and issued veiled threats against Gu. Seeing that she had unwittingly fallen into Wang Lijun's trap, Gu panicked. According to court papers, Gu contacted the deputy police chief without Wang's knowledge and sought his help in destroying evidence. After Wang found out, he grew upset that "Gu Kailai turned up the heat by allowing an increasing number of people to learn about the murder."

On December 14, 2011, Gu Kailai used Wang Lijun's name to invite the four investigators to her house for dinner. Over drinks, Gu expressed her concerns that the evidence relating to Heywood's murder might fall into the wrong hands if not completely destroyed. To give Gu Kailai peace of mind, one officer, Li Yang, sent one of Gu's family assistants to his office and brought all the shredded files back to Gu's house to prove that everything had been obliterated. The next day, all four officers claimed that they could not remember a single thing about what had happened the previous night and they suspected that Gu had put knockout drops in their wine.

Afterward, Wang scolded the four investigators, all of whom were his former colleagues in northeast China who had followed him to Chongqing. Wang told them to guard themselves around Gu. Little did Wang know that one investigator had betrayed him and reported those warnings to Gu.

At the end of December 2011, the paranoid Gu secretly probed several of Wang Lijun's staff members in search of any incriminating evidence that Wang had kept against her. At the same time, Gu also raided Wang's office while he was attending a conference in Beijing, carting away boxes of Wang's shoes, suits, and clothes; bottles of cologne and liquor; packages of cigarettes; name-brand watches and gold jewelry. When Wang confronted Gu, she claimed that Wang was being secretly investigated by the Central Commission for Discipline Inspection and she had tried to protect him by hauling away the soiled goods before investigators from Beijing came in. Afterward, at an informal gathering, Gu allegedly told Wang's daughter that her father was a corrupt police officer like Wen Qiang.

Realizing that Gu was collecting evidence against him, Wang phoned Xu Ming on January 26, 2012, beseeching him to tell Bo Xilai about how his wife had bullied many members of Wang's staff. Xu hesitated, worrying that Wang's words could trigger fights between Bo and his wife. Noting that Xu was reluctant, Wang warned, "If you tell Bo the truth, you are doing a huge favor for the party and for our country. If you don't follow what I say, an explosive and earth-shattering incident would happen. By then, it's going to be irreversible." Wang's remarks indicated that he had pondered exposing Gu Kailai's crime to senior officials in Beijing or to Western governments and media *before* his open split with Bo Xilai.

Henry Chang-yu Lee, a well-known Taiwan-born American forensic scientist, told the New York-based Chinese-language newspaper *World Journal* in May 2012 that Wang had contacted him at the end of January 2002, saying a person was found dead from alcohol poisoning and asking if Lee could offer his help to conduct laboratory tests on the evidence. Lee agreed. Wang promised to send one of his assistants to the US with the sample, but he never did. "Wang had apparently attempted to leak Gu Kailai's case and use Lee to boost his claims," said Lee.

Alarmed by Wang's threats, Xu flew to Chongqing and met with Bo and his wife, but did not broach the subject.

But Wang went ahead and scheduled that fateful meeting with Bo and revealed Gu's role in Heywood's death. He also alleged that Gu was suffering from a mental breakdown because she had ordered him to arrest Bo's ex-wife, his first son, and Gu's fourth sister—for poisoning her.

At the end of that conversation, *Nandu Weekly* reported that Bo shook Wang's hand and thanked him. But after Wang left, Bo questioned his wife, who accused Wang of blackmailing her. Outraged by Wang's betrayal, Bo called Wang and his deputy into his office the next day and delivered the notorious face slap that kicked off the political scandal that led to the destruction of both men.

Wang immediately ordered the four investigators to re-create the Heywood file when the split with Bo became public—before the materials could be detained by Bo Xilai. And this was when investigator Wang Pengfei obtained Heywood's blood sample from Wang Lijun and transferred it to a friend's house in Beijing.

In February 2012—after Wang Lijun entered the US Consulate— prosecutors said they reexamined the evidence submitted by Wang Lijun. Video footage from the hotel security camera showed the appearances of Gu and Zhang on the night of Heywood's death. Fingerprints from Gu and Zhang were found on bottle caps and cup lids at the crime scene. Based on the samples of Heywood's blood and vomit collected at the crime scene, investigators in Beijing determined that Heywood's death was caused by cyanide poisoning and that Heywood had been the victim of homicide. Gu—and her personal assistant, Zhang—were put under residential surveillance on March 15, 2012, and officially arrested in July 2012.

THE NON-TRIAL OF THE CENTURY

IN HER *Winning a Lawsuit in America,* published in 1998, Gu Kailai commented on the O.J. Simpson murder trial and criticized what she considered to be the cumbersome and declining American legal system for paying too much attention to due process:

While developing its legal principles, China has learned a lesson from the pitfalls of the system in the United States, where, even if everyone knows that John Smith has committed the murder, the court can still find the person innocent and release him if the prosecution does not produce the evidence required by law. China has formulated "fact-based" principles. The Chinese law does not play with words. If we know for sure that a certain Mr. Zhang has killed someone, he will be arrested, prosecuted and executed.

Gu Kailai would probably never have imagined that she would one day stand on the other side of the law and experience firsthand the "efficiency" of China's legal system.

Her murder trial took place on August 9, 2012, when most of the world was preoccupied with the summer Olympic Games in London. The proceedings, carefully choreographed like the Olympic opening ceremony, lasted seven hours and the majority of the people I interviewed were not even aware of the trial. They were fixated on an exciting sports milestone. On that day, the country rejoiced at a history-making victory. With the three–nil win over South Korea in the men's team final, China snatched all four ping-pong titles, repeating its results from Beijing four years earlier. The win pushed up China's gold-medal count to thirty-six, two more than that of the US.

The timing of Gu Kailai's trial had other political considerations. It happened a week before an important conference in Beidaihe, a summer resort outside Beijing, where senior leaders would discuss succession plans for the upcoming 18th Party Congress. A guilty verdict against Gu Kailai could effectively justify the ouster of her husband, Bo Xilai.

The government moved the venue of the trial from Bo's home base of Chongqing, the scene of the alleged murder, to Hefei in the eastern province of Anhui so the trial could be free from the interference of local government officials. More important, the venue carried a symbolic meaning for ordinary Chinese—Hefei was home to Bao Zheng, a legendary judge in China's Song Dynasty nearly 1,000 years ago. Legend has it that Bao Zheng possessed an imperial sword granted by the emperor and whenever he displayed it in court, the accused, regardless of their social and political classes, had to bow to its imperial power. With the sword, Bao Zheng could execute any royals who committed crimes without worrying about retaliation. Throughout his life, Bao Zheng had made a name for his uncompromising stance against corruption and he has become synonymous with fairness and justice.

However, the symbolic meanings of Bao Zheng were lost on journalists who covered the trial, which began at about half past eight in the morning. Hefei was battered by torrential rain and wind from a typhoon that had hit the southeast coast the previous day. A Chinese journalist friend who traveled to Hefei said the city had deployed nearly 5,000 police wearing black raincoats over their dark, short-sleeved uniforms. Police blocked all the streets near the courthouse, hustling away a few pro-Bo protesters who identified themselves as residents of Dalian and shouted "Long Live Chairman Mao."

"Those forbidding, dark figures of police in the heavy rain and the secret trial proceedings reminded me of the mafia," quipped my friend. In Chinese, "mafia" is translated as "black society."

The mafia reference could not be more fitting. The so-called open trial was attended by only 140 selected government officials, delegates of the Municipal People's Congress, a few relatives, two diplomats from the British Embassy, and seven state media representatives. No recording devices or pens were allowed inside the courtroom. Outside, several dozen Chinese and foreign journalists as well as other observers were "enduring the pounding rain, under the watchful eye of a roughly equal number of police, some in uniforms and many more in plainclothes pretending to be ordinary passersby," said Keith Richburg of the *Washington Post*.

A month before the trial, Gu Kailai's ninety-year-old mother, who had lived in Chongqing for the past few years, returned to Beijing and tried to rescue her daughter and son-in-law. She hired two high-flying lawyers who had represented disgraced senior officials in corruption cases, but authorities forbade out-of-town lawyers from interfering in the case and declined the request. Instead the court appointed "through meticulous selection" two local lawyers: Jiang Min, chairman of the Hefei Bar Association, and Zhou Yuhao, chairman of the Bar Association in Wuhu, a city near Hefei.

Given the complexities of the case and the tremendous amount of media attention, many expected that the Chinese government would take the case seriously or at least attempt to honor due process for the watching international community. Instead the trial was over in one day. No witnesses were called, so there was no cross-examination. "What is being anticipated as 'the murder trial of the century' is, more precisely, shaping up to be the opposite of a trial," wrote Evan Osnos for a *New Yorker* article titled "The Non-Trial of the Century."

At seven o'clock that night, the public was given some trial details in a brief report on Central China Television during the prime-time evening news. Footage showed Gu Kailai strutting into the courtroom, with her head high and a slight smile on her face, a uniformed policewoman on either side. She wasn't handcuffed. Dressed in a white shirt and black business suit, she acted as if she were a lawyer there to defend a client, rather than standing trial for murder. Having seen photo after photo of her splashed across the Internet—one of her in a bright red Hawaiian shirt strolling next to her husband in what looked to be Honolulu, another in a dark suit, ominous and brooding at her father-in-law's funeral, many observers, including me, were surprised. The once-glamorous thin face with high cheekbones had filled out and the formerly svelte figure was nowhere to be seen. "Sister Gu looked like she just came back from a vacation," one netizen teased. "The food must be really good in jail."

Gu Kailai's weight gain triggered widespread speculation that it was not her in the court but a double. One Chinese blogger carefully compared Gu Kailai's image on TV with previous pictures and listed twenty physical differences, including her eyes, cheekbones, ears, teeth, and even her accent to illustrate that the woman in the courtroom was a fake. Another blogger posted an "exclusive," saying Gu Kailai's double was actually a forty-six-year-old worker named Zhao, who lived outside Beijing. The double was said to have been discovered by the wife of Premier Wen Jiabao, who had paid the woman a large sum of money. The real Gu Kailai, said the blogger, was still in police custody in Beijing.

Those who actually knew Gu Kailai ignored such fabrications, and a Chinese-American psychiatrist told me her weight gain was probably due to the medication she was taking for her depression.

A few hours after the trial ended, Zhao Xiangcha, one of the observers, e-mailed several overseas media organizations his account of the trial after his initial posting on the Internet in China was deleted by government censors. Zhao said his notes were compiled from memory because his pencil was confiscated before he entered the courtroom. Details in his account were corroborated by two other observers and have been incorporated in the previous chapter. The next day, Xinhua news agency issued an official version of the court proceedings, omitting many details laid out in Zhao Xiangcha's version.

"The government faces a dilemma in Gu Kailai's trial," said a legal scholar in Beijing. "If senior officials allow the court to give out too many investigation details relating to the Heywood murder and Bo family corruption, they run the risk of implicating more people in power and generating more public outcry. However, when the court details are too sketchy, people don't believe in the verdict."

Even so, Zhao Xiangcha, who attended the trial, remarked at the end of his observation:

> I feel that the entire courtroom adjudication process was fairly objective and just. There was a slight feeling that things had been rehearsed beforehand. But that didn't affect the ultimate defining of the case. The facts were really clear and the evidence was copious. The prosecutor didn't bully people and the defense lawyers did everything they could. The written testimonies were just and unbiased. To convict these two is absolutely just. In the final statements of the accused, they both admitted guilt and showed relatively sincere repentance. I felt this genuinely came from the heart; there was no trace of acting or of their having been compelled.

But Zhao also noted that he had overheard the sigh of a lawyer, who had originally been hired by Gu Kailai's mother to defend her daughter. The lawyer complained that the defense attorneys were not allowed to do their jobs properly.

LEGAL EXPERTS ASK:
DID GU KAILAI KILL NEIL HEYWOOD?

DESPITE THE GOVERNMENT's meticulous efforts to convince the public at the trial that the cases of Gu Kailai and Wang Lijun were criminal in nature, rather than politically motivated, the lack of due process and transparency failed to change the minds of skeptics.

Gao Guanjun, a US-based attorney who graduated from the Southeast University of Politics and Law in Sichuan, specializes in criminal investigations. He taught the subject for several years at the Chinese People's Public Security University in Beijing. I consulted him about the Gu Kailai trial and interviewed four journalists and legal experts. After combing through the official indictments against Gu Kailai, we have found a dozen important legal issues, which might have resulted in either a dismissal of charges or an acquittal if the defense had been allowed to address them properly.

1. Gu Kailai had been officially diagnosed by court-designated medical experts as suffering from bipolar disorder and moderate schizophrenia. People close to the Bo Xilai family told the overseas Chinese media in April that she suffered from anxiety, paranoia, and depression after the "lead poisoning incident" and that the doctor had prescribed medication for her deteriorating mental condition. Gu sometimes refused to take the medicine due to its debilitating side effects. Moreover, on October 4, 2011, she walked into a conference on how writers should promote the "Smashing Black" campaign in Chongqing wearing a major general insignia that belonged to her father. "First she said that she was under secret orders from the Ministry of Public Security to effectively protect Comrade Wang Lijun's personal safety in Chongqing," a source told Reuters. "It was a mess. She was incoherent and I reached the conclusion that she would be trouble." At Gu's trial, the defense also brought up the

issue of her mental illness. The forensic examination institute under the Shanghai Mental Health Center had given Gu a psychiatric evaluation and concluded that she had been treated for chronic insomnia, anxiety, depression, and paranoia in the past:

> She used to take anxiolytics, antidepressants, and sedative hypnotic drugs, and she also received combined treatment by taking antipsychotic drugs, but the curative effect was not enduring. She developed a certain degree of physical and psychological dependence on sedative hypnotic drugs, which resulted in mental disorders.

Because the indictment is largely based on her confession and in the absence of any corroborating witness accounts, one has to wonder how reliable her memory was, especially relating to the criminal process. Did her mental illness affect criminal intent or capacity?

2. The motivation was not clear. The prosecution stated that Gu Kailai hatched the plot to kill Heywood when she learned that he had detained her son in Britain. Evidence shown to the court only included e-mail exchanges between Heywood and Bo Guagua. However, Guo Weiguo, the deputy police chief in Chongqing who had been briefed on the threats by Gu Kailai (before Heywood's death), examined all the e-mails and said in his testimony that he did not detect any serious threats made on Bo Guagua's life.

3. The indictment said Gu Kailai had illegally obtained the poison from local drug dealers, but no proof was offered that she actually did so. Who were the drug dealers? With the government's tight control over highly toxic materials, where did they get the poison? The indictment failed to clarify such critical issues. According to a police officer in Chongqing, the former district party chief, Xia Zeliang, provided Gu with rat poison he had obtained from a private pest control source. Under normal circumstances rat poison contains cyanide but only a tiny amount—not enough to kill a person. If such questions surrounding the murder tools are unclear, how reliable was the rest of the investigative work?

4. Did Heywood die of natural causes? Gu Kailai admitted getting Heywood drunk and then giving him tea laced with cyanide. However, the initial forensic report displayed no primary signs of cyanide poisoning. A CT scan performed on the victim's body before it was cremated and an initial blood test found no traces of cyanide. All the tests, according to Wang Lijun's testimony, were conducted prior to police knowledge of Gu Kailai's involvement and should be considered objective.

5. From Gu Kailai's description, Heywood's death seemed to have occurred peacefully. He rested his head against the headboard while Gu Kailai fed him poisoned tea. Attorney Gao Guanjun did not believe it was cyanide poison, which normally causes a violent physical reaction—struggling for air, spasms, and incontinence. Because Heywood had a family history of cardiovascular disease and he was not a heavy drinker, could it be possible that he died naturally of a heart attack induced by a bout of atypical excessive drinking?

6. Was Heywood really dead before Gu Kailai left the room? The indictment stated that Gu felt for Heywood's pulse and there was no blood pressure. She was not sure if Heywood was dead or not. By then, Heywood lay in bed, his head resting against the headboard. When the police discovered Heywood's body two days later, however, he was lying flat on the bed, and the mattress showed signs of having been rolled on. Considering this evidence, Heywood was probably not killed by cyanide, which tends to kill quickly, or there was not sufficient poison to kill him right away.

7. According to the defense, strangers' footprints were found on the balcony, left between the time Gu Kailai committed the murder and police discovered Heywood's body, but there were no signs of a break-in. Wang Lijun confessed in his testimony that he had installed bugging devices in Heywood's room. Why did the court not investigate where the footprints came from and to whom they belonged?

8. The prosecution said Wang Lijun took a second blood sample secretly from Heywood's body before it was cremated (the first blood

sample showed no traces of cyanide) and ordered his staff member to transfer the sample to Beijing and hide it in a friend's refrigerator. Four months later, tests on the second blood sample showed cyanide, but this time in an exact amount needed to kill a person. There is no chain of custody to prove the integrity of this second sample.

9. One assumes that as an experienced lawyer, Gu Kailai would have taken a class on criminal investigation, a mandatory course for law students in China. Gu Kailai seemed to act like someone who had no education in this area, let alone legal training. Based on the indictment, Gu Kailai did not wear gloves and left her fingerprints on the water cup and bottle caps. In addition, Gu Kailai spread drug capsules on the floor. With her criminal training, how could she not know cyanide or drugs would be detected in blood tests?

10. During Gu Kailai's trial, the prosecution claimed to have collected 394 witness testimonies and 212 written statements, but there was no direct participation or cross-examination of key witnesses throughout the trial, not even Wang Lijun, the Chongqing police chief, who was asked to cover up the crime and later revealed all after visiting the US Consulate in Chengdu. Gu's son, Bo Guagua, was also considered a key witness. According to CNN, Bo Guagua had submitted a copy of his written testimony to the court, but there is nothing to confirm it was actually accepted.

11. The Chinese government assigned Gu Kailai two defense lawyers a month before the trial. The lawyers, who have been said to have delivered as good a defense as was possible under the circumstances, met Gu Kailai only ten times and had to review 1,468 pages of documents within a short time. Moreover, Gu's lawyers were not even given the chance to question key witnesses during the trial. Even so, the defense identified several discrepancies in the investigation and raised questions regarding Gu's mental competence and the final conclusions surrounding Heywood's death. But the court did not deliberate on any of the issues presented by Gu's lawyers. Lastly, Gu repeatedly called Wang Lijun an "insidious" man and discredited his

accusations. Many saw it as an indication that Gu felt the murder charges had been forced on her. The court ignored her statements. Obviously, Gu's guilty verdict had been predetermined. The presence of the defense lawyers was largely symbolic.

12. Throughout the trial, there was no mention of Bo Xilai, who was the husband of the accused and the boss of police officers charged with covering up the murder. Did he participate? Did he know in advance what was going to happen? Did he order the police to cover up for his wife? Murdering a foreign citizen is normally considered a serious offense because of the likelihood it can explode into an international incident. Therefore, it is inconceivable that Wang Lijun, the police chief, and other investigators did not notify Bo Xilai of the incident until January 28, 2012. As the mayor in Dalian and the party chief of Chongqing, Bo Xilai was known as a hands-on manager, controlling every decision made by his administration that could affect his political future. Story has it that he would even supervise the repair of a leaky bathroom pipe that he had accidentally encountered one night. It would seem preposterous that he did not suspect anything.

Six weeks after the Gu Kailai trial, Wang Xuemei, a top forensic expert in China, brought up similar issues about what she called "glaring inconsistencies" in the theory that the British businessman was killed from cyanide poisoning. Wang rose to fame as the first female forensic scientist to sit on China's highest prosecution body, and her frequent television appearances have made her a household name. In her blog, she said the account of the murder accepted by the Chinese justice system was "seriously lacking in fact and scientific basis."

From the secret recording of Gu's confession to the murder and the court testimony provided by Gu and her assistant Zhang, Wang Xuemei said there was no indication that the perpetrators witnessed a death that "involved the characteristics of cyanide poisoning." According to Wang Xuemei, the symptoms normally include scream reflex that would have occurred during "lightning-fast" suffocation, convulsions that would have been apparent as the cyanide reached Heywood's central nervous system, stupor that would have followed, and eventual cardiopulmonary arrest just prior to his death.

Based on her professional knowledge, Wang pointed out that basic investigative observation and blood work would have ruled out that theory very quickly because of the obvious discoloration of the corpse or the bright red color of the blood samples.

> I believe that the death involving a foreigner at a luxury hotel would have been no small case in Chongqing around that time. The Chongqing Public Security Bureau would have followed the necessary procedure to check the crime scene and conduct forensic tests. They would have invited a relatively senior-level forensic expert to examine the body of the deceased. The blood test result presented in court showed that the Public Security Bureau did conduct its routine procedure. If that was the case, how could the forensic expert fail to detect the obvious hypostasis and blood as an unusually bright red color? If the forensic expert ignored the signs to cover up for the criminal, he or she should be held responsible for listing Heywood's death as "excessive drinking" after the criminal acts were exposed. Four policemen have been convicted for the cover-up, but I don't see the name of the forensic expert on the list of the convicted. In other words, the initial forensic report was correct and there was no signs of cyanide poisoning. . . . I seriously doubt the sudden appearance of cyanide in the blood sample that was under the control of Wang Lijun for three months.

Wang Xuemei did not doubt the conclusion that Gu Kailai possessed a clear murder motive and the murder had been premeditated. But she wondered if the poison that Gu Kailai used was lethal and if Heywood had, in fact, died of cyanide poisoning. Wang Xuemei suggested another possible cause of death: a different person might have caused Heywood's death by placing soft materials around his neck and rendering mechanical asphyxia death. "Such supplemental killing would display signs that are similar to cyanide poisoning, without leaving any bruises around the neck," she said.

Wang Xuemei was not the only dissenter. Back in April 2012, Wang Lulu, Heywood's widow, was also said to disagree that Gu Kailai had killed her husband. She conveyed her skepticism to a few of her friends, but the next day, Wang Lulu received stern warnings from Chinese authorities. The threats were such that Wang Lulu ran to the British Embassy on April 12, seeking permits to live in the UK on the grounds that her safety and that of her children were endangered. The news further fueled the speculation that there was a government cover-up.

These unresolved issues during Gu's trial boosted the argument by skeptics that the murder was part of a wider political conspiracy by senior leaders in Beijing to stop Bo Xilai from seizing power at the Politburo Standing Committee. In addition, new and credible details and analyses that emerged after Gu's trial lead one to believe that the Chongqing police chief, Wang Lijun, was a highly probable suspect.

AN INSIDIOUS MAN

A T HIS TRIAL on September 18, 2012, Wang Lijun—a former police chief who used to claim a number of titles such as "professor of law," "legal expert," and "specialist forensic investigator"—was in his element. He appeared in good health at his trial, and dressed not in the standard orange boiler suit of Chinese prisoners but in a crisp white shirt. While giving his testimony, attendees said, he maintained his usual arrogance and smugness.

Wang had every reason to feel triumphant. By delivering to the US Consulate allegations and evidence that Bo Xilai's wife had murdered Neil Heywood, Wang had exacted vengeance on one of the most influential figures in Chinese politics. Wang's actions also almost derailed the party's leadership transition.

Since Wang Lijun's conviction in September 2012, many police officers and government officials have opened up to overseas Chinese media with startling stories about Wang Lijun, who, they say, personified unbridled ambitions, egoism, brutality, and deception. An official in Chongqing disclosed to me that more than 800 people were executed as a result of Wang Lijun's anti-crime initiatives between 1992 and 2011, and that he had a history of planting and falsifying evidence on those who were accused of having mafia connections. *Nandu*

Weekly, a Guangzhou-based newspaper famous for its investigative reporting, spent a year interviewing Wang Lijun's former colleagues and researching previously-undisclosed court records of Wang Lijun's trial. In December 2012, the paper published a five-part feature examining Wang's life and career. The government banned the article three days later because the paper had cast doubt on the government's handling of the Gu Kailai murder case. More analysts and members of the public are becoming convinced that Wang was the real murderer who, along with anti-Bo forces in Beijing, schemed against Bo Xilai, the former Chongqing party chief.

Wang possessed a clear motive in orchestrating Heywood's murder. *Nandu Weekly* reported that Wang Lijun aspired to join the Municipal Party Standing Committee after he became deputy mayor of Chongqing in May 2011, and asked Gu Gailai to lobby her husband for Wang's promotion. Gu dutifully brought up the issue at home, but Bo was incensed by Wang's relentless requests. Wang never gave up, though, and looked for an opportunity to prove his value to Bo Xilai and make him change his mind.

In the late spring of 2011, families of those who had been imprisoned or executed on corruption- and triad-related crimes during Wang's anti-crime initiatives had traveled to Beijing in droves to petition the senior leadership—accusing Wang of planting evidence, using torture to extract confessions, and violating due process. As the petition movement gained momentum, Wang Lijun became paranoid that some senior leaders in Beijing might have instigated the petitions and conspired against him. According to a police officer in Chongqing, Wang shared his concerns with Bo Xilai, who simply brushed them aside with the promise that if anything happened, Wang would have Bo's full backing. However, in May 2011, when two of his former colleagues in Tieling were under investigation, Wang recognized that the scandal was directly aiming at him. He went to Bo again, entreating him to intervene, but Bo declined. Wang became infuriated and disillusioned. He could see clearly that Bo would have no qualms abandoning him or making him a scapegoat if political troubles occurred. For several months, Wang had to see a doctor because he had been suffering from insomnia. The police chief was also paranoid—he frequently conducted toxicity tests on the food prepared for him at the cafeteria. But in the fall, Wang seemed to have regained his confidence. One of Wang's colleagues suspected that Wang had made a pact with Bo's opponents in Beijing in exchange for political protection, because Wang began showing a strong interest in Bo's personal life around that time and carefully documented his womanizing activities and family finances.

As the conflict between Neil Heywood and Gu Kailai escalated in October 2011, Wang Lijun actively participated in plotting against Heywood, and goaded Gu Kailai into killing him by exaggerating the Briton's threats against Bo Guagua.

On November 12, 2011, Wang instructed Xu Ming to make false charges to the Chongqing police that Heywood was the ringleader of a drug trafficking network in Sichuan and its neighboring provinces. On that afternoon, Wang helped Gu Kailai remove the wax wrapping from the poison at Gu Kailai's house. On November 13, following Heywood's arrival in Chongqing, Wang admitted in court that he had "arranged surveillance and control efforts targeted at Heywood under the pretext that Heywood may have committed drug-related crimes." *Nandu Weekly* claimed that, at eight o'clock that night, Gu was paralyzed with fear and began to have second thoughts. Wang Lijun showed up at her home. "Wang asked why I hadn't gone to see Heywood," recalled Gu. "I said I wasn't feeling well and that I didn't want to do it anymore. Wang told me that I have to do it."

Based on the testimony of Gu's accomplice, Zhang Xiaojun, Wang stayed inside Gu's bedroom for twenty minutes. Gu allegedly begged Wang Lijun to conduct the killing, but Wang insisted that she was the perfect candidate for the job because Heywood would not become suspicious around her. Wang also told Gu that she was eliminating a dangerous British spy for the country. Before Gu left, Wang told the kitchen staff to prepare a bowl of noodle soup to boost her energy. Then, he ordered Gu's driver to get the car ready.

Gu went ahead as planned and arrived at the Lucky Holiday Hotel with Zhang Xiaojun at about nine o'clock. She got Heywood drunk and supposedly added several drops of rat poison to Heywood's tea. However, the rat poison did not contain enough cyanide to kill Heywood.

By the time Gu left the hotel room, Heywood had passed out but was not dead. One version that is widely circulated on the Internet said Gu could not get herself to poison Heywood. Instead, they simply consumed the alcohol and by the time Gu left, Heywood had blacked out, drunk.

According to *Nandu Weekly*, Gu Kailai borrowed her driver's mobile phone and called Wang Lijun, but there was no answer. Gu reached the deputy police chief and asked, "Where is the Devil?" [Wang Lijun's nickname.] The deputy police chief found Wang in his office, informing him that Gu was looking for him. Wang responded impatiently, "Okay, I know." The deputy police chief told the court that Wang Lijun was deliberately avoiding Gu Kailai. A well-connected source with the Chongqing police department claimed that Wang Lijun, who had been monitoring Heywood, became upset that Gu Kailai did not kill Heywood as she had promised.

According to the source, Wang might have driven to the hotel later, sneaked into Heywood's room, and finished him off with a piece of soft material that did not leave any marks around the neck. The unidentified footsteps that investigators found on the balcony might have been Wang's. This scenario also explained why Heywood's body displayed no prominent signs of cyanide poisoning.

"Wang wanted Heywood to die," said my source. "Heywood's death would give Wang the clout to control Gu Kailai and blackmail Bo Xilai."

Furthermore, Wang was well-versed in criminology. If he truly intended to protect Gu, he would have taught her how to destroy evidence, such as removing fingerprints from the mugs and blocking the hotel security camera. "The fact that Wang did not do anything indicated his intention to frame Gu Kailai," continued my source.

On November 14, Wang Lijun went to Gu's residence and coaxed Gu into describing the murder process. Gu admitted killing Heywood and her confession was left on Wang's tape recorder. The taped confession was used as a critical piece of evidence against Gu. The tape was only mentioned, but never played, in court. There is no way of knowing whether Wang had altered or edited the tape.

According to a Chongqing police officer, Gu willingly declared that she had poisoned Heywood because she was worried Wang would blame her for breaching her promise. Also, admission of her weakness could fuel the rumor that she had feelings for Heywood. Therefore, Gu later bragged to Xu Ming that she had added three drops of poison to the tea—even though one was potent enough to kill Heywood.

On November 15, 2012, hotel staff found Heywood's body. Wang Lijun excused himself from the investigation and assigned four police officers without removing any incriminating evidence from the crime scene. Wang's intent was clear—allowing other officers to discover Gu's involvement and clearing any suspicion that he might have framed Gu. In addition, Wang secretly drew some blood from Heywood's body and took it home. Given that Wang was a seasoned forensic expert, there is every reason to suspect that he tampered with the blood work.

One wonders why Wang would take a gamble on killing a Briton, which could turn into a diplomatic dispute and attract Beijing's attention if discovered. A princeling in Beijing whose father used to work for the Ministry of Public Security said Heywood had been on the watch list of China's intelligence agency. As Chongqing's police chief, Wang Lijun was made aware of Heywood's possible connection with MI6, the British spy agency. Therefore, Heywood's death would be a safe bet—the British government would not pressure China to pursue any investigation for fear of exposing Heywood's true identity. On the other hand, Bo Xilai would also beg Wang to cover up Heywood's death because neither Bo nor the Chinese government wanted the public to learn that a British spy had infiltrated a senior leader's family.

After Heywood was cremated and the investigation was closed, Wang Lijun once again broached to Gu the topic of the corruption scandal in Tieling as well as his desire to join the Municipal Party Standing Committee. Gu talked with her husband again, lavishing praises on Wang and beseeching Bo to reconsider Wang's request. When Bo ignored Gu's plea, Gu was said to have fiercely argued with Bo. The two reportedly did not speak for days.

On the night of December 11, Wang's colleagues told *Nandu Weekly* that Wang Lijun had received news that the city was conducting background checks on him for a possible promotion. Wang immediately gathered his subordinates for an emergency meeting. Wang claimed that he convened the meeting to discuss "how to build a clean government," but actually used the occasion to clean up his record. Wang announced that the four cars that had been solely assigned to him could now be used by anyone. "Those are not my cars. They belonged to everyone." In addition, he disclosed that the owner of a big coal mine had donated three floors in a luxury apartment building for his personal use. The property was worth 10 million yuan (US $1.6 million) and he had decided to give it back to the city. All attendees were puzzled by Wang's "generosity" before they found out about his true intention.

A week later, the news about Wang's promotion proved to be false. Wang Lijun stepped up his pressure on Gu, threatening to expose her role in Heywood's murder if her husband refused to promote him. In the face of Wang's blackmail, Gu became paranoid and her mental condition worsened. Then, while Wang Lijun was in Beijing, she raided his office, stating to Wang's staff members and daughter that she was collecting evidence to illustrate that Wang was a corrupt official who lived a decadent lifestyle. Moreover, she said she would report Wang to the Central Commission for Discipline Inspection.

As his relationship with Gu traveled irreversibly downhill, *Nandu Weekly* said Wang decided to report the case to Bo Xilai, and on January 14, 2012, Wang called the four investigators to his office, instructing them to each write a resignation letter, which, he said, should contain four points:

1. They had discovered strong evidence to suggest that the party chief's wife, K, was connected with Neil Heywood's death,
2. K forced them to violate the law by concealing and destroying evidence,
3. K invited them to dinner and allegedly put knockout drops in their liquor, and

4. K had illegally searched the offices and homes of Wang and his staff members.

Separately, Wang Lijun ordered the deputy police chief to attach the internal investigation report on Heywood's death and had the investigators state they could no longer serve the city in good conscience. Wang Lijun told the investigators that he did not really want them to resign. Their letters would simply be used to pressure Bo Xilai to rein in his wife.

Then came the fateful January 29 meeting with Bo where Wang was slapped in the face. On their way back from Bo's office after the incident, Guo Weiguo, the former deputy police chief, remembered complaining to Wang, "We should have pursued the murder investigation from the very beginning. All of our cover-up efforts have amounted to nothing." Wang Lijun disagreed, saying, "I think we have achieved 80 percent of our goal." According to *Nandu Weekly*, Wang Lijun declined Guo's suggestion that they should report the case to the Ministry of Public Security. "Wang tried to use the case for personal gains," said Guo.

The next day, Wang wrote a letter to Bo Xilai and Gu Kailai, apologizing for his "mistakes" and blaming Bo's chief of staff for instigating their split. The letter did not mend fences and Bo fired Wang Lijun. Two days after Wang was sacked, Gu Kailai met with Wang in his office after she had heard from other police officers that Wang had implicated her in seven more murders. Wang allegedly slapped his own face in repentance. Gu sobbed and said she had forgiven him. The two were seen having lunch at police headquarters. But Bo no longer trusted Wang. After Wang had learned that Bo planned to eliminate him, he fled.

If Wang had murdered Neil Heywood, many wondered why he would run to the US Consulate. An official familiar with the case said Wang had no other choice—he had originally intended to go to Beijing, but his friends there talked him out of it. If he had gone into hiding in a remote part of China, he would have been arrested sooner or later. And Wang was certain he could meet the asylum criteria—he had evidence to show that his own life was in danger because he had attempted to expose the murder of a British citizen. Besides, as a senior official, he could provide valuable intelligence to the Americans. If his asylum request was denied, his own attempted defection and revelations about Heywood's murder could provide major headlines in Western countries. The publicity would get Beijing's attention. Wang would also state that Bo had planned a coup to depose Xi Jinping, the designated new party general secretary. The allegation would no doubt cause rifts between Bo and other senior leaders, who would step in and shield Wang from Bo's retaliation. Wang's gamble paid off—he saved his own life and destroyed Bo's political career.

In April 2012, a princeling, whose father was a senior Communist official in the Deng era, contended that Wang Lijun had notified a Politburo Standing Committee member about Gu Kailai's plan to kill Neil Heywood. "This senior leader must have instructed Wang to go along with the plot and make it happen," said the princeling. "Otherwise, Wang Lijun wouldn't have been so bold and relentless." The princeling also pointed out that Wang had planned to travel to Beijing after he was sacked, but the senior official stopped Wang because he wouldn't be in a position to save him. The official advised Wang to try the US Consulate. "Wang had never intended to apply for political asylum," said the princeling. "His sole purpose was to make Bo's scandal an international incident, forcing the party elders such as Jiang Zemin to take action against Bo. Without such stunts, it would be impossible to defeat Bo, who was so well connected in Beijing."

I choose not to disclose the senior official's name because I have not been able to verify the princeling's assertions, but from what happened, it is safe to say the anti-Bo forces in Beijing saw the Heywood murder as a perfect justification to oust Bo. The senior leadership sided with Wang and used Wang's words against Bo and his wife. It was a win-win situation—Bo Xilai and his wife are now safely locked behind bars and a potentially dangerous British secret agent has been eliminated.

At this is being written, the public has not heard Bo Xilai's version of the story. With Gu's conviction, the government will block or ignore any challenges made by Bo's lawyers to the previous court decision relating to Heywood's murder.

In September 2012, Wang Lijun was put on trial for defection, criminal cover-up, abuse of power, and bribe taking. Because he produced "important clues that exposed serious offenses committed by others and played a key part in the investigation of the cases which could be considered as major meritorious service," the government did not make any effort to probe Wang's murder of Neil Heywood. "All that is left to explain the true cause of Heywood's death were the samples that had been taken from a long time before and the related artificial testimonies," said Wang Xuemei, the forensic expert. Thus, the death of Neil Heywood will join a long list of unresolved political mysteries in contemporary Chinese history.

FROM CHINA WITH LOVE

A S PART OF CHINA'S modernization drive under Deng Xiaoping, the government in 1980 encouraged students to learn English. A friend of mine began to take lessons from the radio. One day he encountered a retired American businessman in front of a large hotel and struck up a conversation in his broken English. At the end of their talk, they exchanged addresses. Two months later, the American wrote his new Chinese friend a postcard, describing his adventures in other parts of China. The postcard was intercepted by the street committee, which sent it to the local public security bureau. Officials there immediately contacted an English teacher at a nearby school to translate it. While the letter was being translated, my friend was detained and interrogated. He ended up handing over to the police an English novel that the American had given him as a gift and wrote a lengthy self-criticism for keeping in touch with a foreigner without approval.

Thirty years later, corresponding with a foreigner or inviting a foreigner home for dinner was no longer considered a violation of Chinese security rules. However, for a member of the Politburo, befriending a foreigner can still be taboo. It did not come as a surprise when I heard from a princeling in May 2012 that Neil Heywood had been on the watch list of China's State Security Ministry, China's intelligence agency, for several years.

"The Englishman ran a business consultancy and bragged about his access to Bo and his staff members," said the source. "When Bo Xilai was the minister of commerce, Heywood said he had brought several foreign business groups to meet with Bo. When Bo Xilai moved to Chongqing in 2007, Gu Kailai introduced Heywood to several businesspeople there. She allegedly told friends that Heywood was her 'foreign advisor.' His activities were duly noticed by the Ministry of State Security."

The source added that Bo Xilai arranged for Heywood to meet the then-Chinese vice president Xi Jinping, saying that Heywood came from an aristocratic family and was well connected in the UK. It was not clear when the introduction took place and whether Bo Xilai wanted Heywood to advise on the education of the vice president's daughter, who was studying at a foreign-language school near Shanghai and aspired to pursue her college degree abroad, or on political and cultural issues relating to the UK.

The revelations about Heywood's murky background have added an interesting subplot to the Bo Xilai saga and generated a slew of media reports—journalists cannot resist the lure of being close to an "insider" scandal, particularly one involving members of the secretive Politburo Standing Committee, and the spy angle was just icing on the cake.

According to the *Guardian,* which interviewed Heywood's friends, the Briton drove a Jaguar flaunting the license plate "007" and liked to give people the impression that he was on a secret mission. His friends believed that he was just posturing, creating a fantasy for himself. However, the *Wall Street Journal* revealed that he once worked with Hakluyt, a business intelligence firm founded by two retired MI6 officers that employs a number of former officers from Britain's shadowy foreign spy network and is engaged in covert intelligence gathering along the lines of the CIA in the US. In November 2012, the same newspaper confirmed that Heywood was an "unpaid informant" who regularly provided information on the Bo family's private affairs to an operative of MI6.

Also in November 2012, the *New York Times* confirmed what I had heard in May of that year—China's Ministry of State Security had long suspected Heywood of being a British spy:

A scholar with high-level ties to Mr. Bo and the ministry said Mr. Bo had known of the ministry's official suspicions before Mr. Heywood's death, as had other leaders. Separately, a political analyst with high-level party ties said Mr. Heywood was on the ministry's watch list, possibly for years, as a result of his relationship with the Bo family.

"When a minister-level cadre has such relations with a foreigner, they'll definitely be watched," the analyst said.

Heywood's MI6 ties have given rise to conspiratorial rumors among the public—some details might be true and others are trotted out more for their entertainment value. A November 2012 article on a popular Chinese language forum, creaders.net, said Premier Wen Jiabao, who strongly opposed Bo Xilai's "Singing Red and Smashing Black" campaign, had secretly urged the deputy minister of state security to dig up dirt on Bo Xilai in 2009. Secret agents first targeted Bo's son, Bo Guagua, and tried to identify the funding source for his education abroad.

They soon uncovered the link between Bo Xilai and billionaire businessman Xu Ming, who had channeled money to Bo's son in exchange for government contracts. At the same time, Neil Heywood, who sometimes acted as a middleman for the Bo family overseas, came to their attention. China's secret agents suspected that Heywood could be using his connection with the Bo family to gather intelligence for MI6, but they never found any evidence.

When the deputy minister of state security reported his agents' findings to Premier Wen, he instructed the agents to confirm Heywood's true identity. If they could prove that the English guardian of Bo Xilai's son was a spy, Wen knew that the revelation could be lethal for Bo Xilai. Chinese public security agents began to take a keen interest in Heywood's background. At one point, a member of the National Security Ministry recruited Wang Lulu, Heywood's China-born wife, assigning her to keep an eye on her husband and report on any of his suspicious activities.

In 2010, a friend of Bo Xilai's who was a senior official at the ministry informed him of the Neil Heywood investigation. He warned

Bo Xilai that his political opponents could use his close ties with Heywood to sabotage his political career. Bo Xilai immediately shared the information with Gu Kailai, instructing her and Bo Guagua to break off their relations with Heywood. Since 2010, Heywood had not been allowed to contact Bo Xilai and Gu Kailai, but he did maintain frequent e-mail exchanges with Bo Guagua, who was studying in the UK. The news about Heywood's investigation as a spy aggravated Gu's paranoia. She believed that some senior leaders in Beijing had made up the espionage story to scheme against Bo Xilai. She suspected that Heywood's wife might also have fed information relating to Gu's overseas money transfers to the Ministry of State Security. The creader.net story seems to correspond with a British media report that said Gu contacted Heywood in 2010, asking him to divorce his wife, Wang Lulu, and pledge allegiance to the Bo family. "Gu acted very strangely," Heywood was quoted as saying to his friends.

Also in 2010, creader.net said Bo Xilai submitted a written report to the Politburo, stating that there had been no security breaches in his dealings with Neil Heywood. His report successfully preempted Premier Wen's attacks. In subsequent months, stories started to appear in the overseas Chinese media about how Premier Wen's son and wife had used political connections to accumulate a large amount of wealth. Bo was said to have provided the information in retaliation.

So far, there is no proof that Premier Wen instructed the Ministry of State Security to uncover Heywood's MI6 connection. Chen Xiaoping, a US-based China scholar, believed that Zhou Yongkang, the Politburo Standing Committee member who oversaw the State Security Ministry, had instructed Bo Xilai to get rid of Heywood in 2011. "Zhou had chosen Bo as his successor and he was worried that Bo's connection with a foreigner could give other promising candidates excuses to oppose Bo's appointment at the 18th Party Congress," Chen pointed out. "Killing Heywood in Chongqing, rather than Beijing, could remove any future obstacles and minimize negative publicity." Chen speculated that Bo had used Gu to lure Heywood to Chongqing and assigned the job to Wang Lijun, who choked Heywood to death after Gu Kailai got the Briton drunk. After the Bo–Wang fallout, Wang shifted all the blame to Gu.

A story on Boxun described a scenario where agents from the Ministry of State Security met with Wang Lijun in Beijing in October 2011, ordering him to find a way to kill Heywood, who, they said, was attempting to infiltrate senior party officials. Wang Lijun then used Gu Kailai to ensnare Heywood in Chonqing. After Heywood passed out in bed, Wang injected him with toxic chemicals. He then teamed up with Bo's foes in Beijing and concocted the Gu murder case to retaliate against Bo's refusal to help Wang's friends in Tieling.

These versions, which still lack substantial evidence, could be good material for a John le Carré wannabe looking for a Chinese spin on a thriller novel for the West's publishing industry, which is constantly on the lookout for devious plots in foreign countries. But a source in Chongqing said Heywood's connection with the British intelligence service was an open secret among police. One of the four officers assigned to investigate the Heywood case allegedly said to Bo Xilai, "Gu eliminated a dangerous spy for our country."

The unusual silence by the British government concerning Heywood's death—had he been a merely a British national working in China, his death would have at least been the subject of consular investigation and public statement—further fueled the spy theory. At Gu's trial, the British government sent two diplomats to observe the trial but declined to comment on it after Gu was convicted. The embassy did issue a statement:

> We welcome the fact that the Chinese authorities have investigated the death of Neil Heywood, and tried those they identified as responsible. We consistently made clear to the Chinese authorities that we wanted to see the trials in this case conform to international human rights standards and for the death penalty not to be applied.

In response to the British government statement, a Chinese blogger commented, "What do you expect the British government to say when one of their intelligence gatherers was killed? There is a Chinese saying that best sums up the situation: 'When a mute person accidentally swallows a bitter pill, he feels pain but cannot say it aloud.'"

POISONOUS WATER

GREEK MYTHOLOGY tells the story of Pandora's Box, of how Zeus sent Pandora away to punish men after Prometheus stole fire from the gods. Pandora carried a jar with her and when she opened it, she released all the evils in the world. In the Bible, Eve purportedly ate the apple of knowledge despite God's instructions not to do so, and gave some to Adam, and God expelled them from the Garden of Eden.

In China, people are well-versed in the stories of "poisonous water." For example, in the central city of Xian, not far from the emperor's terra cotta warriors, there is a mountain called Mount Lishan, made famous by two beautiful women who were blamed for wrecking dynasties and gave rise to the phrase "Beauties kill like poisonous water."

The first woman, Bao Si, was associated with a beacon tower built 3,000 years ago on top of the mountain. Legend has it that during the Western Zhou Dynasty, the kingdom was under threat from a hostile aggressive neighbor. As a precaution, the emperor built twenty beacon towers and installed gigantic drums on top of every mountain peak nearby, with the one on Mount Lishan the biggest. If the guard saw the neighbor's troops coming, he would ignite the firewood inside the beacon and beat the drums. The smoke would alert the emperor's allies and they would gather their forces and rush to help. The system worked well until after the emperor died. His son took over and turned out to be a ruthless ruler. One day, the young emperor met Bao Si, the most beautiful woman in the kingdom. He brought her to the palace and made her empress. The young emperor was so in love that he was willing to do anything to please Bao Si, but there was one problem. She never smiled. Her face was locked into perpetual sadness.

One day, the couple toured the beacon tower in Mount Lishan and the emperor hit upon an idea. He ordered one of his ministers to light up the signal fire. Entranced by the smoke and fire, Bao Si burst out laughing for the first time. The emperor was thrilled. Meanwhile, allied troops rushed over, thinking there was a war, only to find out that it was a mere joke.

As expected, when a true emergency happened, the emperor lit the beacon, but nobody came to rescue him. The Western Zhou Dynasty was vanquished. Nowadays, climbers who reach the tower can still see the characters "one smile led to the loss of a kingdom" carved on a piece of rock.

At the foot of Mount Lishan was the Huaqing hot spring, which served as the bathhouse for an emperor's voluptuous concubine in the Tang Dynasty (about 700 CE). As a young man, emperor Xuanzong was a wise and forward-looking ruler, but in later years, he became infatuated with an eighteen-year-old beauty, Yang Guifei, who was originally married to one of his sons. The eunuchs persuaded the prince to give up his wife and the emperor made the former daughter-in-law his concubine. Because of his concubine, the emperor neglected daily duties as the head of his empire and allowed his court to lapse into chaos.

Soon, natural disasters and discontent within the military led to a large-scale rebellion. As rebel forces advanced toward the capital, the emperor and his concubine fled west. On the way, his imperial guards mutinied. Blaming the concubine for the empire's troubles, his guards refused to carry him unless his concubine was killed. Without any choice, the emperor handed over a white scarf to his guards, who strangled the most beautiful woman in the kingdom.

Stories of "poisonous water" are still told in China. Nowadays the famous American quote "Behind every successful man there is a great woman" has been adapted to describe a unique phenomenon in China: "Behind every disgraced Communist official there is an evil woman."

Wang Guangmei was China's first lady. Her husband, Liu Shaoqi, serving as China's president from 1959 to 1969, was the designated successor to Mao, the Communist Party chairman. Wang grew up in the family of a Chinese diplomat and studied at American missionary universities in the 1930s. A science major, she spoke French, Russian, and English. In the mid-1940s, the idealistic Wang escaped to the Communist-occupied territories to work as an interpreter when the American government attempted to negotiate a truce between the Nationalist government and the Communist rebels. At the age of twenty-four, she married Liu Shaoqi, who was nearly twice her age, and initially, after their marriage, served as his secretary. When Liu was made president, Wang Guangmei became actively involved in politics and accompanied her husband on several high-profile trips to neighboring countries. In the 1960s, when women in China were encouraged to dress simply, Wang Guangmei dazzled foreign dignitaries with her *cheongsam*-clad figure and her sophistication. Her pictures graced the front pages of the party newspaper and reportedly aroused the jealousy of Jiang Qing, Mao's wife.

During the Cultural Revolution, Liu Shaoqi and a group of other senior leaders were purged and Liu was denounced as a "traitor and capitalist." Wang was scapegoated and became the public face of her husband's crimes. Her elegant taste for *cheongsam* and jewelry was associated with the decadence of a bourgeois lifestyle. In early 1967, the Red Guards forced her to put on a *cheongsam* and the high-heeled shoes she wore during her diplomatic missions. They wrapped a string of ping-pong balls around her neck as a mock pearl necklace and paraded her at a public denunciation meeting attended by more than 10,000 Red Guards.

Four months later, she and her husband were marched in front of 100,000 residents at Tiananmen Square, where they were publicly humiliated and tortured. After her husband was locked away in a secret location in Henan province, Wang stayed in the notorious Qincheng prison for twelve years. As a child, I read a widely circulated handwritten novel, depicting Wang as an American spy, a counter-revolutionary, and the head of a cult group called "Black Plum," which aimed to blow up many of China's landmark buildings.

In a recent article published in a reputable magazine in China, the author speculated that Wang's beauty might have contributed to her husband's fall, pointing out that Mao had always flirted with Wang in the early 1960s and constantly invited her to swim at his house. Mao's action angered Wang's husband, prompting him to openly challenge

Mao's decisions on several key issues, and the swimming antagonized Mao's wife, who retaliated during the Cultural Revolution.

The charges against Liu Shaoqi and Wang Guangmei were reversed as fabrications after Mao's death.

In September 1971, General Lin Biao, who was enshrined in the Chinese Communist Party constitution as Mao's "closest comrade-in-arms and successor," died in mysterious circumstances. According to the Chinese government, the general had harbored a strong desire to seize supreme power and allegedly plotted to sabotage Mao's train and assassinate the Great Leader. When Mao foiled Lin's coup attempt, Lin, his son, and his wife tried to flee to the Soviet Union, but their plane allegedly ran out of fuel and crashed somewhere in Mongolia. Lin was presumed to have died in the crash.

Following Lin's death, Mao's government declared Lin's fate a state secret and only scant details were released, followed by a nationwide anti-Lin propaganda campaign. Lin's wife became a key target. She was accused of persecuting many of Lin's opponents and pressuring Lin to seize power, even though Lin and his wife had repeatedly begged Mao *not* to name Lin second in line for China's top position. Throughout the 1970s, high-ranking party leaders spread unsubstantiated stories that Lin's wife had forced him to escape China by drugging Lin and dragging him onto their plane.

Jiang Qing, Mao's widow, suffered a similar fate as those who earned her wrath. An accomplished actress in Shanghai in the 1930s, she was influenced by the rising Communist movement and traveled to the Communist headquarters in northern China, where she aspired to rise above the ranks. Mao fell victim to her charms, divorced his wife, a former guerrilla leader, and married Jiang Qing in 1938, over the objections from his fellow Communists, who, according to historians, saw Jiang Qing as a gold digger. After the Communist takeover in 1949, Jiang took charge of China's cultural affairs. When the Cultural Revolution started in 1966, Jiang, with Mao's support, took on a central leadership role in purging their political opponents and intellectuals. She joined the Politburo in 1969 and formed a close political alliance with other radical leftists in the years leading up to Mao's death.

Jiang Qing's political influence dwindled fast after Mao died and as she attempted to invoke Mao's name to build more political support and take power, Mao's designated successor, Hua Guofeng, teamed up with other revolutionary elite and staged a coup in October 1976. Jiang and three other similar-minded senior leaders, collectively known as the "Gang of Four," were arrested. Four years later, she was put on trial on charges of causing the deaths of former president Liu Shaoqi and thousands of other party, government, and military leaders and intellectuals through political persecution during the Cultural Revolution and conspiring to seize power after Mao's death.

Over the course of a month, the Chinese public was riveted by the televised trial of Jiang Qing, who was held responsible for all of China's woes during the Cultural Revolution, as if Mao had simply slept through that period. Even though the trial was politically motivated, one has to give credit to the leadership of the time and the Supreme People's Court for following proper, if not entirely adequate, due process. The trial, in six separate sessions, was broadcast live on China Central Television and lasted a month. Dozens of victims and witnesses stepped up to testify against the defendant. The prosecution presented a large amount of evidence. The defiant Jiang Qing was given the opportunity to deliver an impassioned speech, which included the famous revealing quote: "I was Chairman Mao's dog. I bit whomever he asked me to bite."

Jiang was given a suspended death sentence, which was later commuted to life imprisonment. Like many of the women before her who had been collectively called "poisonous water," she committed suicide by hanging herself in the bathroom of her hospital room in 1991.

Since 2000, each time a senior official was executed on corruption-related charges, the blame has often been assigned to the seductive mistress(es). At a recent anticorruption conference, the deputy director of the Central Commission for Discipline Inspection said, "We cannot always target the mistresses in our anticorruption campaign."

In 1994, Liu Zhengwei, the former party secretary of Guizhou, and his wife, Yan Jianhong, who headed a government-run foreign trade agency, were the targets of a corruption-related investigation. To protect her husband's political career, Yan accepted full responsibility for the crimes and was sentenced to death for abusing power and embezzling public funds, especially from the government's poverty alleviation fund in January 1995. In her will, she famously wrote, "I'm doing this for my husband and I have nothing to regret." At the execution ground, she stood waiting for the bullets, with her head held high like a martyr's. Following her death, her husband was able to keep his job (at one time, he was assigned to take charge of an anticorruption agency) and lived up to the ripe age of eighty-two with his reputation intact.

And as one watched the hastily-conducted murder trial of Gu Kailai, it was impossible not to see the parallels with the fates of those other wives of senior Communist leaders before her.

In May, Bo's supporters distributed an exclusive interview featured in a Japanese newspaper, *Fuji Evening News,* by its reporter, Udagawa, who claimed to have exploited the Ministry of State Security's request for his assistance in the investigation to gain the opportunity to see Bo. Udagawa mentioned in the article:

> Bo began to say something bad about Gu, the suspect. Bo has been separated from Gu for over a decade, though they have not divorced because of "their child and for fear of affecting Bo's political career." Bo did not deny that his wife had killed somebody. He said with regret, "It would have been better if I had divorced her at that time."

Meanwhile, in an August 2012 editorial aired on Radio Free Asia, analyst Liang Jing explicitly brought up the "poisonous water" reference:

> Gu Kailai can be considered "poisonous water" for both the princelings and the party elite. She knew exactly what kind of disastrous political consequences she brought for her aspiring husband. With her dramatic action, she ruined her husband's political career and stained the reputation of the princelings. It is not a bad thing for the country, though.

Gu Kailai willingly took the scapegoat role. At the end of the trial, she expressed her "gratitude" to the court:

This case has been like a huge stone weighing on me for more than half a year. What a nightmare. The tragedy which was created by me was not only extended to Neil Heywood, but also to several families.

The case has produced great losses to the party and the country, for which I ought to shoulder the responsibility, and I will never feel at ease. I am grateful to the humanitarian care shown to me by those who handled the case. I solemnly tell the court that in order to maintain the dignity of the law, I will accept and calmly face any sentence and I also expect a fair and just court decision.

A veteran political journalist in Beijing, who had followed the trial, said that Gu Kailai was smart to understand that the trial's real target was her husband, whom senior party leaders in Beijing hoped to render guilty by association and to destroy for good. If she had contested the murder charges, the government would have initiated corruption charges against her, also punishable by death. In China, corruption is so rampant that no government official is immune, and if such charges were made, more of Bo's relatives and friends could be implicated. Of the two, perhaps the murder charge seemed the better deal. That was probably why Gu Kailai and her family refrained from mounting a vigorous defense: they knew it would amount to nothing. Gu Kailai's fate had already been decided by party leaders in Beijing, not the judges in the court.

By striking a deal with the Chinese government and by actively cooperating with the government—she confessed to the crime that she had not committed and at the same time implicated the police chief and his assistants—Gu Kailai aimed to protect her son from any criminal charges and have her husband's potential death sentence commuted. It is worth emphasizing that Bo Xilai's name was never mentioned once in Gu's trial. Insiders familiar with her trial acknowledged the existence of such a deal between Gu and the government. However, the leadership broke its promises after anti-Bo factions gained the upper hand during the pre–Party Congress power struggles in September 2012. It began to call for tougher sentencing for Bo to diminish his unexpectedly-strong political influences.

As the Chinese saying goes, "As long as the green hills last, there will always be wood to feed the stove." In Gu Kailai's case, keeping her life left open the possibility of a comeback when the political winds shifted, just as her own parents and her father-in-law had done during the Cultural Revolution. So she played along and did what the government expected her to do.

In a sense, Gu Kailai succeeded in what she had hoped to achieve. On August 20, the court sentenced her to death, suspended for two years. Under Chinese law, Gu Kailai's sentence could be commuted in two years. Considering her mental condition, she would be eligible for medical parole.

Even though all the key suspects in the case have been convicted, debate over who really killed Heywood will linger. The vagueness in the official transcripts of the trials and the prevalence of different "insider" stories swirling around provide fodder for more theories.

Regardless of whether or not Gu Kailai killed Neil Heywood, she is forever branded as "poisonous water," along with the likes of Madame Mao and Wang Guangmei. Some bloggers even called her "an evil fox spirit" who attached herself to powerful men and ruined their lives. A political commentator—who claimed that Gu Kailai's greed for money was the source of Bo's political woes—issued a warning to the Chinese Communist Party in his article on the China in Perspective website in September 2012:

Before the Gu Kailai trial, former Chinese president Jiang Zemin urged officials to carefully examine the circumstances for each falling dynasty in Chinese history so they could learn a lesson for today's China. I am certain the "poisonous water" reference weighed heavily on Jiang's mind. One should also take note that a regime rife with greed and political corruption was a breeding ground for dynasty-wrecking women. Therefore, a clean government is the best prevention. At the same time, I hope the wives of senior officials have learned a lesson from Gu Kailai—if they don't act prudently, they will do irreparable damage to their husbands and themselves, not to mention their country.

PART IV

Wang

yu

Kou

The Victor Is King and the Loser a Bandit

Cheng wang bai kou—in the old imperial court, those who emerged as the winner in a power struggle were crowned and the way they seized power became irreproachable. The losers and their friends were killed or exiled.

THE RESILIENT LOSER:
CHINA'S SECURITY CZAR

CHINESE CENTRAL TELEVISION, or CCTV, is China's largest state television broadcaster. Its twenty-two channels of news, entertainment, and educational programming reach more than 1 billion viewers. In recent years CCTV has spread by satellite into North America and Europe and throughout Asia—all part of Beijing's ambitious propaganda efforts to enhance the country's soft power, balancing the West's coverage of China, which is perceived to be mostly hostile.

CCTV's prowess has attracted a large number of the country's most qualified, best-connected, and best-looking journalists, anchors, and hosts. For years, female staff members, especially news anchors and program hosts, have served as a pool of spouses or mistresses for senior Communist leaders. The attraction is mutual. In the movie industry, an actress can obtain a coveted starring role through her "performance" on the casting couch. Inside CCTV, a sprawling state bureaucracy, where political connections are a necessity to get ahead, young women who hope to make it big and have their face seen by a billion people every day are in search of a sugar daddy. There is a popular saying in mainland China now: "Behind every news anchor is a senior Communist leader or a billionaire." The same phenomenon exists in local state television stations across the country as well. The wives of Cao Jianmin, head of the Chinese People's Supreme Procuratorate, China's top prosecution organ, and Zhang Chunxian, governor of Xingjiang and a Politburo member, are both former CCTV news anchors. In December 2011, the director of CCTV was forced to step down after allegations were published on *Mingjing News* that he had pressured female TV personalities to date or sleep with senior leaders to advance his career.

Among the alleged "gold diggers" at CCTV, Jia Xiaohua, a former anchor and journalist on the business and finance channel and an editor at CCTV's *Books and Art* program, landed the biggest fish. Her husband is Zhou Yongkang, dubbed China's J. Edgar Hoover. Zhou had great political and quasi-military power. He served on the Standing Committee and controlled China's law enforcement and judicial authorities including local and armed police, the courts, and the procuratorate, with a budget that is said to be larger than that of China's military.

Though largely unconfirmed, common gossip has it that when Zhou met the CCTV journalist, who was twenty-eight years his junior, he was still married. Soon, Jia Xiaohua claimed she was pregnant and demanded a marital commitment, and Zhou obliged. Just as he filed for divorce in 2008, Zhou's wife suddenly died in a car crash. People suspected that he had personally orchestrated the car accident, though there is no evidence to suggest this was true. At age seventy, Zhou has been the subject of persistent rumors relating to his womanizing activities—his nickname is "King of the Roosters," implying a man with high sexual libido who would not spare any pretty women in his way. At a two-day conference at a hotel in Sichuan province, he was alleged to have slept with several female hotel staff members.

Despite his notoriety among his former colleagues in Beijing, Zhou was largely unknown to the general public. As the country's security czar, he acted mostly behind the scenes, until the Bo Xilai scandal pushed him to center stage. In February 2012, a week after Wang Lijun's visit to the US Consulate, Zhou's name began to surface in many of the online news reports and blogs. Some of those posts were about his sexual prowess, but most discussed him as the mastermind and cohort in Bo Xilai's attempted coup against Xi Jinping, the party's heir apparent.

A source at the Central Party Committee's Secretariat disclosed that the Politburo Standing Committee had held a meeting on February 12 to discuss Wang Lijun's botched defection and his accusations against Bo Xilai:

> Out of the nine members, eight agreed to detain Bo Xilai for investigation and one cast the dissenting vote. That specific member's son and relatives had invested heavily in Chongqing. His son had reportedly obtained 4.2 billion yuan worth of government projects under Bo Xilai. The person was worried the investigation of Bo Xilai could implicate him and adversely affect his family's economic interests. Under the heavy political pressure from his colleagues, he reluctantly agreed to Bo's investigation.

The person who cast the lone dissenting vote apparently was Zhou Yongkang. It was known that his son had made major investments in the oil and construction businesses in Sichuan and that he supposedly had designated Bo as his replacement at the Politburo Standing Committee following his retirement in November 2012.

In February 2012, when Zhou learned that Wang Lijun had entered the US Consulate, he allegedly called Bo Xilai immediately, urging Bo to "get Wang out at any cost." It was Zhou's order that prompted Bo to recklessly send several hundred armed police to surround the US Consulate.

On February 21, Zhou was scheduled to lead a large delegation of Chinese legal experts and entrepreneurs to Argentina, but he canceled the trip at the last minute so he could focus on the Wang Lijun and Bo

Xilai case. One of the orders he issued around that time was to censor domestic blogs and attack overseas Chinese-language media sites. *Mingjing News,* along with Boxun, became a primary target of organized hacker attacks. Insiders from the Public Security Ministry said Zhou was exasperated at reports being published about his womanizing and support for Bo.

When the National People's Congress was in session on March 8 and 12, many senior leaders shunned Bo, whose political future was by then at best uncertain. Zhou, however, visited the Chongqing delegation twice and praised Bo for his achievements in the development of Chongqing. Zhou's praises were viewed as a sign that Bo had procured strong support from senior leaders and he would ride out the storm.

When Premier Wen Jiabao delivered his rebuke of Bo's policies in Chongqing the day before Bo was sacked from his position, some analysts predicted that Zhou was also in trouble. In that week, an insider—who identified himself as a scholar who was briefed by a senior leader on Zhou's situation—posted a story on Boxun saying Zhou had been barred from leaving the country because the senior leadership had found out that Zhou and Bo had conspired to topple Xi Jinping, the party's heir apparent. According to the scholar:

> Zhou Yongkang and Bo Xilai held five meetings over the past year to strategize on how to get Bo elected to the Politburo Standing Committee to succeed him as the country's top security chief. They had conspired to topple Xi Jinping in two years. If necessary, Zhou urged Bo to dispatch armed police forces to arrest Xi. Zhou said multiple times to friends that Xi was too weak and unfit to be China's top leader and that Bo had the capabilities to take over. They would rally national and international media to support Bo and the takeover should be no later than 2014.

The scholar further alleged that Wang Lijun had procured imported electronic surveillance equipment from Israel and Germany with Zhou's help to monitor the telephone conversations of senior leaders, while Zhou had instructed Wang to establish secret files on senior leaders. He wanted them investigated for transgressions in their private lives and economic "crimes" so he could release the information to more than two hundred journalists and scholars after the Lunar New Year in 2012, but the Wang Lijun incident disrupted his plan.

According to the scholar, Zhou enjoyed a steady supply of young, beautiful women, including singers, actresses, and students from Minzu University of China. Bo Xilai made a "gift" to Zhou of a singer with whom he'd slept.

This scintillating article, clearly aimed at discrediting Zhou, went viral on the Internet, even though the majority of the details were not substantiated. On March 22, the Politics and Law Commission held a series of ideological training sessions in Shanghai, but Zhou, its leader, was absent, leading people to believe that all the previous reports about Zhou's downfall were true and that he was under investigation.

As news about Zhou's absence spread wildly, the state media were ordered to stem the rumors. The next day, CCTV aired a clip about Zhou meeting with the Indonesian foreign minister in Beijing—an unusual choice given that Zhou's portfolio covers domestic affairs. Two days later, Zhou was seen on TV again, planting trees with other senior leaders and then giving a speech to a group of law enforcement officers, calling them to solidify the ruling position of the Communist Party. But despite the sudden flurry of media appearances designed to suggest business as usual, insiders still claimed that he was being investigated and continued to leak unsubstantiated information to overseas media.

On April 17, two days after the government officially detained Bo and his wife, an official who said he was familiar with Zhou's status e-mailed me, stating that the Politburo had held a secret two-day meeting and reached consensus on two decisions: launching a secret investigation into Zhou in relating to his involvement in Bo's scandal; and postponing the 18th Party Congress, which was scheduled from mid-October to November 2012, to focus on the Bo–Zhou investigation. Soon, other overseas Chinese-language outlets reported the same information. By April, Zhou had become one of the most searched Chinese officials online, next to Bo and his wife.

ZHOU YONGKANG, born in 1944 in the southeastern province of Jiangsu, got his start in the oil industry. In 1962, he was enrolled in what is now the China University of Petroleum to study geophysical prospecting, an obscure five-year degree program that many urban students chose to skip because a career in geophysical prospecting would require living most of one's life in the wilderness. Fortunately for Zhou, he was assigned a job at the Daqing Oil Field in northeastern China, a model state enterprise.

In the 1960s, the China University of Petroleum was not considered a prestigious university in Beijing, but many years later, a large number of its graduates have emerged as influential figures, controlling much of China's energy industry.

Having grown up in China's warm south, Zhou struggled with the icy weather in the northeast. But he soon became acclimated to both the natural and political environment. He began as a technician and was subsequently promoted to regional director. By 1983, he headed the Liaohe Petroleum Exploration Bureau and was concurrently the mayor of Panjin, an oil city of 1.2 million people.

In 1985, when the group of revolutionary veterans including Bo Yibo, the father of Bo Xilai, were preparing for their retirement, the Party Central Committee scouted for young, educated party officials nationwide and transferred them to Beijing to be trained for senior positions. Zhou, who turned forty-three that year, was chosen to be the deputy manager and subsequently general manager in 1996 of the China National Petroleum Corp., or CNPC, the country's largest state-run enterprise, which manages oil and natural gas exploration and production projects in China and some thirty other countries.

With China's growing appetite for oil and other energy resources, Zhou's career soared. He found himself in great demand. In the late 1980s and early 1990s, Zhou headed a large oil field in the far western province of Xinjiang while simultaneously leading a state-run petroleum bureau and serving as municipal party chief of a city in the central eastern province of Shandong, 2,000 miles from Xinjiang.

China's state monopoly of the oil industry, which included an almost unlimited budget, was a breeding ground for corruption. As general manager of CNPC, Zhou was involved in his share of scandals. He was known for being a state oil tycoon who was ideologically dogmatic, bullying people around him, and possessing an insatiable need for young women. He obtained his "Rooster King" nickname from this period. During his tenure at CNPC, Zhou often ignored international criticism: he visited Sudan fourteen times to cement ties with its corrupt and genocidal government.

In recent years, Chen Tonghai, who served as president of CNPC and chairman of the state-owned oil refiner Sinopec Corp., received a suspended death penalty for accepting 200 million yuan (US $32 million) in bribes, and Li Rong, who headed an oil field in northeast China, was sentenced to death for embezzling nearly 40 million yuan. Zhou had close ties with both officials, but somehow was untouched by accusations of corruption.

When the State Council was in search of a candidate in 1998 to take charge of China's newly formed Ministry of Land and Resources, which manages the preservation and development of land, mineral, and ocean resources, Zhou was picked for his background in geophysics and his rich experience in the oil industry. At that time, China's economic boom had just taken off. Land and energy were two of the most contentious and challenging areas, triggering numerous disputes over resource distribution.

"Zhou felt like he was sitting on a powder keg and he spent most of his time on conflict resolution," recalled a former official at the Ministry of Land and Resources. "Even so, he was the constant target of personal attacks from people who were involved in the conflicts. Zhou was paving his road to the top with his blood."

In December 1999, one year and nine months after he assumed the top position at the Ministry of Land and Resources, he was transferred again, ending his thirty-two-year career as a technocrat in the energy industry. Zhou was asked to replace Xie Shijie, the party secretary of Sichuan province, who had just retired.

If Zhou's previous jobs at CNPC and the Ministry of Land and Resources were based on his highly specialized technical knowledge and experience, his stint in Sichuan was purely political. He was on the fast track to the Politburo. Ruling China's largest province provided him an opportunity to showcase his political leadership skills and accumulate political capital.

In the past, Sichuan, with more than 80 million people, had served as the launching pad for many aspiring leaders. Former premier Zhao Ziyang rose to prominence for his reform initiatives that greatly improved Sichuan's industrial and agricultural output in the late 1970s. Zhou followed a similar path. In his official biography, he is credited for introducing a series of innovative initiatives to rejuvenate Sichuan's economy even though no official records indicate what those innovations were. To many human rights activists, Zhou gained a reputation for his brutal crackdown on Falung Gong practitioners—a meditation group declared a cult by the government after it staged a flash protest in Beijing in 1999, marshaling 10,000 practitioners within hours by using cell phones and catching the police entirely by surprise. Zhou Haiying, a medical researcher at Harvard University, filed a lawsuit in the US against Zhou in 2001, accusing him of ordering police to persecute and torture his family members for practicing Falun Gong.

In addition, Zhou was also criticized for his mistreatment of Tibetans in western Sichuan, which is home to a large population of Tibetans. According to overseas reports, Zhou never hid his disdain for Tibetan culture during his reign. In March 2000, he reportedly criticized the Tibetan religions for encouraging people to pay too much attention to the afterlife, rather than the current life, and opposed the Tibetan practice of donating money to temples. In the summer of 2001, the Sichuan provincial government put pressure on the abbot at Serda Lharong monastery to remove the Dalai Lama's pictures and reduce the number of monks enrolled at the monastery. When the abbot refused, the government expelled more than 1,000 monks and nuns who had come from other parts of mainland China, Hong Kong, and Singapore to worship and study there, forcing them to sign a document denouncing the Dalai Lama and then demolishing their apartments.

At the same time, Zhou implemented policies to force Tibetans to give up their religion and accept Communism. He said:

> The Dalai Lama attempts to split China. Most of his anti-China activities are underwritten with donations from Tibetan people. We

need to stop there. We need to propagate atheism and advocate science so they can give up their religions.

In 2002, the year he turned sixty, Zhou joined the Politburo and in December he was appointed minister of public security. Many people wondered about the rationale for Zhou's new post. But the oil industry has always been run like a military unit and leaders have always adopted a quasi-military management style, with employees obeying orders without question, like soldiers. Zhou's ascension to the post of the country's top policeman was a logical progression.

As minister for public security, he sought to root out sloppy practices and enhance the reputation of the police force. He sacked hundreds of public security officers who were involved in excessive drinking. Zhou also ordered the arrest and kidnapping of many political dissidents in Sichuan, vowing to crack down on any protest movements instigated by "Western hostile forces."

At the 17th Party Congress, he emerged as a dark horse and was elected to the Politburo Standing Committee. In *Xi Jinping PK Li Keqiang,* a book about China's new leadership, author Xia Fei believed Zhou's rise was part of the push by then president Jiang Zemin. "Before his retirement, Jiang Zemin installed three of his loyal supporters to take over the military, the Central Guards Bureau and the public security apparatus, which has access to armed police. The arrangement boosted his [Jiang's] influence after retirement."

There are reports that Zhou is related to former president Jiang Zemin's wife. Although many say this is no more than a rumor, one thing is sure: Jiang Zemin and Zhou were close political allies. An official at CNPC said Zhou had befriended Jiang Zemin back in the days when Zhou dominated the oil industry. Zhou might have preferred to be China's vice premier, which could fit with his technical expertise, but Jiang secured him a more powerful position.

Like Russia's Vladimir Putin, who posed bare-chested with a horse to show his good health and stamina before an election, Zhou, at the age of sixty-four, pulled a similar stunt on the eve of his ascension before the 17th Party Congress. On August 31, 2007, he visited a local police station and walked into a gym, where officers had their regular training and workouts. In front of the cameras, he performed ten sit-ups in one breath.

Zhou's appointment was said to have triggered widespread opposition from other Politburo members, who cited his lack of experience in internal and external security matters and his scandal-tainted past. Still, Jiang's opinion eventually prevailed.

In a speech at his inaugural ceremony to assume the head of the Politics and Law Commission, Zhou stated his three priorities: solidifying the ruling status of the Communist Party, maintaining stability of the country, and protecting people's safety. Overseas analysts criticized him for putting the people's interests last.

The Politics and Law Commission was formed in 1949 to enhance the party's control over the country's legislative, law enforcement, and judicial functions as the Communists tried to bring the diverse elements of a war-torn country in line with the directions of the new Communist government. But the head of the commission was a symbolic title without much substantial power.

During the Cultural Revolution, when the Red Guards, instigated by Mao, destroyed China's legal system, the commission was abolished. China was plunged into lawlessness. Under Mao's social legality theory, any local party organizations or the police could arbitrarily arrest citizens and conduct impromptu trials on the spot. Death sentences were handed down frequently by the so-called revolutionary committees for petty crimes such as "creating mass panic" and looting, as well as more serious ones, such as burglary and rape. In Beijing, Mao could throw any of his senior leaders into jail without any legal justification.

In the post-Mao era, Deng Xiaoping and a group of revolutionary veterans who had suffered tremendously during the Cultural Revolution called for the restoration of legal reforms. The Politics and Law Commission was reinstated and its status was elevated within the party. Even so, in the early 1980s, holders of the commission chair were typically revolutionary veterans at the end of their careers. The position was more a consolation prize for past services, suggesting it carried little innate power. When reform-minded leaders under party secretaries Hu Yaobang and Zhao Ziyang attempted to enhance the functions of the legislature and enhance judicial independence in 1988, the commission was downgraded again and renamed: the Central Politics and Law Group. With its limited power, the work group reinvented itself by shifting its focus to antismuggling operations.

The political winds soon changed once more. After the government cracked down on the student protest movement of 1989, the conservatives pushed Jiang Zemin, the new party secretary, to elevate the organization to "strengthen the party's leadership role in the legal arena." It again became a commission and its responsibilities were considerably expanded.

When, in June 1999, the Chinese government moved against the Falun Gong as a political cult, the authorities responded by creating what was known as the "601 Office" under the commission to specifically target Falun Gong. As social unrest escalated due to government corruption, illegal seizure of land, unpaid wages to migrant workers, and employment and pension issues for laid-off workers, the party added "maintaining stability" to the commission's remit.

Starting in 2002, the head of the commission was elevated to the Politburo Standing Committee and Zhou became the third–most important person in China, after the president and the premier. His direct control over police and armed police made him nearly invincible.

It is estimated that Zhou supervised a staff of 10 million—far exceeding China's standing army of 2.5 million troops—and his annual budget to maintain China's stability has allegedly reached as high as 700 billion yuan (US $112 billion). Zhou's expanding empire, known as China's fourth power—besides the party, the government, and the military—encompassed the nation's public security departments, that is, the police, the procuratorate, the state agency for prosecution and criminal investigation, the courts, justice departments, civil affairs agencies that register nongovernmental organizations, and national security departments, which are responsible for intelligence gathering. More important, Zhou controlled the country's large contingent of armed police, a paramilitary force of former soldiers, specifically charged with handling social unrest.

During the past decade, in the name of maintaining stability, the Politics and Law Commission under Zhou has turned China into a de facto police state, similar to those that operated in the former Soviet Union and former East Germany. Armed police have been used to suppress pro-independence protests in Tibet and to persecute Christian underground church members and political dissidents, and arbitrarily arrest and torture petitioners and human rights lawyers. In the 1980s, the commission resorted to the use of this paramilitary force only once in ten years. Under Zhou, it was deployed on average fifteen times a year to crack down on group protests or riots. In recent years, the commission, in violation of Chinese law, has ruled that police involved in "maintaining stability," or controlling group protests, do not have to document their actions. This unwritten rule was widely adopted by local law enforcement organizations throughout China, prompting them to take extreme measures, such as kidnapping, torture, and illegal confiscation of personal property without having to justify their actions. The judiciary passively condones the practice. There is now a saying among the public that the party operates like a triad: the police are worse than the bandits.

With such expansive power, Zhou thought he could wrap up his tenure smoothly and pass the baton to his friend, Bo Xilai, whose experience in running a police state was second to none in the country. However, Wang Lijun's defection disrupted Zhou's plan, plunging him into a deep crisis.

In April 2012, the state news agency, Xinhua, engaged in a furious campaign to counter negative coverage of Zhou by the overseas media. Within one month. Xinhua ran ten long articles about Zhou, making him the most featured Politburo Standing Committee member—on April 6, Zhou received a delegation from Austria and on the same day, in a separate article, he was attending a conference on "Cleaning up the Internet." On April 17, he participated in a seminar organized by the Ministry of Public Security, and on the same day met with a visiting leader from Cuba.

At the same time, Zhou's name appeared with equal frequency in the overseas media, which continued their follow-up with previous reports that President Hu Jintao and Premier Wen Jiabao were keen to purge Zhou and his allies. One article revealed that several retired officials—including Zhou's mentor, former president Jiang Zemin, and former premier Zhu Rongji—were said to be unhappy with Zhou's high-profile alliance with Bo.

An overseas Chinese website carried an exposé of how Zhou's son used his father's influence in the legal arena to extort "protection" fees. One source told Boxun that Zhou's son received 20 million yuan (US $3 million) in bribes because he managed to get a key triad leader released from jail, even though he had been charged with brutal murders in Gansu. In another case, Zhou's son bailed out a police officer who killed a criminal suspect by pouring buckets of scorching hot water over his body. He pocketed more than 100 million yuan (US $16 million), paid for by the suspect's relatives.

Ji Weiren, author of *The Enigma of the Bo Xilai Incident*, said in June that Zhou had made a tearful apology at a Politburo Standing Committee meeting for backing Bo, but vehemently denied the allegations that he was plotting against future party leaders. Zhou was eventually barred from a three-person work group handling the Bo Xilai investigation. "Based on the Central Party Committee regulations, if a senior official is implicated in a certain case, he has to be excluded to avoid conflicts of interests," said author Ji Weiren.

Because many of the overseas stories about pending investigation into Zhou's connection with the Bo Xilai scandal were based on leaks from inside the decision-making bodies in Beijing, Shi Zangshan, a China expert, wondered if Beijing was flying a test balloon to determine public reaction to decide whether to take action against Zhou.

After Wang Lijun went to the US Consulate, it took thirty-five days for his boss, Bo Xilai, to lose his job and freedom. Many wondered how long it would take for the party to unseat Zhou, Bo's boss in Beijing. But as the 18th Party Congress approached, it was apparent that the resilient Zhou Yongkang had survived.

A Beijing-based Chinese journalist put it this way:

Zhou Yongkang's foes inside the Politburo Standing Committee spared him any punishment because he was at the end of his term. Any attempts against him could cause unnecessary disruptions and distract attention from Bo Xilai. By leaking negative information to the overseas media, the Politburo Standing Committee effectively put Zhou in a defensive position, limiting his ability to make any political maneuvers and harm others before his retirement. The power struggles in Beijing have taken on a new form—you hit the opponent's internal organs and destroy his ability to attack without any visible outward injuries. This has avoided much public embarrassment for Zhou and at the same time, protected the party's image of unity.

This analysis is only partially accurate. One should not forget about the consensual rule made in the 1980s when Deng Xiaoping was in power. The rule stated that members of the Politburo Standing Committee should always act as a coherent unit, or at least maintain a facade of unity to prevent chaos and preserve the stability of the party. As the ancient Chinese saying points out, "Punishment does not extend to the emperor's advisers and ministers." For the sake of the collective unity, members of the Standing Committee have been granted immunity from criminal investigations and prosecution. So Zhou was spared.

Even though Zhou was allowed to retire peacefully, his power base diminished after he had lost the opportunity to install an ally as his replacement. Barely a month after he retired, the new party leadership under Xi Jinping opened an investigation into one of Zhou's protégés, Li Chuncheng, the deputy party chief of Sichuan province. Li was said to have brokered several transactions in oil and real estate businesses for Zhou's son in Sichuan. The current investigation, related to charges of embezzlement and selling government and party positions, is seen as part of a broader plan by the new leadership to weed out Zhou loyalists from key party positions and further erode his influence.

More important, at the 18th Party Congress, the status of the Central Politics and Law Commission was downgraded, and the head of the commission no longer holds a spot on the Politburo Standing Committee. The move could somewhat restrict the expansive power of this gigantic state machine, leaving more space for future reforms to improve judicial independence and alleviate social tension. However, until real political reforms are initiated, Zhou and his menacing legacy will continue to loom large in China, further aggravating social and political problems that will eventually, if left unchecked, topple the Communist Party.

THE BILLIONAIRE LOSER:
BO XILAI'S SECRET WALLET

BILLIONAIRE BUSINESSMAN Xu Ming sensed catastrophe when he heard on February 2, 2012, that Wang Lijun had been sacked from his police chief's position. Xu, a close friend of Bo Xilai's, immediately flew from Dalian to Chongqing.

Xu had just visited Chongqing a week before, at the request of Wang Lijun, who had sought his help to broker peace between Wang and Gu Kailai. Xu was unsuccessful. Then, on January 28, Wang went directly to Bo and complained about his wife, Gu Kailai. Afterward, he told Xu that the conversation with Bo went well. After Xu returned to Dalian, he heard of the subsequent meeting and face slap. Xu contacted Wang immediately and urged the police chief to apologize and reconcile with Bo. Wang agreed. But Xu did not anticipate how dramatically things would deteriorate in the next days.

Radio France International, quoting a friend of Xu's, reported that the Dialan businessman spent an hour at Bo Xilai's office, persuading Bo to reconsider his decision, but Bo refused to back down. Xu then went over to Wang's apartment, advising him not to do anything rash. Wang, still smarting from the face slap and dismissal, remained defiant.

Knowing that the Bo–Wang conflict could lead to disastrous consequences affecting everyone around them, Xu, who had been involved in the plotting of Heywood's death, became overwhelmed with fear. He tried to connect with Bo Xilai again over the next three days. When his last-ditch efforts failed, Xu boarded his private jet on the night of February 5 and journeyed south, in the direction of Australia, where he holds residency status. Many top businessmen in China have foreign residency permits as a form of insurance against government policy changes.

The drama that unfolded in the following weeks, with Wang Lijun's visit to the US Consulate and the revelation of Neil Heywood's murder, justified Xu's initial concern.

BORN IN 1971, Xu Ming grew up in a small village outside Dalian. For years, his family lived inside a fifteen-square-meter mud hut. Known among his friends as "Fatty Xu," an endearing nickname reflecting his stocky build, Xu was remembered by a fellow villager as a timid and shy boy with a shrewd business sense. *Southern Weekend* reported that Xu would buy different types of stationery and snacks from a wholesaler and resell them to his high school classmates. He used the profit to supplement his pocket money. His friends said when it came to girls, he was relentless. He pursued a classmate, a pretty girl who knew how to play the piano, for five years before she consented to marry him in 1993.

After high school, Xu claimed that he had attended Shenyang Aerospace University in the provincial capital of Shenyang, but a college friend pointed out that he had actually attended the university's three-year adult extension program, for which the government offered no tuition subsidies and graduates had to find jobs on their own. Xu's first job after college was with a cold-storage firm that specialized in frozen shrimp exports to Japan. As the company's representative, he had an office in Dalian to handle requests from Japanese customers and coordinate the shipping. In his spare time, he would hang out inside a dance hall with his cell phone, then a novel device in China that helped attract many girls to his side.

A year later Xu quit the shrimp export company, rented an office space inside a hotel in Dalian, and started his own shrimp export business. In those days, the government imposed restrictions on raw shrimp, but not cooked ones. Xu took advantage of the policy loophole to export frozen cooked shrimp. His friends recalled that his business was a total failure; he did not complete a single transaction. Disappointed, he returned to his native village and set up a small factory to make circuit boards for a South Korean company.

In early 1992, he became restless and went back to Dalian. A profile in a Chinese magazine said he began to wear a suit and would practice his Mandarin for hours to conquer his local village accent. He was determined to learn a foreign language, improve his calligraphy skills, and learn to drive. Of the three things, he accomplished only one: driving.

It was in Dalian that he was introduced to Gu Kailai, wife of the then acting mayor of Dalian. The connection with Gu Kailai and her husband, Bo Xilai, paid off handsomely.

In the 1990s, the government offered preferential treatment to Chinese joint ventures with foreign entities. Many took advantage by simply enlisting a foreigner's name in their company directory with a fake joint-venture contract. Xu traveled to Macau and met three Macau businesspeople, who agreed to let him use their names in return for a stake in future profit. Xu took them out to dinner after the contract was signed and on the way back from the restaurant, the intoxicated driver, who was one of Xu's business partners, lost control of the car and got into a serious accident. All of Xu's business partners were killed. Xu was the only survivor in the car, with a few broken ribs.

Undeterred by the freaky accident, Xu continued with his plan upon his return and set up a foreign trade company in his county, and he appointed himself general manager and legal representative. Though his foreign partners were dead, Xu Ming used his joint-venture contract to obtain a large loan from the China Agricultural Bank and purchased an office building, which would later become his company headquarters.

In 1993, the city of Dalian under Bo Xilai initiated a series of large-scale public construction projects. Xu smelled opportunity. He teamed up with a Hong Kong businessman, who purchased used excavation equipment from Japan and the US. They formed Shide Machinery Industrial Limited and, with Gu Kailai's help, Xu received his first government contract: digging a large pit for the foundations of the city's Victory Square. He earned 3 million yuan from the project. When Bo Xilai decided to construct Asia's largest public square near the Xinghai Bay, Xu's new company was contracted to undertake a land reclamation project that required the filling of 600,000 cubic meters using concrete and mud excavated from other parts of the city. During Bo Xilai's reign as mayor of Dalian, Xu was awarded more than thirty such construction projects.

Xu's business hit another milestone in 1994. As part of his "Greening Dalian, Brightening Dalian, and Beautifying Dalian" program, Bo Xilai ordered commercial and residential buildings along Dalian's main roads and highways, as well as residential complexes, to install plastic steel window and door frames, which he believed were decorative, sturdy, and environmentally friendly. (Plastic steel is a composite plastic that's as strong as steel but lighter and transparent.) Xu was one of the two bidders on the project. He took a trip to Europe, where he studied the most advanced methods of plastic steel manufacturing and found a German partner. They jointly established the Shide Plastic Steel Industrial Ltd. With 120 million yuan (US $19 million), Xu built twelve door and window frame assembly lines. Official records show Xu took out a loan of 30 million yuan to form the Dalian Shide Plastic Steel Door and Window Factory, the only one of its kind in Dalian.

Orders from Bo Xilai's municipal government poured in. City officials went all out promoting the use of plastic steel door and windows. For residents who could not afford the installation, the government provided subsidies. Within a short time, Xu's products could be seen all over the city; the majority of the government and commercial buildings in downtown were fitted with plastic steel windows and doors. So were newly built residential buildings.

In 1998, Shide Plastic Steel Industry Ltd. produced four tons of plastic steel a year and by 2001, the company's annual production capacity reached forty tons, serving clients all over China and South Korean, Japan, the US, Canada, and the EU. Company assets exceeded 2 billion yuan (US $320 million).

Xu's fortune rose with Bo Xilai's soaring political career. With continued support from Bo, Xu expanded his business and entered into hot-water heaters, electric appliances, and real estate. At the urging of Bo, who saw Dalian's nationally known soccer team as an "attractive business card" for the city, Xu invested 60 million yuan (US $ 9.6 million) in the city's club in February 1999 and became its sole owner a year later, changing its name to Dalian Shide Football Club. Xu admitted he was clueless about soccer. Before taking over the club, he had seen a total of twenty minutes of a live match. "In the first year, Xu did not come for a single match," a player said to Ji Weiren of *The Enigma of the Bo Xilai Scandal.* "When we issued invitations to him to attend matches, Xu turned us down every single time."

At the beginning of Xu's takeover of the soccer club, Bo and other municipal leaders never missed a home match. Xu enthusiastically invested time and money, making sure his team won. He was determined to turn the sport into a real business. In 2000, Xu initiated a structural change for the club. Many veteran players and coaches under the previous ownership retired and resigned. Xu formed a complete new team. In 2001 and 2002, Xu gradually built a soccer empire with the purchase of six additional clubs in China. In all, he had seven teams in two major leagues. An avid gambler, Xu allegedly engaged in match-fixing schemes—if one of Shide's star teams needed to win a match, the other teams would have to let it happen. If one team was required to win certain games to stay in the league, others, including star teams, would conveniently lose. In the aftermath of the Bo scandal, many fans in Sichuan province blamed Xu for ruining their professional team, which was bought by Xu and was riddled with match-fixing scandals. "It's time to settle scores with Xu Ming," wrote one fan in his blog.

In recent years, the government launched a crackdown on match-fixing schemes in response to public outcry. Two senior officials at the Chinese Football Association received more than ten years in jail. Xu's close ties with Bo and Zhou Yongkang gained him a reprieve.

In addition to soccer, Xu also entered the realm of real estate. In 2001, when Chinese banks tightened lending policies, the Shide Group was on the blacklist of many banks, which were concerned that Xu had too many risky investments and that a collapse of his company could trigger a severe crisis. Again, with the help of his friends in the government, Xu weathered the storm through a windfall in the real estate market and other capital investments.

In that year, Xu sold a factory, along with equipment and land, to a large chemical company for 256 million yuan (US $41 million). Soon after, an insider told Xu that the government was planning to purchase the land for a development project. He quickly bought up a majority of the shares in the chemical company to control its management and moved the land back to his company at a much cheaper price. As expected, when he sold the land to the government, he netted a profit of 230 million yuan (US $37 million). After the land transaction was completed, Xu sold out his stocks in the chemical company and made an additional 14.6 million yuan.

One of Xu's childhood friends told *Southern Weekend* that Xu had an insatiable desire for money. In 2002, his excessive drinking—a prevalent practice for businesspeople who have to spend lavishly on drinks and dinners for clients and government officials—led to cirrhosis of the liver. He was on the brink of death. His friends were told that a bear's gallbladder, when dried, ground into powder, and mixed with herbs, could save his liver. They searched around China for the cure and finally found one in Hong Kong, where a bear in the zoo was dying. Xu's friends immediately flew over and obtained the gallbladder at a hefty price.

Xu Ming gradually recovered—whether by luck, Western medicine, or the death of a bear is not clear. His friends assumed that the near-death experience would give him a new perspective on life. On the contrary, Xu was greedier than ever. "I need to earn more money," he was quoted as saying. "In this way, I can afford to buy a healthy bear and kill it to get its gallbladder, rather than having to wait for it to die."

He quickly returned to his desk and started several ventures in 2002, including forming a life insurance company, and buying stakes in three banks. In 2004, when Bo was minister of commerce, Xu obtained a license to build a petrochemical company in Dalian, but the plan never took off.

By 2005, Xu owned three public companies, three commercial banks, two insurance companies, and a hedge fund, as well as more than ten enterprises, covering seven industries, including plastic steel, automaking, petrochemicals, and pharmaceuticals. In 2011, Shide Group ranked as the sixty-sixth-largest privately owned firm in China, with annual revenue of 1.2 billion yuan (US $190 million). Curiously, Xu dropped on the *Forbes* China Rich List from 8th in 2005 to 253rd in 2011, leading many to speculate that Xu was following the path of discretion, as most businessmen in China do, hiding his assets to avoid being the target of a government probe, which had toppled a majority of those on the *Forbes* list. Others believe his business shrank significantly after Bo Xilai moved out of Dalian.

An official Chinese media report in May 2012 said Xu's electric-appliance company was facing the challenges of rising costs and low profit margins. The government revoked his automobile production license in 2005. His soccer enterprise was hit with scandals and sponsorship dried up. There were constant stories about Xu's failure to pay his players and Shide Group was billions of yuan in debt. In 2011, he was also forced to give up his CEO position at Shide Group, though he remained president.

His diminishing fortune probably drove Xu closer to Bo's circle. More than anyone else, he pinned his hopes on Bo's ascension to the Politburo Standing Committee, which carried huge political and economic power. Based on an account from an official with the Central Commission for Discipline Inspection, Xu and another of Bo's business friends carried boxes of cash to Beijing to lobby other Politburo members and bribe the media to support Bo's political bid.

In February 2012 Xu was believed to have spent two weeks in Australia, watching the Bo Xilai scandal unfold. Late that month, Bo allegedly got ahold of him, called him a coward, and urged him to return. With Bo's reassurance, Xu assumed that the coast was clear and came back to China.

Like Bo, Xu had grossly miscalculated the political situation. Premier Wen Jiabao delivered his scathing criticism of Bo' s policy in Chongqing on March 14, 2012, and an official in Chongqing said that within an hour about seventy municipal leaders were under escort to Beijing for an important briefing about Bo's pending political demise. Xu disappeared that night. A source at the Public Security Ministry said Xu had attempted to flee the country for the second time on March 16, but was intercepted by immigration and customs officers.

Over the next week, I combed the Chinese official media for clues relating to Xu's whereabouts but came up with nothing.

At the end of March, a financial magazine affiliated with Xinhua confirmed Xu's arrest. The report said Xu was "under the control of the Central Commission for Discipline Inspection" for his alleged involvement in economic crimes. At the same time, the commission sent a team to Dalian to investigate Xu's business activities. Even though the article did not provide any details, the public knew that Xu's detention was related to Bo.

Dalian Shide Football Club lost miserably in a game in Nanjing city on March 30, and after the game a reporter asked the players about Xu. They shook their heads but said nothing.

Xu's company, the Shide Group, issued an internal circular on March 31, acknowledging that company officials had not heard from Xu since March 14 and that no government agency would officially say what had happened. According to the circular, the company had submitted a written report to the Dalian municipal government about Xu's disappearance and his brother had stepped up to temporarily take over Xu's responsibilities as board president. The company pledged to abide by party policies and keep the business running as usual. The internal circular was first posted on the Internet portal Sina but was soon deleted.

After Xu's arrest was gradually made public, more information has come to light. Xu allegedly paid the tuition and living expenses of Bo Guagua, the son of Bo Xilai, and covered most of Gu Kailai's overseas travel expenses. In addition, Xu had shelled out millions of yuan for actresses and models to sleep with Bo. In one incident, when a news anchor in Dalian became pregnant after having an affair with Bo, Xu paid her 10 million yuan to keep quiet. One official media report said Xu was facing charges of match-fixing and violation of China's financial regulations—one accusation was that in 2009, he had mortgaged a plot of land that did not belong to his company to obtain a loan of 150 million yuan (US $24 million), from a local bank.

During the trial of Chongqing's former police chief, Wang Lijun, on September 9, 2012, Xu was named in the official transcript:

In April 2009, one of Wang's immediate family members was transferred to a working position in Beijing. Not having a residence in
Beijing, the family member of Wang received two apartments in
Beijing bought by Xu Ming at a price of 2.85 million yuan [US
$449,583]. The apartments were registered under the name of
Wang's father-in-law. After the deal, Wang gave his thanks to Xu in
person. In July of the same year, Wang, at the request of Xu,
instructed law enforcement departments in Chongqing to release
three people who were under detention.

Xu's name also appeared in both of Gu Kailai's confessions, alleging he had helped plot Heywood's murder by filing false charges that
Heywood was a drug trafficker. These mentions herald tough sentencing for Xu in the coming year. Xu's story is a reminder that many Chinese billionaires have followed a similar curve. The most recent was
Huang Guangyu, who traveled to Beijing in 1990 from his rural village
in Guangdong province. With 4,000 yuan (US $645) in his pocket, he
started his Gome Electrical Appliances Holdings, which became
China's second-largest home appliance retailer. He was ranked as
mainland China's richest person by Hurun's China Rich List from
2005 to 2008, with assets reaching 4.3 billion yuan (nearly US $700
million). In 2008, when he was forty-one, a Beijing court sentenced
Huang to fourteen years in prison for illegal business dealings, insider
trading, and corporate bribery, charging that Huang directly bribed or
instigated others to bribe five government officials with 4.5 million
yuan (US $725,000) in cash and properties from 2006 to 2008 in
exchange for corporate benefits.

Huang's sentencing led to the downfall of a group of senior officials
at the economic crime investigation bureau of the Ministry of Public
Security, the State Administration of Taxation's inspection bureau,
and the economic investigation division of the Beijing municipal public security bureau. The assistant minister of public security was also
investigated for accepting bribes from Huang.

Before Xu's detention, several of his friends expressed their concerns to him. One day in 2000, Xu had a business meeting with a

colleague in his office. Over the course of the conference, Xu's phone rang. It was from a deputy district chief in Dalian, who asked if Xu was willing to talk to Bo Xilai in an attempt to secure him a promotion. The colleague, who overheard part of the conversation, quit a few months later. "I knew that Xu Ming would get into trouble someday," he told *Southern Weekend*. "He was tied too closely with the interests of certain leaders." The colleague warned him, but Xu ignored his words.

The misfortunes of Xu and other prominent Chinese businessmen highlight the close and yet precarious relations between Chinese government officials and businessmen. In China, businessmen rely heavily on government officials. It is not uncommon for a millionaire to bow to the needs of a tiny government agency director, who might control the local policies and resources, and could make the businessman's wealth evaporate overnight. During a recent visit to central China, I learned that the owner of a local supermarket chain had offended a senior official at the municipal People's Congress by refusing to donate money to one of the official's pet projects. A year later, the businessman was notified that the shopping center, where his flagship store was located, would be demolished to make way for an office building. The notice came right after he had renewed a ten-year lease and invested heavily in the store. Even though the city government would compensate him for part of his costs, the loss of the prime location effectively destroyed his business.

Because politics and businesses are so intertwined, many businesspeople in China are more politically astute than scholars. Many who visit New York would invite me out for dinner to discuss politics. During our conversations, I've noticed, they are very well informed and have a deep understanding of intricate political issues. When I inquire about the types of political connections they have in China, most of the big businesspeople are friends with the provincial party chief, the governor, the mayor, or Politburo members.

The attraction seems to be mutual. Officials are increasingly dependent on businesspeople to underwrite their own family expenses. Officials realize that unless they can find a way to convert their power into cash, they will end up with nothing after they retire. In the 1980s and 1990s, bribes from businesses came in the form of a red envelope with several hundred yuan of cash or a gift card or unlimited access to a certain bank account. That has evolved into diverse methods of bribery, where a wealthy businessperson is treated like an official's private treasurer or underground office manager. He quietly pays for big purchases made by the official's family members. Some officials, such as Bo Xilai, even ask their business partners to purchase houses or pay their children's tuition abroad. In some cases, a businessperson will make an official or his family member a silent investor in an enterprise. The deal is a win-win situation—the official obtains a certain percentage of the company for nothing and without the knowledge of the public or the party, and the businessperson gets the necessary political protection or a certain government contract.

In the 1980s, the Communist Party forbade children of senior leaders to engage in business. But now it is rare to find officials whose children are not using their parents' connections to do business. This happens at all levels of the government. Sometimes, a businessperson becomes an official's secret lobbyist, bribing senior leaders on behalf of the official for promotions and pays the media to write positive stories. As a consequence, corruption permeates every level of the party and the government. If an official attempts to stay clean, he or she would be considered a rule breaker who could soon be purged.

With their shared interests, businesspeople and government officials are tied together in one boat. If one side gets into trouble, the other one will go down with it. At the time of writing, Xu is still being detained in an undisclosed location. As the ruling elite is building a strong case against Bo, Xu's testimony will no doubt play a big role. However, with so much attention focused on Bo, the world seems to have forgotten Xu Ming, the legendary billionaire who once headlined many business and financial publications. Xu's situation illustrates a sad fact in China—once a businessperson loses the protection of power, he can be crushed like an ant. That was also the very reason Xu Ming clung so closely to Bo Xilai, but unfortunately, Xu was barking up the wrong tree.

THE UNEXPECTED LOSER:
"PEOPLE'S PREMIER" OR THE "KING OF SHOWBIZ"?

IN MID-OCTOBER, when an editor at the *New York Times* reached out to the Chinese government for comments relating to an upcoming article that investigated the financial assets held by Premier Wen's family members, the officials declined. But Zhang Yesui, the Chinese ambassador in Washington, DC, and the Chinese consul general in New York City personally visited the *New York Times* headquarters, trying to block the publication of the article, penned by David Barboza, the *Times'* Shanghai business correspondent.

"Chinese officials raised six points in the conversation," said a businessman close to Premier Wen. "They explained the cultural and political differences in both countries and demanded that the *Times* kill the article about the Chinese premier. The ambassador also threatened that publishing such a negative article about Premier Wen before the Party Congress could seriously damage Sino–US relations."

Such arrogance and a lack of basic understanding of Western journalistic institutions on the part of Chinese officials only confirmed the importance of the article. On October 25, the *New York Times* published Barboza's lengthy investigative report on its English- and Chinese-language websites. The article confirmed in considerable detail the rumors about Premier Wen Jiabao's wife and son circulating on Chinese Weibo and in overseas Chinese media since 2011.

Many relatives of Wen Jiabao, including his son, daughter, younger brother, and brother-in-law, have become extraordinarily wealthy during his leadership, the *New York Times* investigation revealed. A review of corporate and regulatory records indicated the premier's relatives—some of whom, including his wife, have a knack for aggressive deal-making—controlled assets worth at least US $2.7 billion. In many cases, Barboza found, the names of the relatives were hidden behind layers of partnerships and investment vehicles involving friends, work colleagues, and business partners.

Barboza's untangling of the financial holdings provides an unusually detailed look at how politically connected people have profited from being at the intersection of government and business as state influence and private wealth converge in China's fast-growing economy.

The article alleged that Wen's wife, Zhang Peili, had grown rich through her involvement in the diamond trade, while their son, Wen Yunsong, made large profits through private equity and other business deals. Barboza said he found no record of holdings in Premier Wen's name and that it was not possible to tell from records whether he had assisted his relatives' business dealings.

The story about Wen Jiabao was picked up by the foreign media around the world, but most Chinese were kept in the dark. The Chinese government blocked the *New York Times* websites in China three hours after the article was posted. The Chinese Foreign Ministry spokesperson castigated the *New York Times* as "harboring ulterior motives and blackening China," while the state media attacked the *Times* with claims that "there has been an explosion in plagiarism and fabrication by its journalists." Online discussions that contain the phrases "$2.7 billion" or "Wen Jiabao" were quashed, but bloggers cleverly skirted government censors by replacing Wen Jiabao's name with *baobao,* the Chinese word for "baby." One blogger even brought up Wen's frequently quoted lines that "people should have the right to access information and supervise the government" to point out the brutal ironies of the situation.

For the general public, it was hard to reconcile the image of the pro-people premier, supposedly one of the cleanest in the Politburo, with that of a man who would allow his family to use his political status to amass $2.7 billion in assets. Although some discarded the report as pure fabrication to smear their beloved premier, many felt duped. "Wen Jiabao is a hypocrite," wrote a Shanghai-based blogger with the user name of "tusingan." A Beijing-based journalist agreed: "It's been a well-known fact among the political community here that Wen's family is wealthy," she said. "Even former president Jiang Zemin reportedly teases Wen, calling him the wealthiest person in China. Yet, he howled the loudest during anticorruption campaigns. The article shows how pervasive corruption is. The Chinese proverb, 'When a man attains enlightenment, even his pets get to ascend to heaven' sums up the situation well. Officials are now converting political power into money. The *New York Times* is doing a job that domestic media cannot do."

Coincidentally, the *New York Times* article was released on the day the Chinese state media announced that Chinese lawmakers had stripped Bo of his position as a delegate to the National People's Congress at a bimonthly session, thus removing Bo's immunity from prosecution. Twenty minutes before midnight, Xinhua issued another news report that the country's highest prosecution organ had "decided to put Bo Xilai under investigation for alleged criminal offenses, as well as impose coercive measures on him in accordance with the law."

The timings of these two events led to claims that Bo Xilai supporters and other conservatives had supplied the newspaper with negative and false information to retaliate against Premier Wen for bringing Bo down. Back in February 2012, two weeks after Wang Lijun's attempted defection, a party insider alleged that Bo Xilai had hired several Chinese journalists and scholars to dig up dirt on Wen's wife and son. A large-scale media attack against Wen had been planned in early 2012 to embarrass Wen and weaken his ability to influence his replacement on the State Council. In an Internet article posted on October 23, the anonymous author, who had apparently learned about the pending *New York Times* article after the newspaper contacted the Chinese government for comments, stated again that more than ten English- and Chinese-language media outlets, including mine, had received stacks of documents relating to Wen's family in October. "Party conservatives had meticulously organized this despicable smear campaign through foreign media for quite some time to discredit the country's righteous premier and even the president elect," said the anonymous author. "The documents included hundreds of pages of company reports and internal memos. Without the help of party insiders, it would not be possible to obtain such confidential material."

In addition, the article said the documents contained false evidence and speculative statements to mislead the media. In the case of Premier Wen Jiabao, the anonymous author pointed out that the conspirators deliberately attributed other people's assets to Wen's family members to sensationalize the impact.

Because David Barboza adopted a Chinese name, Zhang Dawei, during his tenure in China, a blogger searched the Internet and found several online articles with the byline Zhang Dawei about Bo Xilai's accomplishments in Chongqing. The blogger quickly concluded that David Barboza, aka Zhang Dawei, had been wined and dined by Bo Xilai in Chongqing, and that the facts in his articles should be called into question. A few hours later, other bloggers indicated that it was a mistaken identity and Barboza had never visited Chongqing.

After reading the anonymous writer's online posting, I contacted several overseas media outlets. None had received "stacks of documents" about Wen Jiabao. During an e-mail exchange in December 2012, Barboza also vehemently denied obtaining any information from party insiders. He said he had started working on the story a year before and his information had come from public records. In addition, he stated in his blog, "Not only were there no leaked documents, I never in the course of reporting met anyone who offered or hinted that they had documents related to the family holdings. This was a paper trail of publicly available documents that I followed with my own reporting, and if I might hazard a guess, it was a trail that no one else had followed before me."

I also disputed the rumor through an editorial on *Mingjing News*. "The important issue is whether the *Times* has presented the facts accurately and fairly," I wrote. "From the article, we can see that the *Times* has conducted meticulous research and provided a balanced report. The paper offered opportunities for the Chinese government and Premier Wen to respond and comment on the story, but no one did."

Even so, some political analysts and the Chinese public remain unconvinced. One analyst charged that the *New York Times* had degraded itself by becoming a tool of China's power struggles. Gao Xin, author of *The Biography of Premier Wen Jiabao,* argued during an interview in Chinese on Radio France International:

I cannot vouch that Wen Jiabao's family members are innocent. However, if we look around, we'll see that the families of the majority of the senior Chinese leaders are in business. Why was Wen Jiabao, who is retiring in 2013, singled out? It is simple. By repeatedly advocating democratic reforms, he made many party senior leaders and elders nervous about their future. At the same time, Wen's high-profile role in the anti-Bo campaign made him the number-one enemy among Bo supporters. Both groups want to destroy his legacy and credibility, making it harder for his successor to continue his liberal policies. Wen has become a vulnerable victim in a new round of power struggle.

However, political analysts acknowledged that there had been persistent rumors about Wen's family finances since 2010 and the volume of such noises started to pick up after Wen had taken on a prominent role in the Bo case. Chen Xiaoping, a US-based scholar, noted:

> Since Bo's dismissal, Wen gave several high-profile talks about the party's anticorruption efforts, calling for the implementation of laws that require officials to declare their assets. It is natural that Wen's family finances drew greater media scrutiny. Insiders might have leaked some news tips to the overseas Chinese media. When Western reporters captured the leads, they started to conduct their own independent research. This thoroughly investigated story in the *New York Times* has put Wen in a politically precarious position, hitting home the message that Bo Xilai was not the only senior official tainted with corruption scandals. Those who threw him out, including the seemingly most pro-people premier, are equally guilty.

KNOWN FOR HIS compassionate and unassuming personality, the seventy-one-year-old Wen Jiabao was seen by the public as an affable, scholarly official who quoted ancient classics in his speeches and understood the needs of ordinary people. He was not a member of the princeling group. Wen mentioned many times in his talks his humble origins: he grew up in an ordinary family in the northern city of Tianjin, his parents were schoolteachers, and they had a hard life when he was young. Journalists addressed him fondly as "Grandpa Wen." On

Chinese New Year's Day, a time of family reunion, Wen would either celebrate the holidays with a family in the remote rural areas in the country's far northwest or eat dumplings with coal miners, deep underground in central China. He shed tears and bowed to the families of victims during a mining accident, and held the hands of an AIDS patient in a village devastated by the epidemic due to government denial and inaction. For years, people noticed him wearing the same worn-out down jacket and a pair of broken sneakers during his visits to factories and villages.

Wen Jiabao began his career as a geologist and then was an administrator in the northwestern province of Gansu. After he was transferred to the Ministry of Geology in Beijing in the early 1980s, his connections with the reform-minded party general secretary, Hu Yaobang, helped him rise to chief of the General Affairs Office of the Central Party Committee, which oversaw the day-to-day operations of senior party leaders. He survived the purge of Hu Yaobang in 1988 and continued to serve in that position until Hu Yaobang's successor, Zhao Ziyang, took over.

In 1989, when a million protesters occupied Tiananmen Square, the then party general secretary, Zhao Ziyang, who aimed to take advantage of the anticorruption movement to advance his reform agenda, instructed Wen to send a telegram to Wan Li, head of the National People's Congress who was visiting the US. Zhao had hoped to team up with Wan Li and stop the conservative faction from imposing martial law. Wen never sent the telegram. Instead, he reported Zhao to the Politburo Standing Committee. Zhao was eventually overthrown by veteran revolutionaries and put under house arrest. On the day of Zhao's departure, Wen accompanied him on his visit to Tiananmen Square, where he delivered a tearful farewell speech. In the aftermath of what has come to be known as the Tiananmen Massacre, Wen emerged unscathed—his critics called him an opportunist—and went on to serve the next party general secretary, Jiang Zemin. In 2003, with the help of Jiang and the retiring premier Zhu Rongji, Wen ascended to the premier's post.

Wen came to power at a time when China was facing serious social problems during its unprecedented economic boom. In the 1990s, party leaders had pinned their hopes on high economic growth, believing that a robust economy would justify the legitimacy of the Communist Party. As a consequence, the party's lopsided economic policy led to the overuse of natural resources and deterioration of the environment. In addition, government figures showed that China's industrial growth centered mostly in the coastal provinces and cities. The vast inland region—71 percent of China's total area and home to 30 percent of its population—accounted for just 17 percent of GDP in 2003. Growth on the coast and continued stagnation in the interior meant that development and income gaps between urban and rural areas, and between the wealthy and the poor, widened dramatically.

Globally, many economists use the Gini index to measure the degree of equality with respect to distribution of assets or income. The value index ranges from zero to one—zero expressing total equality and one for maximum inequality. China's Gini index in 2003 was 0.47, way above that of its neighbor Japan (0.24) and the US (0.4). It was ironic that workers and peasants, who helped underwrite the Communist revolution and were called by Mao Zedong "masters of the country," had dropped to the bottom rung of society. The party, which held itself up as champion of the workers and peasants, was under pressure.

To address the disparity in development and income distribution, Wen, along with President Hu Jintao, adopted a series of pro-people policies, such as abolishing agricultural tax in 2005, establishing social security systems, and promulgating rules to protect small and medium-size private enterprises. These policies proved to be ineffective and the urban–rural gap further deteriorated. In the face of widespread social discontent, Wen and Hu stepped up high-profile campaigns against corruption, which Wen believed had gravely undermined the people's trust in the party. In 2003, the party's anti-corruption bodies launched extensive investigations, putting more than 3,000 government officials behind bars on corruption-related charges. Wen also attempted to push for regulations that would require senior government leaders to divulge family finances. The move encountered strong resistance and was never implemented.

In his second five-year term, as President Hu launched measures to support failing state enterprises to prop up the economy, along with brutal suppression of dissent to maintain social stability, Wen started to slip away from the party line in favor of bold liberal rhetoric on democratic reforms. He frequently gave press conferences to foreign media, impressing reporters with his straightforward answers on previously politically sensitive topics. At the end of the National People's Congress in 2010, when a French journalist asked Wen about an article he had published in a government magazine regarding democracy in China, Wen replied:

> A core value of socialist democracy is to let people be the real masters. This means that we need to guarantee people's rights to elect their own officials, participate in decision-making, and manage and supervise the government. This means we have to create conditions for people to criticize and supervise the government and offer people the opportunities for them to fully develop and utilize creative and independent thinking.

At the 2012 National People's Congress, Wen mentioned the word "reform" seventy times. He said that China must "press ahead with both economic structural reforms and political structural reforms, in particular reforms of the leadership system of the party and the country."

Chinese dissident writer Yu Jie, who had left China after he was detained and repeatedly beaten by police for his writings, called Wen the "King of Showbiz" in a recent book. Yu charged that Wen's prodemocracy rhetoric was insincere and empty, and that his many shows of visiting poor families in his old down jacket were purely publicity stunts for the Chinese media. Yu Jie was one of the first writers to reveal that Wen's wife and son had built a vast business empire with their political connections. He charged that Wen had no intention of promoting political reforms, which could jeopardize his own family economic interest.

Wen was also criticized for his dual-faced role in the May 2008 Sichuan earthquake, which killed nearly 70,000 people. Among those killed were 5,335 schoolchildren. A few hours after the earthquake, Premier Wen Jiabao appeared. Despite his own injuries from the debris, he spent days and nights commanding the rescue efforts and tearfully consoling survivors. The unprecedented disaster and the immediate response by the government ignited an unprecedented display of concern. Within days of the earthquake, the public rallied to offer donations and many traveled to Sichuan to help with the excavation. The government granted unprecedented freedom for journalists to cover the disaster, which effectively prevented rumor and speculation that could cause chaos.

However, the unity and positive energy generated by the earthquake relief efforts did not last long. Soon, officials resumed their normal corrupt and bureaucratic practices. Control over the media returned. Many heartbroken parents who had lost their children gathered to urge local officials to investigate the shoddy construction of school buildings. When their requests went unanswered, frustrated residents staged a series of protests. Police were called, arresting and imprisoning many parents and human rights advocates. Wen never intervened. One parent wrote to Wen:

> Do you really believe in the accusations lodged by local officials that we harbored evil intentions to subvert the government? President Hu and you used to study engineering in colleges. You know very well that some school buildings had been made with substandard construction. Nonetheless, you turned a blind eye to the issue because you are afraid that we could cause instability.

For political analysts, Wen's liberal rhetoric resembled Bo's "Singing Red and Smashing Black" campaign. Both men were, in essence, populists trying to win the hearts of the disgruntled public, and neither believed in what he preached. Premier Wen was said to be a fan of Bo Xilai when the latter was minister of commerce in 2004. They went on several trade missions together and Wen even recommended Bo for the vice premier's position. However, their relationship grew strained after Bo moved to Chongqing. An official with the Chongqing Municipal Party Committee said Bo started to move closer to other princelings and distanced himself from Wen. On several occasions, he publicly berated Wen. At a local party conference, Bo praised his partner, the mayor of Chongqing, calling him "more competent" than the premier of China. Bo's remarks put the mayor and many attendees in an awkward position.

In 2011, when Bo's Chongqing model grabbed national attention as a seemingly effective way to combat rampant corruption and achieve common prosperity, Wen became an outspoken critic. He refused to offer his endorsement. As other senior Chinese leaders traveled to Chongqing and heaped lavish praise on Bo's Chongqing model, Wen backed Bo's political rival, the party chief of Guangdong province, who advocated greater market reform and political liberalization. Wen made it clear in published articles that he was a disciple of reformists such as Hu Yaobang and Zhao Ziyang, whereas Bo Xilai unabashedly positioned himself as a descendant of veteran Communist leaders such as Mao and his own father.

So there was a great deal of significance in the fact that in March 2012, it was Wen who became the first senior leader to criticize Bo harshly at a press conference during the National People's Congress, accusing Bo of trying to restore the practices of Mao's Cultural Revolution, under which millions of people were persecuted to death. In April, when the Politburo Standing Committee was divided over whether to slap Bo with an internal reprimand or undertake a full-blown legal investigation, Wen, along with former president Jiang Zemin, was reportedly adamant that Bo be tried as a criminal and receive severe punishment.

Wen's tough stance toward Bo was not all ideologically driven, said a retired official in Beijing. Having heard about Bo's harsh tactics against his political foes and private businesspeople in Chongqing, "Wen was determined to destroy Bo to protect himself and the interests of his family before his term expires in 2013." At the same time, Bo felt that Wen attempted to sabotage his chance to join the Politburo Standing Committee and reportedly vowed to imprison Wen's relatives in the name of corruption after he seized power.

In September 2012, after Bo Xilai was expelled from the party and was facing a criminal trial, many hailed the seventy-two-year-old Premier Wen as the clear winner. However, the *New York Times* report on the Wen family's wealth all but wiped out Wen's political gains from

Bo's downfall. He found himself a target of public anger and ridicule. I wrote in an editorial in *Mingjing News*:

> If proven to be true, the Wen Jiabao corruption is far more damaging to the Communist Party than the scandal surrounding Bo Xilai, which only involved a regional leader and bribe-taking of 20 million yuan. As the second-highest leader, who has ostensibly positioned himself as a man of the people, the Wen scandal will undermine the credibility of the party and directly challenge the party's legitimacy.

Feng Shengping, a US-based analyst, saw the Wen scandal from a different angle. To Feng, Bo Xilai represented the far Left and Wen the Right. Both of their policies were seen as a threat to the interests of the party establishment. Bo's weakness was his police chief, who used the US Consulate to launch his attack, and Wen Jiabao's was having greedy relatives. Two strategies were at work: Bo's removal would clear an obstacle to a smooth leadership transition at the Party Congress; Wen's downfall would appease the conservatives who worried about losing the party's monopoly.

Chen Xiaoping, the US-based scholar, was more acerbic. "Wen chose to punish Bo for his political ambitions and policies with the crimes of corruption and immoral lifestyle, all of which would please the public, which hated corrupt officials. Wen did not realize that the same weapon that gunned down Bo Xilai was aimed at him. Now, Wen's opponents intend to attack his legacy with similar excuses of corruption. The Wen story added a new twist to the party's intense power struggle before the Congress."

Two hours after the Wen story appeared, a person who identified himself as a friend of the Wen family contacted me from Beijing. He asked if I could interview a wealthy businesswoman, Duan Weihong, who was quoted in the *Times* story. She wanted to tell *Mingjing News* that the majority of the assets listed in the *Times* article were erroneously attributed to Wen family members. I assigned a reporter to conduct the interview.

Then I received another e-mail, from another source close to the Wen family. This second source disclosed that the Wen family had hired lawyers who would issue a statement soon. I was asked to post it on *Mingjing News*. According to this source, Premier Wen emphasized four key points after reading the *Times* article.

First, his family has never engaged in any illegal commercial activities. Second, the US $2.7 billion mentioned in the *Times* article did not exist. Third, all of his family members would disclose their financial dealings and cooperate with any audit or investigation by the relevant government agencies and judicial organs. Last, all of Wen's family members, friends, and colleagues would stand accountable for their own businesses and actions.

I soon received a statement from Junhe Law Office and Grandall Law Firm, both of which are based in Beijing. The statement echoed similar arguments I had heard from Wen's friend, except the lawyers added the threat of legal action against the *Times*. All of this was posted on *Mingjing News* and later widely reported by the international media. In the period of two days, I received pictures and documents from Wen family members and business associates in vigorous defense of Premier Wen. Legal experts I consulted said the documents were too vague and the arguments too weak to serve as evidence of innocence or guilt.

What was unusual, and perhaps more significant than the scandal itself, was the approach taken to defend Wen. I was accustomed as an editor that each time a negative story about a senior leader had been published, government censors would harass reporters and attempt to block the article through intervention on the Internet, and the Chinese Foreign Ministry would issue a terse statement, accusing the media of "harboring ulterior motives and demonizing Chinese leadership." There was never any response from individuals named in the article. In June 2012, when Bloomberg ran a story about president-elect Xi Jinping's family, Xi's friends took an unusual step by sending me meticulously researched facts to dispute the Bloomberg report, which was not broadcast inside China. In Wen's case, he effectively promised to face the public and defend himself after the Party Congress. The active interaction with the media was entirely unexpected and spoke volumes about the potential for more media freedom to participate on the political stage.

In addition, Premier Wen's relatives conveyed a message through *Mingjing News* that Wen would respond in writing to the *New York Times* allegations. "No matter what happens, my family and I are ready to take full responsibility, even if it means sacrificing my career and life," Wen said.

Wen's decision elicited positive responses online. "If he and his family have violated regulations, he should willingly face the consequences," posted one resident of Sichuan. "Even if he ends up in jail, he would go down in history as a respected politician, whose honesty and courage would help bring about true political reforms."

In my editorials on *Mingjing News,* I reminded Wen's friends and his supporters of the opportunity that the *Times* article had presented for China:

> For years, Premier Wen has pushed for such financial disclosure regulations. If he is confident that he has nothing to hide, I would recommend that he defend his name by releasing his family financial records to the public, just as politicians do in democratic countries. By divulging such information, he will set a new standard in Chinese politics and an unprecedented example for other senior leaders. Transparency is an effective way to stem corruption and rescue the party from being toppled.

My article also urged senior leaders not to obstruct Wen's efforts. I predicted that some senior leaders inside the party would prohibit Wen from going public about his defense, thereby setting a dangerous precedent, and some of his own family members might silence him before he damaged their economic interests:

> A critical issue here is that if Premier Wen bows to the system, ignores public outcry and sticks to his denials until his retirement, he and other leaders will prove to the world that the party is incurably corrupt and rotten to the core. They would all end up tragically like the other corrupt dictators in the world.

The Chinese leadership takes pride that their country has emerged as an economic and political superpower. However, being a superpower also means that China has to subject itself to scrutiny by the Western media because every political and economic decision made by China has global consequences.

The *New York Times* story about Wen's family has led to broader scrutiny of the records of other senior leaders—Bloomberg released an article about the billionaire offspring of revolutionary veterans in December 2012—and spawned a new round of attacks among political opponents who compete to expose each other's dirt to the overseas media. In a refreshing way, the foreign media, including the Chinese-language media overseas, now plays the civic role of supervision that should belong to the Chinese domestic media. The party will either improve with increased media scrutiny or be toppled by a better-informed public.

In an interview with Fareed Zakaria on CNN's Global Public Square television program aired in October 2010, Wen made the following statement: "I will like to tell you the following two sentences to reinforce my view. I will not fall in spite of the strong wind and harsh rain, and I will not yield until the last day of my life."

At the time of this writing, we have not seen any response from Premier Wen. He has either encountered opposition from the new leaders, as I predicted in my editorial, or he has simply realized that he can never clarify the issues raised by the *New York Times* about his family finances because what has been reported is largely accurate.

HU IS A LOSER:
THE PRESIDENT AND HIS CHIEF OF STAFF

DESPITE THE PARTY'S repeated claims that the Bo Xilai scandal would be handled as a legal case, not a political one, the public still sees the party chieftains, such as President Hu Jintao and Premier Wen Jiabao, as the de facto judges, rather than those in the courtroom.

The public perception is based on the fact that in China, the party controls police, prosecutors, and judges, and decides the outcomes of politically sensitive trials in advance.

Therefore, President Hu Jintao and Premier Wen Jiabao became the proxies of Bo's adversaries within the party who orchestrated the political drama that had unfolded since February 2012. In many overseas media reports, the case was positioned as Bo versus Hu and Wen. In July, an anti-Bo activist even hailed the removal of Bo Xilai as one of the key accomplishments during President Hu's otherwise uneventful tenure.

As I have described in the previous chapter, among these two proxies, Premier Wen probably deserved the title of Bo's true public enemy. On the other hand is President Hu, who many analysts say was a reluctant participant. If one examines Hu's policies during his rule, one can see clearly that Hu felt a deep kinship with Bo—they both strove to be true disciples of Mao.

ON DECEMBER 5, 2002, a heavy snow fell on the vast expanse of northern China, turning the mountainous regions outside the capital of Beijing into an icy wonderland, resembling what Mao Zedong had described in one of his poems the country had to memorize during the Cultural Revolution: "The mountains dance like silver snakes and the highlands charge like wax-hued elephants." On that cold, snow-flurried day, many people were advised to stay indoors because of treacherous road conditions. However, the inclement weather did not deter sixty-year-old Hu Jintao, the new party general secretary, from traveling. He went to Xibaipo, one of the Communist Party's "holy sites"—the temporary headquarters for Mao Zedong and his troops in 1948, before they won the civil war in 1949 and took over China.

With a head of jet-black hair—a dye job, as commonplace among senior Chinese leaders as the Mao suit once was—and a face purposefully pious, the new party chief came flanked by several of his cabinet members. It was his first public appearance since he was officially installed as the party's general secretary. Though he had been a "crown prince" for ten years, Hu was an enigmatic figure. Most people had no idea who he was, or where he stood on issues facing the party and the country. Using China's former Communist neighbor as a reference, people wanted to know if he was going to be China's Gorbachev, or a Putin.

He chose Xibaipo to set the tone for his upcoming rule because, on the eve of the Communist victory in 1948, Mao had formulated many of the ruling strategies for the party in Xibaipo and commanded the three crucial battles against the Nationalist forces. Xibaipo, which fell into obscurity and disrepair for many years, was restored in the early 2000s and has become a popular tourist destination. Being close to the capital, it is frequently visited by group tours organized by local party branches. People who grew up under the rule of Mao Zedong— essentially anyone under sixty years old—feel a nostalgic connection there. Exhibits and pictures in Xibaipo specifically feature the plain living conditions of the hardworking senior Communist Party leaders in the early days of the revolution. Visitors are regaled with legendary tales of how senior leaders like Marshal Zhu De helped locals plow the land and harvest crops, and how he volunteered to be a coffin-bearer at the funeral of his barber. The grindstone that Mao used while working in the mill house, the kerosene lamp that Premier Zhou Enlai carried when he rescued a villager from an accident on a rainy night, and the wooden wheel that senior leader Dong Biwu used to spin yarn are on prominent display. Their simple lifestyles are a stark contrast to those of the current leadership.

During his short visit, Hu reviewed the successful experience of Mao's Communist revolution in the 1940s, searching for inspirations and ideas that would help shape his answers to China's contemporary problems. He took the unusual step of doing so in front of members of the government-controlled media, so the entire country could mark his "pilgrimage." Xinhua reported Hu spent time at a makeshift auditorium and listened attentively to the guide's briefing on the seventh Party Congress, which had been held there. At that congress, Mao had addressed the challenges of being a ruling political party by warning the whole party, especially the senior leadership, against complacency and corruption. He said:

> Winning the war is only the first step of a 10,000-mile-long march. I urge all of our comrades to continue keeping their modesty,

prudence, humility, and honesty. I also urge you to keep up with the spirit of hard work and plain living.

Based on Mao's recommendations, the party leadership drafted the following guidelines: Do not host lavish birthday parties; do not accept gifts; do not toast each other with liquor frequently; do not applaud each other frequently; and do not name a place or a street after a leader.

A tour guide told a reporter with a foreign media organization that visitors would always giggle sarcastically at such references because wining and dining at public expense, and accepting gifts, have become the least corrupt activities among officials today, in comparison to the millions of yuan embezzled each year at all levels of the party.

Journalists following Hu during the trip noticed that he had spent 30 yuan, or $5, on food out of his own pocket. He also insisted on staying overnight in Xibaipo even though his aides advised against it because the conditions of the local government guest house might be rudimentary. Hu wanted to experience how ordinary people in this old revolutionary base lived their lives. The next day, Hu and his entourage visited the homes of several villagers and advised local officials "a Party that does not cherish the spirit of hard working and plain living cannot survive and thrive."

After Hu Jintao left the village, a reporter asked a villager, surnamed Han, who had chatted with the new party chief for fourteen minutes, "What do you think of party General Secretary Hu Jintao?"

"He is a very nice person," Han said, with a beaming smile. "He specifically told us not to make any preparations before [his visit]."

The villager's comment—"he is a nice person"—reflected what the public in general thought of Hu in 2002, when ordinary people were full of hope and cautious optimism. Unlike his predecessor, Jiang Zemin, who was perceived to be too flamboyant, showy, and elitist, Hu fit the traditional image of a young emperor—poised, humble, prudent, with a cultured and composed demeanor. He was seen as a true commoner who understood ordinary people's needs. During his rule, Hu repeatedly appealed to public sentiment for Mao Zedong, pushing the resurgence of Mao-worshipping to a new height. He admonished party members by reminding them that the party was first and foremost the people's party and from those roots the party derived its legitimacy to rule. He also tried to imitate Mao by establishing tighter political control, as Vladimir Putin did in Russia after the fall of the Soviet Union. Many of his pro-people policies and his brutal crackdown on dissent clearly reflected Mao's influence. Bo Xilai's "Singing Red and Smashing Black" campaign in Chongqing was a logical expression of Hu's leftist philosophy.

Unlike the princelings, Hu was born into a small tea merchant's family in China's southeastern province of Jiangsu in 1942. His mother died when he was very young. His father's family business was wrecked by wars and natural disasters. After the Communists came, Hu's father joined a state retail cooperative as an accountant and supported his three children on a meager income.

In 1959, through his own intelligence and diligence, Hu Jintao entered Qinghua University, similar to MIT in the US, to study hydraulic power stations on rivers and was assigned a job in 1968 as an engineer at a hydroelectric station in the impoverished province of Gansu in northwestern China. In Gansu, he overcame adverse political conditions in the Mao era and gradually moved up the hierarchical ladder of the party, from engineer to administrator and junior party official.

Chinese journalists liked to recount an incident in his early career to illustrate Hu's humble origins and his solidarity with those who had suffered injustices in the hands of corrupt officials. In 1978, Hu's father passed away in his hometown, but there was some unsettled business Hu wanted to conclude. During the Cultural Revolution, his father had offended some city officials, who in retaliation charged him with "embezzling public money" and locked him up for a short period of time. The imprisonment ruined his health and became a stigma for his family for years. In the aftermath of Mao's death, the local government agency had promised to revisit his father's case and reverse the verdict against him. While preparing for his father's funeral, Hu contacted local officials, requesting that they clear his father's name before the burial so he could rest in peace.

Acting on the advice of his friends, Hu hosted a lunch at an expensive restaurant in his hometown and invited the county chief to "have a heart-to-heart talk" over food. For the meal, Hu paid 50 yuan, almost equivalent to Hu's monthly salary. Two tables were set, but no one showed up. Two hours later, a junior official from the county chief's office arrived with the news that the county chief and other leaders were too busy to attend. Feeling insulted, Hu shared the food with the chefs and waitstaff at the restaurant. Hu was said to be so disgusted and hurt he never visited his hometown again.

The local pols in Hu's hometown had totally misjudged Hu's political potential. In 1980, when the Communist Party under Deng Xiaoping revised its charter and abolished life tenure for senior party officials, Hu's career took off dramatically. In March of that year, the party unveiled a series of succession plans calling for the central and local governments to promote university-educated individuals with science and technology backgrounds to key leadership positions. In Gansu, Song Ping, the provincial party chief, was Hu's fellow alumnus. He noticed Hu, a junior manager at the Provincial Construction Committee, during a presentation at an urban planning conference, where Hu's amazing memory and his familiarity with statistics left an indelible impression on Song. He later appointed Hu deputy director of his organization. In 1981, when Song was called back to Beijing to head the State Planning Commission, he arranged for Hu to attend a training session for cadres at the Central Party School in Beijing. While Hu was undertaking his one-year training program, Deng Xiaoping issued a challenge to the party's personnel department: he wanted to see at least fifty new leaders under the age of fifty on the Party Central Committee at the upcoming Party Congress.

Deng's request was duly met and a large group of relatively young university graduates entered the Party Central Committee in 1982. Hu Jintao was chosen as an alternate member and was made deputy secretary of the China Youth League Secretariat, a potentially powerful position. He and his family moved from Gansu to Beijing.

The China Youth League is a Communist Party–led organization for young people between the ages of fourteen and twenty-eight. The league, with an estimated 73 million members, is structured like the Communist Party and is responsible for guiding the activities and ideologies of young Chinese. Hu served first as the deputy and then secretary general at the China Youth League for more than two years, during which time he became acquainted with the then party general secretary Hu Yaobang. The two of them made many visits around the country to mobilize young people for the party's modernization drive. In the mid-1980s, the reformists and Maoist conservatives within the senior ranks of the party fought fiercely over China's future. Both factions reached out to the China Youth League, trying to gain influence over the next generation of Communists. Although it was a challenge for Hu Jintao to decide which faction he should support, he cautiously chose the middle path, actively implementing activities initiated by reformists and promoting programs to preserve and solidify the Maoist ideology advocated by the conservatives. Hu thrived in the center.

In 1985, with the recommendation of reformist leaders such as Hu Yaobang and Zhao Ziyang, Hu Jintao was transferred to China's southwestern province of Guizhou, a poverty-stricken region where the per capita GDP in 2011 was only $1,502, the lowest in China. As the provincial party chief, Hu told the media that Guizhou provided him with a rare opportunity to understand the real China and the lives of people at the bottom rung of society. In Guizhou, Hu displayed his signature political personality—he quietly focused on the local economy and education, and dutifully followed Beijing's directives without openly siding with either political faction. His prudence again served him well. When his mentor, Hu Yaobang, was forced to resign in 1988 for what were deemed by the party to be "liberal pro-Western" programs, Hu Jintao was spared the purge that consumed many of his contemporaries, though his prize was to be appointed party chief of Tibet, a volatile and internationally sensitive region that needed a stable leader.

A few months after his arrival, Tibet's pro-Beijing spiritual leader, the Panchen Lama, died of a heart attack. His sudden death fueled all kinds of rumors, one of which claimed that the party had assassinated him because of his criticism of the party's Tibetan policies. It was a time of political and social uncertainty. As the new party chief, Hu appealed to social and religious leaders to maintain peace. Despite his efforts, rioting became commonplace and, on March 7, 1989, the State

Council declared martial law in Lhasa. The next day, the *Tibetan Daily* published a large photo of Hu Jintao wearing a helmet and directing troops called in to restore order. This was Hu's first media exposure in Tibet and the face he showed the Tibetan public was clad in a menacing helmet. It was a carefully calculated political posture. Judging from the severity of the situation, Hu knew that if he was too soft, pro-independence forces being championed in some overseas media might gain advantage. He needed to project the image that China would not back down an inch from its claim to sovereignty over Tibet, which was incorporated into China in 1951 and classified as the Xizang Autonomous Region in 1965. The news photograph of Hu in a helmet reached Beijing and changed the perception of senior party veterans. There is an unconfirmed story that after his aide showed him a picture of Hu in the *Tibetan Daily*, Deng Xiaoping commented, "I'm pleased that Hu is tough and stands firm on principles."

Martial law in Lhasa shocked the world. The European Parliament, the US Congress, and many human rights organizations voiced their strong condemnation of China's brutal suppression. There would be geopolitical ramifications for China, but Hu held firm and ended the rioting. To Hu's supporters in Beijing, it was a spectacular beginning.

The 14th Party Congress in 1992 marked the last chance for Deng Xiaoping and his contemporaries to serve on the Party Central Committee. Before giving up their power, the veterans became obsessed with the party's succession plan for 2000, when a new leadership would be appointed. The country was still reeling from the aftermath of what the official media called the "Tiananmen Incident" of 1989. The new leaders would decide the direction for China for the next century, and the octogenarians wanted a smooth system of succession that would ensure the party retained its ruling status and that the country would not abandon Communism. Of immediate concern for Deng Xiaoping, who was retiring, was to select a reliable leader who could complement Deng's successor, Jiang Zemin, one capable of checking and balancing Jiang's power while continuing the reforms Deng had initiated and championed.

During the search, Hu Jintao appeared on Deng's radar. Hu's handling of the riots in Tibet was still fresh in the memories of Deng and many veterans and they were convinced that the young man would be a tough leader. Deng reportedly liked the fact that Hu was prudent and practical. Hu's humble family background made it easier for the public to accept him, and Hu had skillfully cultivated relationships with both factions within the party, so his promotion would not disrupt the status quo and polarize the party.

The choice of Hu surprised the public and political analysts; the party chief of Tibet, largely an unknown entity, was designated as Jiang Zemin's successor at the 15th Party Congress, the "crown prince" of China. But, Hu was soon depicted as boring and humorless by the public because he could not speak his mind freely or act according to his own will. He was constantly caught between two masters. On the one hand, he needed to curry favor with Deng Xiaoping and the other veterans who had installed him. Though the veterans had supposedly retired, they remained active and influential in political circles. Hu knew that they could lift him high or destroy him. On the other hand, he had to tread carefully around Jiang Zemin, his current boss, who similarly held his fate in his hands. Hu felt the need to please all sides.

Quietly, Hu used his position as head of the party's personnel department to promote his own people, especially former colleagues at the China Youth League at both national and local levels. As a result, a significant number of youth leaguers joined the Party Central Committee. The trend continued after Hu's official takeover. Even though Hu never openly admitted it, he was known within the party as the "spiritual leader" of the youth league faction, which, along with the princelings, now dominates China's political arena.

In prevailing terms, "youth leaguers" refers to those who start their political careers at youth league organizations and were born and grew up under Communism. The China Youth League charter defines it as a provisional army of the Communist Party. The youth league has long been considered a training school or a launching pad for young people who aspire to rise within the ranks of the Communist Party. Unlike the princelings, who owe their rich political and social resources to their parents or relatives, the majority of youth leaguers, such as Hu Jintao, grew up in ordinary families and rose to power on the strength of their talent, connections, or pure luck.

Over the past decade, the youth leaguers have formed a relatively cohesive political force within the party. They do not have a set political platform or agenda, but they are bound together by shared experiences working in the same organization or on projects in the field. When one is promoted, he or she will normally create opportunities for others.

The princelings feel entitled and believe they are China's political elite. While princelings are more pro-business and pro-development—Bo Xilai might be considered something of an aberration—youth leaguers tend to advocate social and economic equality, and see themselves as representatives of the interests of the masses. They are supportive of equal opportunities in education and are more likely to advocate the interests of the weaker social groups. Because they have worked with high school and college students, most youth leaguers are excellent community organizers and are ideologically driven.

Most of the youth leaguers Hu Jintao promoted were born in the 1950s and grew up together during the Cultural Revolution. More than 80 percent have advanced degrees. Hu Jintao and many of his contemporaries majored in natural sciences, though a large number of the youth leaguers studied law, economics, finance, philosophy, and education. Because they start very young at different levels of youth league organizations and gradually move up the party hierarchy, they are commonly referred to as professional bureaucrats. Hu Jintao might be a true follower of Maoism, but Gao Falin, a former youth league official, said many other youth leaguers treat Communist ideology as a tool to help advance their careers and will bend with the winds of change.

Whereas the princelings are closely connected with the business community—their families have amassed huge fortunes through their political connections—Kang Xiaoguang, a researcher at Qinghua University's China Study Center, said most youth leaguers are relatively "clean" and possess a stronger sense of justice when it comes to handling party corruption cases. Kang said many youth leaguers, including Hu Jintao and Li Keqiang, the former party chief of Henan and Liaoning and China's premier-in-waiting for the spring of 2013, were promoted largely on the basis of their untainted records. Kang attributed uncorrupted youth leaguers to the nature of their former jobs at the China Youth League, which seldom involved financial dealings. That albeit simplistic characterization fits with Hu Jintao, who insisted on having simple meals and refused extravagant food and drinks during his visits. Li Keqiang, a known workaholic, is said to slurp on instant ramen noodles while working during the weekends. Still, a series of scandals involving high-profile youth leaguers, such as Hu's chief of staff Ling Jihua, prove that factional lines are no obstacle to corruption, which has infected virtually every single official.

During Hu's reign, the other youth leaguer to burst onto the national scene besides Li Keqiang was Wang Yang, who worked for a youth league organization in Anhui province before becoming the party chief of Chongqing in 2005 and Guangdong province in 2007. Like Bo Xilai, he was a strong contender for the Politburo Standing Committee. Hu's efforts to elevate youth leaguers, who shared his experiences, values, and political vision, illustrate his concern about the tremendous challenges he faced during his rule. Economically, the country benefited from the efforts of Hu's predecessors, Jiang Zemin and former premier Zhu Rongji, whose bold reforms ushered in a period of rapid growth. In the Jiang Zemin era, the government emphasized GDP growth, believing that if the pie could be made bigger, everyone could have a piece and be happy. In this way, the party's ruling status would be secure. By the time Hu came to power, segments of society were notably wealthier than before—China produced more millionaires than at any other time in history—while the reemergence of significant inequality did little to legitimize the Communist Party's founding ideals. But the country faced increasing social unrest as disgruntled urban residents and migrant workers staged wave after wave of large-scale demonstrations, protesting against forced relocation, striking over unpaid wages and pensions, and coming together over rampant government corruption. In the pursuit of higher economic growth, China was consuming resources such as land and the environment without any consideration for future generations. And the vast hinterland was being left behind.

Hu realized that something had to be done to bridge the widening economic gap and ease social conflict. He also knew that overly ambitious political reforms could disrupt the power balance, offending the political elite. If not prudent, he could trigger an implosion of pent-up conflict. The party and the country could easily slip away from him. Hu drew lessons from his predecessors, notably former party general secretaries Hu Yaobang and Zhao Ziyang. Hu Yaobang was known for his courageous efforts to reform the Chinese political systems and Zhao for his refusal to suppress the peaceful Tiananmen demonstrations with force. Both were ousted before their tenures had expired.

Instead, Hu came up with a political philosophy that combined Mao Zedong's totalitarian maintenance of one-party rule at all cost with Confucian "pro-people" values. The result was the well-known "developing a harmonious society" mantra or the three "pro-people principles" by which the government should "use power to help people, use compassion to care for the people, and use welfare to benefit people."

Under Hu, the party switched from the country's previous focus on "development is the hard truth," or making the cake bigger, focusing instead on how to divide the cake equally and fairly for each social group so everyone might benefit from the economic boom. Under Hu and his premier Wen Jiabao, agricultural taxes were eliminated for farmers, more flexible policies were promulgated to improve the living and working conditions of migrant workers living in cities, more investment was made to cultivate China's inland regions, minimum-wage laws were enforced in cities, and the government subsidized affordable housing developments. Generally speaking, these policies have been well received by the Chinese public. Ironically, Bo Xilai further expanded those programs in Chongqing but was accused of "straying from party lines" by his political foes after his downfall.

Hu rejected any drastic ideas to revamp the political system, but he implemented cosmetic changes. He wanted the party to be more open and started by publishing details of some Politburo Standing Committee meetings. He urged the state newspapers and TV stations to reduce coverage of party leaders' activities and focus more on ordinary people, and he banned lavish send-off and welcome-back ceremonies of Chinese leaders when visiting abroad. For the public, the new policies represented a welcome trend.

Commentators were not persuaded, however. One said, "Improving the people's livelihood can stabilize the economy, but the practice proved that for every one-yuan increase in welfare Hu gave the poor, the money the bureaucrats placed in their own vaults increased by ten yuan, or even more." Dissidents within and outside China believed that without fundamental political change, the political system in China could not guarantee governance that was compassionate about people's welfare and that respected the people's will.

As the party promoted Hu's new "harmonious society," the public security apparatus stepped up efforts to silence any voice that was not "in harmony" with that of the party. Under Hu Jintao, the government designed a nationwide surveillance system and planted plainclothes policemen all over China. Police could have people disappear, detain them indefinitely, or beat them up. Dissidents were not the only targets. Party officials were not ignored. Their cars and homes were bugged and, during political power struggles, officials could be taken away and interrogated in the name of anticorruption. Authorities invested heavily in censoring the Internet to isolate China from the rest of the world by restricting free flow of information. Many websites were blocked by firewalls and authorities tried to monitor personal computers by preinstalling filter software. Many journalists and bloggers were abducted and imprisoned for writing that criticized the government. Shi Tao, a former editorial director at the Changsha-based newspaper *Modern Business Daily,* was sentenced to ten years in jail in April 2005. He was charged with "providing state secrets to foreigners" after sending an e-mail on his Yahoo account to Democracy Forum, a US-based website. The e-mail detailed instructions issued by the local propaganda department on how to restrict coverage of the government-banned Falun Gong group and the fifteenth anniversary of the 1989 Tiananmen Square protest. Such heavy-handed measures made the public highly cynical: they called Hu's politics "selling dog meat under the label of a goat head."

Netizens in China interpreted the concept of "building a harmonious society" as demanding "be obedient, do what I tell you and shut up if you don't like it." If the government shut down a website or censored online posts, skeptics would say, "The website has been *harmonized*."

In 2008 and 2009, when the global financial crisis ravaged virtually every economy in the world, Hu was credited with helping China survive the meltdown by delivering a surge in GDP from a low of 6.8 percent in fourth-quarter 2008, to a full-year 9.2 percent for 2009. A large stimulus package helped boost urban infrastructure spending, and authorities in Beijing stepped up support for state-run enterprises with financial subsidies and favorable fiscal policies, reversing a trend initiated by Deng Xiaoping and Jiang Zemin to encourage private enterprises and allow them to grow, while letting inefficient state enterprises fail. In 2008, state enterprises, with the injection of government funds, emerged as leaders in steel and iron, coal, chemistry, aviation, food, and real estate. Enterprises under the control of the central government—*yangqi* in Chinese—associated with inefficiency and loss a decade before had by 2009 become the symbols of rising fortune. *Yangqi* (yang-chee) became a buzz word, embodying a new Chinese economic model. Many Chinese economists began to question the direction of the country's market reforms and wonder if the rapid growth of state enterprises would suppress the development of private enterprises, eventually stifling the budding market economy in China.

The global financial crisis boosted the status of China, which played the unexpected role of a "white knight" riding to the rescue of the world's economies whereas the US was blamed for causing the world's economic woes. The universal values of democracy and freedom lost their attractiveness. Hu began to see the capitalist world in a different light. As Western governments toned down their criticism of Beijing's human rights abuses in exchange for more business opportunities for their countries, Beijing became emboldened and started to tout the superiority of a limited market economy under a tough totalitarian rule. At the Frankfurt Book Fair in 2009, where China was guest of honor, an official declared, "We are not here to be taught a lesson in democracy. Those times are gone forever."

In the Jiang era, China would occasionally release some political prisoners and send them abroad in exile as "goodwill" gestures or bargaining chips to extract concessions from Western governments on other issues that could benefit China. The practice stopped under Hu. Many dissidents or civil rights advocates remain imprisoned and, despite condemnation from the international community, he did not grant any high-profile releases. Instead, the government went all out to defend its bottom line, arresting and imprisoning anyone who dares to challenge one-party rule. In 2009, the government arrested and imprisoned Nobel Peace Prize winner Liu Xiaobo for his role in the drafting of "Charter 08," a manifesto calling for political change in China. During the Arab Spring in 2011, public security forces picked up writers, artists, and human rights activists, including Ai Weiwei, and detained them for weeks without notifying relatives of their whereabouts.

Jiang Zemin used to recite Abraham Lincoln's Gettysburg Address and would go out of his way to explain to the media that he was not a dictator. Hu never bothered. Human rights activists castigated him as a truly evil Maoist dictator.

In January 2011, Hu Jintao paid his third and last visit to the US as the president of China. At the welcome ceremony on the south lawn of the White House, US president Barack Obama's beaming smiles exuded confidence as the leader of the world's largest superpower. In contrast, the Chinese president, leader of the second-largest superpower, looked stern and menacing. After nearly nine years in office and ten years as the president-in-waiting, Hu still found it hard to relax. Whether he was the host or the honored guest, he carried the same facial expression—constrained and cautious. As the number one of China, former guerrilla leader Mao Zedong had the flair of a lawless rebel. Party veteran Deng Xiaoping radiated experience and power. English-speaking Jiang Zemin demonstrated the showiness of a performer. But Hu Jintao was a stiff.

In the Hu era, politics moved from social to economic—different economic groups control and manipulate decision-making. The economy under Hu was a power economy. Political power and businesses banded together to form strong interest groups that control the market and monopolize the profit.

The scale of corruption during Hu's rule was unprecedented. Power and money bred greed. Rampant corruption wormed its way into the ranks of police, taxation, court, auditing, quality control, and petition handling. Though Hu launched one campaign after another to purify the ranks of the party, nothing worked. He might have gotten rid of one corrupt official, but thousands more emerged. Corruption and social disparity created a volcano of widespread social discontent that could erupt at any time. Hu tried to save the system, but his efforts were superficial—a case of too little, too late.

Before the end of his rule, the state media heaped praise on Hu, calling his ten years in office China's "golden age," but insiders say many in the party, including retired officials, characterized Hu's tenure as "a decade of stagnation" and "a decade of inaction." Some princelings, who consider Communist China a "big house" their parents built with Mao, called Hu "an incompetent housekeeper" and a "failed student of Mao."

Hu's perceived incompetence created room for opportunists, Wen Jiabao on the right and Bo Xilai on the left, to emerge and expand their power bases. Politically, Hu is seen, erroneously, as a reformer who sided with Premier Wen and opposed Bo. But after we have examined Hu's past history, it's not difficult to see Hu identified more with Bo, whose programs in Chongqing mirrored or carried on to the extreme what Hu had initiated for China. If Bo was a phony Maoist, Hu was a true disciple of Mao.

In the final three years of his rule, Hu expanded the powers of the Communist Party, which monopolizes the country's resources and controls the government, the military, the legislature and the judiciary, the media, and all government enterprises, and extended its reach into private and foreign enterprises, to the point where many private and foreign companies now have employee party branches. The party used taxpayer money to boost village party organizations, strengthening its control over the rural areas. At an internal meeting, Hu reported to party leaders that China should be tough on dissidents and learn from North Korea and Cuba.

Bo practiced what Hu preached. Insiders say Hu's chief of staff would arrange for Bo to see the president each time he visited Beijing to brief Hu on the latest accomplishments in Chongqing. Without Wang Lijun's dramatic and history-changing visit to the US Consulate, Hu Jintao would have traveled to Chongqing, thrown himself behind Bo, and taken credit for Bo's "common prosperity" policy. There is also no doubt that Hu would have supported Bo's bid to join the Politburo Standing Committee. The rise of Bo could have checked the powers of Hu's successor, Xi Jinping, and the powerful princeling faction supported by Jiang Zemin. Any challenge to Xi would enhance Hu's authority after he relinquished the presidency.

For that reason Hu expressed ambivalence about punishing Bo in February 2012. It was only in mid-April that Hu allied himself with liberals who opposed Bo's radical policies, corrupt officials who felt threatened by Bo's aggressive and ruthless campaign against organized crime, and party elders and princelings who would not allow anyone to disrupt the coronation of Xi Jinping, and businesspeople who were victimized by Bo's sweeping anticrime initiatives.

The fall of Bo Xilai was initially seen as a fatal blow to the princelings, aggravating the public's resentment against the group and weakening their political power ahead of the Party Congress. But in fact Hu lost more than the princelings from Bo's fall, because he was one of the last to abandon Bo. Then Ling Jihua, Hu's confidante and chief of staff, was caught up in a scandal. The ensuing political crisis washed away any political gains from Bo Xilai's misfortune that might once have accrued to Hu, and instead strengthened the hands of former president Jiang and other party veterans. Hu was left with hardly any allies in the forthcoming new administration.

The Ling Jihua scandal burst into the open in the early hours of March 18, when a black Ferrari 458 Spider spun out of control and crashed into a concrete bridge support on a highway in Beijing. Due to its high velocity, the car bounced back from the concrete before crushing steel safety fences and landing on the side of the road. Press photographs showed the car had virtually disintegrated in the impact. The engine landed five meters from the main body of the car. There were three occupants. The driver, who was naked when his body was cut from the wreckage, was pronounced dead on the spot. He was identified as twenty-three-year-old Ling Gu, the son of Ling Jihua. Two women were freed from the wreck and had suffered critical injuries. Both were ethnic Tibetans and both reportedly semi-naked. An anonymous source told *Mingjing News* that the inebriated Ling Gu was apparently engaging in what has become known in China as *che zhen,* or car sex. One semi-naked woman was sitting in Ling's lap and controlling the steering wheel while the other lay across the front passenger seat engaged in a sexual act with Ling. A passerby took a picture of the accident and called the police. Fifteen minutes later, the Beijing traffic police arrived at the scene and cordoned off the road to conduct investigations.

The two women were sent to the hospital. *Asiaweek* said one woman was Tashi Dolma, a graduate of Mingzu University of China and the daughter of the deputy police chief of China's northwestern province of Qinghai, and the other, Younge, attended the University of Politics and Law in Beijing and her father was a well-respected lama. Tashi Dolma suffered injuries to her stomach and returned to her hometown after treatment. Younge's legs were severed in three parts and her arms were broken. Her upper body, including her scalp, was severely burned. She was in a coma for two weeks, but survived her injuries; apart from the loss of her legs she was paralyzed from the waist down.

"Anonymous" sent me the secure e-mail detailing the accident three months later. *Mingjing News* posted the account, with a note at the end, saying we could continue to investigate and provide follow-up coverage. The news attracted waves of interest and criticism from readers. While some asked how a salaried government leader could afford a $200,000 Ferrari and expressed disbelief at the decadent lifestyle of young princelings, others dismissed the news as pure fabrication produced by supporters of Bo Xilai. One person wrote in the comment section, "Many people hate Ling Jihua, who is a close friend of President Hu Jintao, because he has personally signed the order to dismiss and detain Bo Xilai. It is so obvious that Bo Xilai's supporters are desperate and retaliating by making up this cruel and vicious story about his [chief-of-staff's] son." A senior official in Guangzhou called me after reading the story, saying the source was "an imaginative fiction writer."

Hong Kong media, including the pro-Beijing English-language daily the *South China Morning Post,* gradually confirmed many of the details through their own sources in September and October.

Asiaweek reported that on the night of the accident, the three victims had left a private party and were on their way to another. The Ferrari 458 could carry only one passenger but the two women squeezed in regardless. When the car was making a sharp turn, the woman sitting in the middle was thrown out on top of the driver, blocking the steering wheel. Allegations of car sex have not been substantiated.

Fifty-five-year-old Ling Jihua was born in Shanxi, Bo Xilai's ancestral province. *Mingjing News* revealed in December 2012 that the Bo and Ling families had very close ties. When he was alive, Bo Xilai's father treated Ling Jihua as an adopted son. Like Bo, Ling married a wife with the last name of Gu, who is a legal professional by training and has been rumored to have used her husband's political connections to engage in lucrative land and property investment and accumulate a large amount of wealth for the family. Ling's wayward son had attended Beijing University, one of China's elite schools, through his father's connections. According to an official at the university, the son's grades were far from ideal, but the university leadership still hired him as head of the school's youth league organization after he had graduated a year before. Ling's son was a notorious playboy and had expensive taste in cars.

Ling started working for the China Youth League in a small county in Shanxi province in the mid-1970s. After Bo Xilai's father was reinstalled as China's vice premier in 1980, he brought Ling to Beijing. The twenty-three-year-old was elevated to the propaganda department of China's Youth League Central Committee, where Ling had stayed for twenty years in different capacities within the organization before becoming chief of Hu Jintao's office in 1999.

"Ling's close relation with the Bo family makes us understand President Hu's initial position that Bo should be isolated from the Wang Lijun incident," said *Mingjing News*. "Ling was Bo's 'deep throat' in Beijing. His secret support gave Bo the confidence that he would survive the crisis. It explains why Bo was so cocky during the National People's Congress."

Known for his uncanny ability to navigate the complex political issues in Beijing, Ling was familiar with every department inside the Central Party Committee and the central government. When Hu became the party general secretary, Ling became his "housekeeper," taking care of often-overlooked minor details, such as checking venues where Hu was due to speak to ensure everything went as planned. Ling was put on the fast track for promotions and Hu made him chief of the General Office of the Party Central Committee, which took over handling the daily affairs of the senior leadership in 2007. Premier Wen Jiabao served in that function on his rise to seniority. Hu had intended to promote Ling and another youth leaguer, Li Yuanchao, who was in charge of the party's personnel department, to the Politburo Standing Committee to balance the influence of the princelings.

When the Bo Xilai scandal broke, Ling, in his position as chief of the General Office of the Party Central Committee, coordinated the investigation. His son's accident on March 18 came three days after he signed the order to sack Bo Xilai. Ling immediately suspected it was a political assassination by pro–Bo Xilai forces and ordered members of the Central Guards Bureau to surround the Beijing Public Security Bureau on the night of March 19, demanding his son's body be released before any investigation was completed, and ordering that they capture his "murderer." The confrontation reportedly lasted more than an hour and some residents in Beijing wrote on Weibo that they had heard gunshots. Mobilizing members of the Central Guards Bureau to threaten the Beijing Public Security Bureau without authorization from the president is tantamount to staging a military coup. Zhou Yongkang, the head of the Law and Politics Commission at the Politburo Standing Committee and a close ally of Bo Xilai, was called and he rushed over to the Beijing Public Security Bureau building. He agreed to launch a thorough investigation.

Realizing that the freak accident could ruin his political career if news of it leaked out, Ling was forced to strike a deal with Zhou, who allegedly agreed to have the Beijing traffic police erase the victim's identity, bury details of the accident, and hide the crash in the usual traffic accident report. Zhou further agreed to support President Hu's efforts to bring Ling onto the Politburo Standing Committee. In return, Ling would continue to lobby President Hu and Premier Wen Jiabao to limit the investigation of his friend Bo Xilai to ensure Zhou was not implicated.

Ji Weiren, author of *China Coup*, wrote on *Mingjing News* that Zhou and Ling formed a team to handle the accident. Through Zhou, Ling contacted Jiang Jiemin, who was chairman of PetroChina, the world's fourth-largest company. Jiang transferred from his company a large sum of money to compensate and silence the two surviving women. In the next twenty-four hours, police in Beijing received instructions from Zhou to destroy the original accident report. The name on the death certificate was changed to Jia, which is both a common family name but also sounded the same as the word for "fake." In the following days, several Weibo postings by witnesses were deleted. Words such as "Ferrari accidents," *"che zhen,"* or "car sex," were blocked on major search engines. Two weeks later, *Asiaweek* carried a news story claiming that Ling Jihua's son was actually alive and his Weibo account was still active. Because the victim's name on the death certificate was Jia, some bloggers suggested that the crazy driver was the illegitimate son of Jia Qinglin, a prominent Politburo Standing Committee member.

It looked like the cover-up might work. In exchange for Zhou's help, Ling persuaded President Hu not to investigate Zhou's involvement in the Bo Xilai case. He even ordered mental evaluations on Wang Lijun, the former Chongqing police chief, hoping to support the claim that Wang's allegations against Bo were pure fabrications because Wang was deranged.

At the same time, Zhou helped Ling manipulate the nomination process for the Politburo Standing Committee. Under normal circumstances, President Hu would solicit input through an informal vote from members of the Central Party Committee before the leadership transition. The balloting was originally planned to take place at a scheduled session on June 18. Fearing that his son's Ferrari crash could leak out anytime, Ling persuaded President Hu to reschedule the voting for May 7, 2012. Prior to the informal vote, Zhou and Ling campaigned vigorously among members of the Party Central Committee. Ling's chances looked good. The May 5 vote ranked him as the third–most electable candidate on the list, well positioned to win one of the five seats to be vacated.

However, Ling's action infuriated many who felt that the schedule change for the informal voting was done without a full explanation to members of the Politburo Standing Committee and without consulting retired leaders, such as former president Jiang Zemin. Some were said to have questioned Ling's motives in letters to President Hu.

In June, the cover-up of the Ferrari accident was exposed and former president Jiang Zemin reportedly called President Hu to his house, and asked if Hu was aware of it; Hu shook his head, saying he had been completely kept in the dark. Upon hearing that Ling had placed his son's body in a morgue for months without allowing his wife and relatives to visit for fear that people would find out, Jiang called Ling "a person devoid of human nature" and former premier Zhu Rongji said derisively that "Ling was worse than a beast."

An *Asiaweek* report later revealed another startling fact about Ling. By August 2012, Younge, one of the Tibetan women, had gradually recovered. As she was going through physical therapy in Beijing, she allegedly became bored and started texting and chatting with her friends about the accident. A month later, Younge suddenly lost consciousness and died. Her doctor attributed her death to complications from her injuries. Her parents, who had decided to bring her back to her hometown in the winter, were devastated, but told reporters, "If she failed to survive, it's fate." An insider told *Asiaweek* that officials had warned Younge's family members who came to look after her at the hospital not to talk with anyone about the accident. "It's a complex situation and the whole world wants to know the stories behind the accident," the official was quoted as saying to Younge's father. One of Younge's friends saw the young woman's death as suspicious. "In our country, a senior leader's wife would even dare kill a foreigner with poison and the police chief would willingly cover up. So, killing an ordinary Chinese is no biggie to those in power." Younge's body was cremated immediately. There was no autopsy. A simple funeral was held and Younge's family members were monitored and well provided for while they were in Beijing. They were told that her ashes had to remain in Beijing.

In August, party elders such as Jiang requested a thorough investigation of Ling Jihua. But with the Bo Xilai case still pending, the Politburo Standing Committee considered it politically risky to handle two high-profile corruption cases before the 18th Party Congress. As a compromise, Ling Jihua was banished from the political center. On September 1, 2012, Ling Jihua was demoted to director of the Central United Front Works Department, a largely ceremonial post.

There are rumors Ling may be prosecuted after Hu's retirement. A source connected with the General Office of the Party Central Committee told me at the Carnegie Club in New York City that many youth leaguers, and princelings, accused Ling of deceiving President Hu and misleading him on many key decisions. For example, he allegedly formed a secret alliance with Bo Xilai back in 2011—if both were elected to the Politburo Standing Committee, they would seize power from Xi Jinping, the new party general secretary. Ling had also allegedly arranged for President Hu to visit Chongqing and endorse the Chongqing model, but was forced to change the plan after the Neil Heywood case emerged and the majority of the Politburo Standing Committee joined the anti-Bo camp. In addition, the family members of both Ling Jihua and Bo Xilai are said to have engaged in illegal coal mining in Shanxi province and profited from their political connections. Ling's fall dealt a fatal blow to Hu and the youth league faction. In the final years of Hu's rule, Ling allied with another prominent youth leaguer, Li Yuanchao, who was in charge of the party's personnel and expanded his own influence by promoting, without President Hu's knowledge, a large group of youth leaguers, many of whom were his personal favorites. In the aftermath of the Ferrari accident, the princeling faction, led by the new leader Xi Jinping and backed by Jiang, used Ling's investigation as an excuse to purge youth leaguers connected with Ling, and Hu lost his leverage to intervene.

Li Yuanchao, a strong candidate for the Politburo Standing Committee, was kicked out in the October reshuffle. Li Keqiang, the premier-in-waiting, was the only youth leaguer left with any power on the Politburo Standing Committee. Ling had, however, over the past three years, made it difficult for Li to see or talk with Hu and pushed Li more and more toward the princelings' camp.

At the end of the 18th Party Congress in November 2012, Hu stepped down from all party posts: party general secretary and chairman of the Central Military Commission, which commands China's armed forces. Hu's decision came as a surprise—many had speculated that he would keep control of the military for two years, like his predecessors Jiang and Deng Xiaoping had done, so he could install more of his allies in key positions and protect the interests of his family and his loyalists, such as Ling Jihua.

In exchange for his full retirement, the Japanese newspaper *Asahi Shimbaum* reported, Hu wanted a systematic ban on intervention in the political sector by retired leaders, including the long-retired Jiang Zemin, age eighty-six, who had hovered over Hu for years after retirement. "It was a courageous move by Hu Jintao," claimed the paper. "Hu's action led to a second tidy transition since the Communist takeover in 1949, making it easier for the new leadership to initiate reforms."

To some Beijing observers, such as journalist Gao Yu, Hu's full retirement might have been forced—in the months leading up to the 18th Party Congress, Hu had indicated numerous times that he would stay around for two years. Gao Yu wrote:

> Over the past two decades, the Communist Party leaders and minions have accumulated a large amount of economic gains while they were in power. They see themselves on a big boat trying to navigate in treacherous water. Oftentimes it is not up to the leader to decide whether he leaves the boat or not. He is controlled by members of his own interest group. If he plunges headlong into the water, others would also drown.

Even though Hu might have been reluctant to relinquish power, the Ling Jihua scandal had weakened Hu's bargaining power, leaving him without many choices.

Throughout his career, Hu expressed no desire for posthumous fame. He was a technocrat who wanted only to complete his tenure peacefully and smoothly, without triggering an internal implosion. His famous slogan *Bu-zhe-teng* best illustrates his philosophy: "Don't rock the boat, don't make any changes." But what Hu has passed on to his successor is a country rife with scandal and on the verge of political collapse.

THE ULTIMATE LOSER
"WE'LL NEVER ALLOW HIM TO WALK OUT ALIVE"

SOME TRADITIONS are so deeply rooted that even the Chinese Communist Party knows better than to mess with them. The Ghost Festival is one such tradition, honored wherever Chinese people live, be it San Francisco or New York, London or Bangkok. By the Western calendar, it occurs around mid-November, when the spirits of the dead can cross over and visit the living. On that day, ancestors are honored with food and burning incense, and people burn stacks of fake money, intricately cut paper clothes, even paper TVs and exquisitely made paper houses at the graves of loved ones or on street corners (if the offerings are being made far from the hometowns). The Ghost Festival in 2012 marked the first anniversary of British businessman Neil Heywood's murder. Perhaps Wang Lulu, Heywood's Chinese widow, and his two children, twelve-year-old Olivia and eight-year-old Peter, followed the Chinese tradition and burned fake paper money for him, a man whose greed had led to his tragic end in Chongqing. At the time of writing, Wang and her children lived in London, but she has received promises from the Chinese government that she is free to visit China whenever she wants.

A week after the Ghost Festival, my coauthor paid an anonymous visit to the Lucky Holiday Hotel, which outwardly seemed to maintain an air of normalcy. A young female clerk at the front desk shook her head warily when asked if she had heard about Heywood. An insider later said all the staff members had been replaced after the murder was made public. At the villa where Heywood was killed, it was business as usual but when my coauthor poked his head into a downstairs room, the maid, who was making the bed, seemed quite nervous—almost as if Heywood's ghost had just appeared. She dialed the manager immediately.

It is part of Chinese traditional belief that if a ghost is angry, it will not leave the world of the living until it has exacted revenge on its enemies. One can only wonder whether Heywood's ghost has been lingering in Chongqing. Would he be able to find a medium and unveil the whole truth about the November 15 murder?

Would Heywood take comfort in the fact that his death triggered one of the biggest political crises in the history of Communist China? That his murder set in motion a sequence of events that toppled Bo Xilai, a ruthless political maverick, and almost derailed China's once-in-a-decade power transfer?

If this were a Shakespearean play, the convictions of Gu Kailai and Wang Lijun would set the stage for Bo, the main character, to reveal himself. Bo's dismissal from his powerful official posts in March 2012 and his detention in April heightened public suspense and fueled speculation. How would Bo's political foes finish him off? Would his career end with a bullet in the back of the head?

In late August 2012, political observers and Bo supporters published articles on *Mingjing News* speculating that Bo would make a soft landing. He would simply be kicked out of the Politburo and the Party Central Committee, in addition to losing his position as the Chongqing party chief—serious punishments for one who had devoted his life to climbing the party hierarchy, but also a slap on the wrist in comparison with the prospect of years of languishing in jail. The assumption was not completely off-base. During Gu Kailai's trial, Bo's name was never mentioned, as if he had never existed. In addition, no corruption charges were filed against the Bo family. An analyst commented that Bo was not aware of his wife's crime until later and that investigations into Bo's family finances had not yielded any concrete evidence. In September, Wang Lijun's lighter sentencing prompted more analysts to suggest that Bo would not face a criminal trial.

"Members of the Politburo are very divided over Bo's future," said an official to *Mingjing News* after the Wang Lijun trial on September 17:

> Bo's friends, including many princelings, still believe that he was unjustly punished for his courageous pro-people programs. Some

powerful figures, such as Zhou Yongkang, and even President Hu Jintao, are reluctant to punish Bo. Even though Bo's enemies want to destroy his chances of a comeback, they worry that an expanded investigation would implicate more people and create new political rivalries. Besides, with the volatile political situation in China, many officials understand very well that they could all end up like Bo someday. Come to think of it, who doesn't have a skeleton in their closet?

Such optimistic assessments pervading the Internet and private conversations must have energized Bo's supporters. On September 18, 2012, anti-Japan protests swept across China, with thousands of young people smashing made-in-Japan products and surrounding the Japanese Embassy and consulates to mark the anniversary of Japan's brutal invasion eighty-one years before. Demonstrators used the occasion to protest Japan's sovereignty claims over the Diaoyu Islands (Senkaku Islands in Japan), which the Chinese insisted were theirs. As Chinese security forces turned out en masse to contain demonstrations, they noticed some unexpected images: several hundred protesters, dressed up in Red Guard uniforms, carried portraits of Mao Zedong.

"The spectacle of hundreds of Mao portraits held aloft recalled the days of traumatic upheaval during China's Cultural Revolution and appeared to shock some," said the *Washington Post* when describing a demonstration in Beijing.

During an interview also with the *Washington Post,* a retired worker vigorously defended Bo Xilai: "In the history of the party, lots of cadres, including Chairman Mao, they all made mistakes, but everyone deserves a chance to correct the mistake. A comrade who has corrected his mistake is still a good comrade."

In Chongqing, protesters held banners that read, "Diaoyu Islands belong to China and Bo Xilai belongs to the people" and "We kick out the Japanese and welcome back Bo Xilai."

Such a show of support for Bo Xilai was said to have spooked China's senior leaders, who realized they had underestimated Bo's popularity. An official connected with the Central Party Committee revealed in a secure e-mail to *Mingjing News* that those pro-Bo images and slogans strengthened the position of the hawkish wing of the anti-Bo alliance, making them believe that severe punishment would send a stern message to Bo's supporters that the party was united in its decision against Bo. Any attempts to bring Bo back would be futile. "Those protesters meant to pressure the senior leadership to release Bo Xilai, but they ended up harming him," said the official.

A source close to Xi Jinping, the new party general secretary, doubted that the appearance of Bo supporters at the anti-Japan demonstrations had any impact on the party's decision relating to Bo's punishment. During our conversation at a Chinese restaurant in Manhattan on September 22, the source acknowledged that Bo's case had caused division among senior leaders in the early phase of the investigation, but many Politburo members were appalled by the mounting evidence of corruption presented by the Central Inspection and Discipline Commission. They changed their minds and opted for tougher punishment. Additionally, Wang Lijun shared with his handlers more negative information about Bo's conspiracy against several Politburo Standing Committee members to seek leniency after charges against him were published.

Two days later, *Mingjing News,* based on another tip provided by a senior official traveling in Europe, announced that Bo could face "double expulsion"—he would be expelled from the party and removed from public office. This meant that Bo could face criminal charges. Meanwhile, I had learned from three journalists with state media that Bo's double-expulsion request had been submitted to the Politburo for approval at an upcoming meeting. If the twenty-five Politburo members endorsed a decision, the state TV would broadcast the news on the night of September 29, 2012.

Over the next three days, news about Bo's upcoming double expulsion spread quickly on Weibo, rattling many of Bo's supporters. "I won't believe it until I hear it on CCTV," tweeted one person from Chongqing. "When Bo Senior was persecuted during the Cultural Revolution, Mao kept his party membership."

On the late morning of September 28, *Mingjing News* confirmed that the Politburo had approved Bo's double expulsion. After the story was posted, the stock markets in Shanghai and Shenzhen jumped 1 percent and 1.5 percent, respectively, in afternoon trading, following a sluggish start in the morning. Investors believed that the consensus by the Politburo on the Bo case meant that the power struggle would soon be over, and the country's focus would be redirected to its economy.

As expected, detailed charges against Bo headlined CCTV's prime-time news program that evening. Based on the state media, Politburo members "deliberated over and adopted an investigation report submitted by the party's Central Commission for Discipline Inspection." The report listed six charges against Bo Xilai:

1. Bo seriously violated party disciplines while heading the city of Dalian, Liaoning province, and the Ministry of Commerce and while serving as a Politburo member and as party chief of Chongqing municipality.

The report did not dwell on the specifics of Bo's violations, but the line conveyed clearly that the party had negated his whole political career, from 1984, when he became the deputy party chief of Jin County, to his most recent stint in Chongqing. Ironically, Bo had been touted as an official of "integrity" as recently as 2007, when he was transferred to Chongqing. At the changeover ceremony, the head of the party's personnel department presented Bo as a person who was "honest, upright, and dedicated to his career" and who was "politically mature; possessing strong principles and pioneering spirit." Over the past decade, the state media carried numerous features about Bo, portraying him as a rising political star. "What a difference six months make," commented an editorial on RedChinaCN.net, a popular leftist website in China. "It seems only yesterday that Bo was a core member of the senior leadership team. Overnight, he has turned into a total villain."

Gao Yu, a journalist in Beijing, echoed similar sentiments. "The report gives one the impression that Bo has been committing evil deeds from the very beginning of his career," she said. "If that was the case, how was it that he kept getting promoted? Who is lying here, the party or Bo Xilai?"

2. Bo abused his power, made serious mistakes, and bore major responsibility in the Wang Lijun incident and the murder of Neil Heywood.

The most striking charge in the report was to link Bo explicitly to the murder of Heywood, even though he was not referenced in the trial of Gu Kailai. Based on previous state media coverage, charges against Bo seemed to be largely based on the following: (a) At the end of December 2011, Bo illegally detained four police officers who had been assigned to investigate the Neil Heywood case and forced them to pledge that his wife was framed for murder. (b) When Wang Lijun notified him that his wife was a murder suspect, he sacked Wang from his police chief's position and illegally detained three of Wang's staff members for interrogation. (c) Bo allegedly plotted to have Wang killed, making it appear that Wang was mentally ill and had committed suicide. Until new evidence is presented at Bo's trial, it is not clear if and how Bo was involved in the plotting and cover-up of Heywood's murder. The charge further confirmed the speculation that Gu's trial was a political conspiracy to criminalize and justify Bo's ouster.

3. Bo Xilai used his position to seek profits for others and took bribes either directly or through family members. His position was also abused by his wife, Gu Kailai, to seek profits for others.

How much money did Bo embezzle over the span of his political career? Before September 28, 2012, there were several figures online, from US $6 billion, claimed by a Japanese newspaper, to US $1 billion, as reported on Boxun. The Chinese-language service of Deutsch Welle stated Bo had taken bribes in the amount of nearly 100 million yuan, one-third of which was provided by his billionaire friend, Xu Ming.

Meanwhile, a Beijing-based analyst who had read the full investigative report submitted by the Central Commission for Discipline Inspection listed the amount at 26 million yuan (US $4 million)—Bo accepted 6 million yuan directly and his family members took 20 million yuan on his behalf. This figure was later corroborated by the Hong

Kong–based *Ming Pao* newspaper, which was briefed by different sources in Beijing. After *Mingjing News* published the 26 million figure, a blogger with the alias "Chinese Injuries" wrote, "Only 26 million yuan? Bo Xilai is truly one of the cleanest officials in China. A county chief can easily embezzle that amount."

Others suspected that the amount of bribes Bo took was much higher and that the government had reduced the number to mask the severity of corruption within the party and minimize damage to the party's reputation. Since February 2012, there had been numerous stories about how his son lived a luxury life abroad—he attended elite schools that charged exorbitant tuition, and drove expensive cars. In addition, the Bo family supposedly owned a US $3.75 million apartment in London and another apartment that is being rented out at US $3,500-a-month in Cambridge, Massachusetts.

Upon hearing about Bo's embezzlement charges, a Chongqing resident dug out excerpts of Bo's past speeches and posted them on the Internet. One excerpt was taken from his remarks at the press conference in March 2012: "The media have spread rumors about me and my family. In fact, my son, my wife, and I have no personal assets. It's been like this over the past decade." Another was from his inspirational quotes, which were widely distributed in Chongqing when he was party chief: "Integrity is a kind of happiness. A person lives a stress-free life if he is not greedy and doesn't take bribes. He is at ease and focuses wholeheartedly on his work."

A commentator on Voice of America remarked with sarcasm, "How can you not be touched by such noble teachings? On the same note, how much trust should we place on other senior leaders who are preaching similar messages?"

4. Bo had or maintained improper sexual relationships with a number of women.

According to a source who had close ties with the Politburo, investigators presented a status report on Bo Xilai at a Politburo meeting on September 28, 2012. While chronicling in detail each bribe Bo and his family members had taken over the past two decades, the report also described Bo's "perverted lifestyle" and listed the names of women with whom Bo had had improper sexual relations. As expected, the "perverted lifestyle" description grabbed the most attention. "Nobody seemed to care how much money Bo Xilai had embezzled," said the source. "Many members carefully perused Bo's womanizing file, trying to figure out how 'Erection Bo' could do something that they were not capable of," he joked.

The line "Bo had improper sexual relations with a number of women," even though vague, also caught the imagination of the prurient and the curious public. Stories of Bo's affairs—he gained the reputation of "Erection Bo" when he was still mayor of Dalian—had been around for many years. In 2005, a magazine in Hong Kong carried an open letter by a victim who accused Bo of "biting and bruising a model's nipples" in the early 1990s. A recent report on *Dongsen News* alleged that two of Bo Xilai's staff members had been assigned to arrange pretty young women to sleep with Bo. His womanizing continued when he moved to Chongqing in 2007 and Wang Lijun allegedly secretly recorded many of Bo's trysts. Boxun reported that Bo slept with more than one hundred women and on several occasions, he allegedly pimped his "girlfriends" to his friends after he was tired of them.

Investigators identified twenty-seven of the one hundred women, many of whom were models, well-known actresses, anchors at CCTV, and pop singers. *Mingjing News* obtained a partial list on September 29 and published it with only their last names.

The Bo Xilai "mistress list" spread quickly on the Internet, causing panic among female celebrities whose last names happened to match the ones on the list. Several actresses and models declared on Sina Weibo that they never knew Bo and had never been to Chongqing. Xu Xin, a legal scholar in Beijing, told the Hong Kong–based *Apple Daily* that PR agents for several female celebrities were instructed to monitor Weibo and work to have posts mentioning their clients deleted posthaste.

Once again, rumors about Zhang Ziyi, star of *Memoirs of a Geisha* and *Crouching Tiger, Hidden Dragon,* resurfaced because her last name was mentioned prominently on the list. As I mentioned in the previous chapter, Zhang's lawyers lodged lawsuits in the US and Hong Kong against Boxun and *Apple Daily* in June 2012, after the outlets ran salacious reports about Zhang's alleged encounters with Bo. On September 29, Zhang Ziyi lost her cool. On her Weibo, she wrote an angry note: "I have already responded to those who harbor ulterior motives five months ago. My response today is: 'Go ask your mother. If she was there [with Bo Xilai], so was I.'"

Many political analysts I know were surprised that details of Bo's sexual transgressions had been included in the official investigation report and listed as one of Bo's offenses. In China, although wife-swapping or having private sex parties is considered a criminal offense, adultery is not. It is not clear from the official statement whether Bo had participated in any group sexual activities that could be considered "assembled imprudence."

Liu Lu, an exiled Chinese lawyer in the US, believed the party had fanned the flames of the womanizing accusations with the sole intent of destroying Bo's reputation and diminishing his popularity. Liu called the party's practice despicable and hypocritical: "Womanizing is a common trait among senior Communist Party leaders," Liu told *Mingjing News*. "In the modern era, movie studios and TV stations have become harems for party leaders. Why do they single out Bo? It's quite obvious. The party tries to use Bo's sexual misconduct to masquerade the true nature of his case—it is a power struggle." A blogger named "Old Unemployed Peasant" agreed: "If you maintained a proper relationship with the party, your relations with numerous women would be proper. If you have lost favor with the party, your relationship with numerous women would be improper."

5. Bo has violated organizational and personnel disciplines and made erroneous decisions in the promotion of personnel, resulting in serious consequences.

When commenting on this charge, which obviously refers to Bo's hiring and promotion of his former police chief, a professor at Beijing

University who refused to disclose his name during an interview on October 4, 2012, said sarcastically, "Bo Xilai is blamed for making erroneous personnel decisions. Then who should we blame for promoting Bo? When he was promoted from the mayor of Dalian to the minister of commerce and the party chief of Chongqing, did the leadership conduct any audits or background checks? How come they never found anything? Who should be held accountable for creating Bo, such a monster?"

6. The investigation also uncovered evidence that suggests his involvement in other crimes.

This vague and yet all-embracing statement leaves the door open for prosecutors to add more charges later. For years Bo was known to be responsible for the deaths of two of his opponents when he was in Dalian and two of Wang Lijun's staff members in January 2012. In addition, relatives of those who had been targeted during Bo's anti-crime campaign claimed that the Chongqing police had used torture to extract confessions and many innocent people had been executed on false charges. Analysts say these could all be dredged up if the other charges fail to convict Bo.

The Communist Party hailed the double expulsion as an illustration of its efforts to "rule the country in accordance with the law." In announcing the charges against Bo, the senior leadership moved fast to clear the way for the high-profile trial. On October 25, ten days before the 18th Party Congress, China's top legislature expelled Bo, stripping him of his legal immunity from criminal charges. The news raised false expectations that Bo could be on trial before the leadership transition on November 8, 2012, because President Hu Jintao was pressured to resolve the case before his imminent retirement. But the trial never materialized. News of intense power jockeying in the days leading up to the Congress, the Ling Jihua scandal, and the *New York Times* exposé of Premier Wen Jiabao's hidden family wealth might have delayed the proceedings. "The party did not want any more distractions before the Congress," said a source in Beijing. However, at a pre-Congress meeting, members of the party's Central Committee ratified

Bo's double expulsions, which finally put a period on Bo's twenty-eight-year political career, even though he had not yet been convicted in court. With his party membership revoked, Bo's chances of a comeback have become very remote.

Although the party declared the end of Bo's political life, Wang Juntao, a prominent Chinese dissident in New York City, believes in the opposite. "The rampant corruption and widespread social injustices have generated discontent and hatred among the public," said Wang. "Many saw Bo as their leader who dared challenge the status quo. They understand that Bo is no angel, but they still worship him because those who brought him down are more evil and despicable."

Wang said Bo has been made a martyr, a banner and symbol of a potentially powerful political force: "The party has to address these legitimate concerns and give them a voice within the party. Suppression will only marginalize them, turning them into a lethal opposition force and a formidable political challenge."

In October, nearly 400 activists, academics, and dissidents, some of whom didn't even consider themselves in Bo's corner, wrote an open letter to the National People's Congress demanding that China's legislature allow Bo to defend himself before lawmakers. "Whether Bo Xilai broke the law or not should be based on facts; we ask for openness and fairness," the letter said. "If the legitimate rights of . . . former Chongqing Party Secretary Bo Xilai . . . can be violated as if by lightning, then how much hope is there that the rights of ordinary citizens will be protected under the law?"

To Tie Liu, a writer and journalist who suffered tremendously during Mao's anti-rightist campaign in the late 1950s, dismissed the open letter as a desperate stunt by leftists. "The open letter will only put more nails in Bo's coffin," he said. Tie Liu also felt Bo's removal represented a significant step forward. "This is a triumph for those who support Deng Xiaoping's open-door and economic policies," he commented in an article online. "This is a triumph for those who promote freedom and democracy in China. The imprisonment of Bo will deliver a death blow to the rising Maoist group, marking China's farewell to the 'red' disaster. I hope the country will start a new wave of reassessing Mao's policies and uncovering the brutal truth about

Mao's rule. At the same time, the fall of Mao will create a favorable condition for China's political reforms."

Tie Liu's views were consistent with those of the party, but could go only so far. The news did not bring public cheers or raise the public's hopes for the party. "Before a new king is crowned, a giant scapegoat has to be slaughtered as a sacrifice," said Yang Haipeng, a well-known blogger and former reporter with *Caijing* magazine. A tweet by @penyuangzhong summarized the views of many: "Bo Xilai abused power and employed tyrannical means to get rid of his political opponents. In the end, a bigger tyrant came in and toppled him. It has nothing to do with reformists or Maoists. The Bo Xilai case shows that a power without checks and balances is corrupt; a power that is above criticism [is] shameless; a power without supervision [is] dictatorial."

Lu Di, a UK-based political analyst, provided his straightforward answer: "Bo Xilai's vaulting political ambition and his Chongqing model are seen as a threat and blatant attempts to seize power and split the party. For the leadership, that's a cardinal sin."

Lu Di's remarks accurately summed up the essence of Bo's demise. He has broken the taboo by challenging the party's mantra of "uniting tightly around the Party Central Committee, led by the party general secretary."

Taikungpao, a pro-Communist newspaper in Hong Kong, described Bo's political style in a September 28, 2012, article:

> Surrounded by bodyguards, Bo shook hands with the cheering crowd. He delivered stirring speeches without a script and peppered his media sound bites with personalized language. These scenes remind one of a candidate during a presidential election in the US.

This couldn't be a more apt description. Bo used the gimmicks of a Western politician and reached out to the public with a populist agenda, which made the president of China look incompetent. The criticism by Zhang Dejiang, his successor in Chongqing, was more revealing. Zhang accused Bo of being self-important and self-absorbed, claiming that Bo had attempted to establish another political center in Chongqing: "We should always remember that the accomplishment in

Chongqing will not be possible without the leadership of the Central Party Committee and the State Council."

In a culture where parents advise their children to behave according to the adage "The gun will shoot the head of the flock," Bo's relentless self-promotion and maneuvering also alienated many of his fellow princelings, who increasingly felt that Bo was usurping too many political "shares," leaving them with little to grasp. Thus, when Wang Lijun escaped to the US Consulate, the leadership finally had had enough. "In the end, all factions abandoned Bo because the crisis poses a challenge to the legitimacy of the party itself," said Li Cheng, a senior fellow at the Brookings Institution. "The stakes are very high, and the challenge facing the party leadership is intimidating."

At the time of this writing, Bo had been placed under a new round of investigation by the state prosecutor for his alleged offenses. "Coercive measures would be imposed on him in accordance with the law," reported the state media. Once the judicial investigation is completed, legal experts say Bo will face a criminal trial. Since the courts are subordinate to the party, Bo's trial will likely be a mere formality; a highly choreographed affair. The charges will largely be based on recommendations provided by the party's Central Commission for Discipline Inspection. No matter how vigorously his lawyers defend him, a guilty verdict will almost certainly await Bo.

"Bo's trial will now matter less to the Politburo Standing Committee, which has already moved on," a Beijing-based legal scholar said recently. "But the new leaders will use Bo's punishment for another purpose—showcasing the party's determination to clamp down on corruption and abuse of power."

Gao Zicheng, a well-known Chinese lawyer, told Deutsch Welle's Chinese-language service that Bo would receive lifelong imprisonment, if not the death penalty. At present, an official could face up to ten years in jail if he or she embezzles 100,000 yuan (US $16,000). Bo has allegedly taken more than 26 million yuan in bribes, according to overseas media reports. He Weifang, a professor at the Beijing University Law School, also predicted during an interview with Voice of America that Bo would get at least twenty years or even a suspended death penalty.

Regardless of what type of prison sentence Bo might receive, his opponents have one goal in mind—crushing any future chance of Bo's comeback. A source who is related to a top leader in Beijing whispered to me—nonchalantly over dinner during a recent visit to New York City—that "It doesn't matter how Bo's case is handled. We'll never allow him to walk out alive."

THE BACKSTAGE WINNER: LONG LIVE THE KING FATHER

EMPEROR KANGXI lived between 1654 and 1722 in the Qing Dynasty, ascended the throne at the age of eight, and ruled China for sixty-one years, becoming the longest-reigning emperor in Chinese history. During his reign, his wife and concubines gave birth to more than fifty children—thirty-five of them were boys. Such a big contingent of princes spawned a fierce power struggle. Over time, nine of the sons emerged as powerful political and military figures, fiercely contending for the title of crown prince. Yinzhi was his eldest son, but the honor went to Kangxi's second son, whose mother was Kangxi's first and favorite spouse, who died in childbirth.

Displeased with the decision, Yinzhi attempted to sabotage the transition and, in 1708, when the crown prince was temporarily deposed after he fell out of favor with his father, Yinzhi was assigned to take custody of his younger brother. Lured by imperial power, Yinzhi urged his father to have the deposed crown prince put to death, and to install him instead as the next emperor. Yinzhi's raw ambition reportedly shocked and disgusted Kangxi, who called his eldest son a "treacherous subject." Other princes deserted Yinzhi, alleging he had once used sorcery to try to unseat the crown prince. Kangxi stripped Yinzhi of his princely title and placed him under life-long house arrest to prevent future disruptions in the succession plan.

If Bo Xilai resembles the overly insidious and ambitious first prince Yinzhi, the modern-day version of Kangxi is former president Jiang Zemin. When Wang Lijun disclosed to the senior leaders after his botched defection that Bo had attempted to disrupt the previously negotiated transition and threaten the ascension of the designated successor, the powerful patriarch, or the king father, intervened. Jiang rallied Bo's political foes and had Bo locked up, even though Bo was widely believed to be one of his protégés.

More than a decade after he notionally retired to Shanghai, Jiang's words still hold sway among senior Chinese leaders, like a king father in imperial China. His long absence from the public view softened his image, making memory grow fonder for a large sector of the populace that had disliked him intensely when he was in power. In comparison with President Hu Jintao, many of Jiang's former critics have started to see the former president in a different light, someone who was a stabilizing force, like a monarch.

Jiang's influence was most evident in the media hoopla over reports of his "premature death."

In April 2011, Jiang visited his hometown of Yangzhou, a city near Shanghai. Knowing that he fancied calipash, the green gelatinous substance found under the shell of the turtle and a local delicacy, city officials commissioned farmers to catch wild turtles in the river and brought them to Jiang's favorite restaurant to be cooked and served. A few days after Jiang returned to Shanghai, he began to suffer from very high fever. His staff members checked him into the Eastern China Hospital, but doctors there could not figure out the cause. When the leadership in Beijing was contacted, they ordered officials in Shanghai to transfer Jiang to the Beijing 301 Hospital, an army hospital where senior leaders generally received treatment.

As doctors frantically searched for a diagnosis, rumors started to swirl. Several media outlets in Hong Kong quoted insiders as saying that Jiang had liver cancer and his heart had stopped. One story even claimed that Jiang had been struck with a virus from mosquitoes while in the southwestern province of Guangxi and the virus had caused severe complications. The story claimed that senior leaders had brought Jiang back to Beijing, where preparations were already under way for a grand funeral ceremony.

The speculation peaked on July 1, when Jiang was absent from the celebration of the ninetieth anniversary of the founding of the Chinese Communist Party. At noon on July 6, a local government news site in mainland China featured a portrait of Jiang Zemin with a caption that read, "Eternity to Our Beloved Comrade Jiang Zemin." At six o'clock that evening, ATV, an influential TV station in Hong Kong, interrupted its regular programming and announced that Jiang had died. When the spokesperson at the Chinese Foreign Ministry declined to respond to a question by a BBC reporter about Jiang's health, media outlets around the world started to speculate that something had gone wrong. Many analysts expressed concerns about Jiang's demise and how it would affect the power transitions in 2012. The next day, as the ATV announcement was reposted on thousands of websites around the world, the Chinese state news agency Xinhua, quoting "authoritative sources," declared that overseas media reports were "pure rumor."

News about Jiang's death was finally put to rest in early October when he appeared at a public event. Subsequently, an official explained to *Mingjing Monthly* that Jiang's illness had not been serious. A young Chinese doctor who had been trained at Johns Hopkins Hospital in the US found the cause of Jiang's fever—a parasite in the wild turtle that Jiang had consumed in his hometown. Medicine was rushed from Japan and Jiang was cured. Whether he was kept abreast of the international media storm surrounding his illness is not known.

But the media attention focused on his personal health underscored Jiang's influence as the king father, especially in the days leading up to the Party Congress. In February 2012, after Wang Lijun went to the US Consulate, Bo Xilai was said to have contacted Jiang, seeking his help in putting out the fire, but Jiang refused to see him. According to an insider, President Hu consulted with Jiang frequently after Bo's removal. The king father urged Hu to build a criminal case against Bo and "hold him accountable for the party and the people." Jiang's position played a decisive role in Bo's final demise.

Jiang Zemin, whose name means "benefitting the people," came to power in 1989, after Deng Xiaoping and a group of revolutionary veterans brutally crushed the Tiananmen Square protests and removed Zhao Ziyang, the reform-minded party general secretary. Jiang appeared to be the perfect alternative. He was the party chief in China's second-largest city of Shanghai and had closed down a liberal-leaning newspaper, the *World Economic Herald*. When students marched on the street in protest of his decision, Jiang had stood firm. Deng Xiaoping and the party elders were reportedly impressed with Jiang's conservative sensibilities and strong principles in his fight against the invasion of "Western liberal ideas." More important, he was raised in a revolutionary martyr's family—his uncle was a famed national hero during the resistance war against Japan in the 1940s. While in Shanghai, Jiang had the reputation of being respectful and compliant, someone Deng Xiaoping felt he could control. Deng made him the new party general secretary.

The promotion came as a shock to the sixty-three-year-old Jiang. An article in the Beijing-based *New Legend* weekly magazine described Jiang's sudden meteoric rise, offering a glimpse of the erratic succession process:

In 1989, Jiang Zemin, who was the party chief of Shanghai, turned sixty-three. After retirement, he had planned to leave politics and become a professor at his alma mater—Shanghai Jiaotong University.

In mid-June, Jiang Zemin received an urgent notice from the Central Party Committee Secretariat, urging him to come to Beijing right away. When he rushed to the airport, he noticed a private jet waiting for him on the runway. But when he arrived in Beijing, the car that came to pick him up was an ordinary Volkswagen Santana. By then, he was told that it was Deng Xiaoping's private car and the paramount leader was waiting for him at a château in Beijing's West Mountain resort. . . .

On June 24, news of Jiang's appointment was announced to the whole world. His relatives and family members were equally as shocked as China watchers in the West. Jiang Zemin himself felt unprepared. At the subsequent Fourth Plenary Session of the 13th Party Congress, Jiang was officially elected to be the party general secretary and to the Politburo Standing Committee.

On September 4, at a conference with Jiang and the new leadership team, Deng Xiaoping brought up the topic of his retirement and disclosed that he was ready to give up his baton. Then Deng quickly moved to a new topic—the transition plan. Deng Xiaoping scanned the room and fixed his eyes on Jiang, who had been in his party general secretary's position for barely one hundred days. "The Military Commission needs to have a chairman," he said, emphasizing every single word. "I propose that Jiang Zemin be confirmed as chairman of the Military Commission." After the conference, Deng Xiaoping officially submitted his full resignation.

The article failed to mention that Deng not only chose Jiang to succeed him, but also picked a successor for Jiang to ensure smooth leadership transition over the next two decades.

During Jiang's first year in office, nobody believed he would last: First, he was elevated to the country's top post without prior political accomplishment and without a strong power base inside the party. Second, even though Deng had retired, he still wielded significant power as a king father and he could depose Jiang anytime. Last, many felt that Jiang did not have the stature of such "red emperors" as Mao Zedong and Deng Xiaoping. He liked to show off his English and Russian skills, belt out karaoke songs, and play the piano when he got close to one. Westerners might see those qualities as charming, but the Chinese public frowned upon his "flamboyancy," some calling him a "member of the Communist performance troupe."

Jiang had a shaky start but survived. He first cultivated the support of powerful party elders, including Xi Zhongxun, whose son is Xi Jinping, the current party general secretary, and Bo Yibo, the father of Bo Xilai. In an effort to appease the conservative wings of the party, he followed a leftist agenda in the first year, vowing to fight against "bourgeois liberalization" and stick with the path of socialism by suppressing growth of capitalistic ventures. Jiang's leftist policies went against Deng's belief that the only way for the Chinese Communist Party to survive in the aftermath of the collapse of Communism in Eastern Europe was to develop the country's economy. In 1992, Deng was said to have become impatient with Jiang's lack of leadership in economic reform, but by then, his debilitating Parkinson's disease deprived Deng of the energy and influence to topple Jiang. Instead, Deng slapped Jiang's face, metaphorically, by taking a high-profile tour of southern China where he had first ignited the country's economic reforms and stated in no ambivalent terms that the pace of reform was not fast enough, and the "central leadership" bore direct responsibility.

Deng's words awoke Jiang, who did an about-face to promote Deng's reform agenda and save his precarious political career. Starting in 1993, Jiang Zemin embraced capitalism with both arms. Jiang was an overnight convert to the pursuit of economic growth and the development of a socialist market economy—turning a centrally planned socialist economy into a government-regulated market economy became his trademark accomplishment. He even created the "Three Represents" formula, allowing Communist Party membership to capitalists.

Under Jiang and Premier Zhu Rongji, a vibrant middle class emerged. Though strictly speaking capitalists, the nouveau riche gradually became a formidable political and economic force able to influence government policies, and the Internet turned into an effective alternative to government-controlled media. More people were allowed to leave China and pursue their studies abroad and experience the West's much-touted "freedom."

Jiang Zemin and Zhu Rongji were considered pro-West. They grew up in the pre-Communist era and were well versed in Western science. Both experienced the horrors of Mao's Cultural Revolution and saw the pressing need for China to embrace Western civilization, if not its "democratic" system. Jiang was frequently criticized for being image conscious, but his supporters argued that Jiang boosted China's international status and image by orchestrating the country's successful bids to join the World Trade Organization and to host the 2008 Summer Olympics.

Jiang and most of his contemporaries in the senior leadership team were technocrats, not creators, but implementers. They copied Deng's economic reform agenda and carried it to the extreme. In the Mao era, people were fanned to frenzy by Mao's revolutions and, under Jiang in the 1990s, the whole nation became obsessed with making money. Little else mattered. The government's single-minded strategies of reforming state enterprise and stimulating growth led to the bankruptcies of thousands of state companies, leaving millions of workers unemployed. Public assets fell into the hands of a small group of well-connected entrepreneurs, some of whom were princelings. Unbridled capitalism under a totalitarian system spawned massive corruption within the government and led to a moral vacuum as Communist beliefs collapsed. The widening gap between the rich and poor, and between the developed coastal region and the underdeveloped hinterland, caused widespread social discontent.

Jiang rejected calls by dissidents and party liberals to revisit the issues raised in Tiananmen Square in 1989—corruption and accountability within the party. However, many jailed dissidents and protesters were released and some were allowed to leave the country. There are those who argue that Jiang effectively used prodemocracy activists as hostages in exchange for Western support for the country's other political initiatives, but often overlooked is that many party hardliners who played a prominent role in the bloody suppressions of June 1989 were quietly purged from the Jiang administration.

His relatively enlightened approach to the events of 1989 was canceled out by his persecution of practitioners of Falun Gong. Falun Gong, which claimed to have millions of adherents worldwide, alleged that thousands have died of torture during incarceration. It has gone so far as to allege that, in some cases, the government harvested their organs. Jiang has been portrayed by Falun Gong as an "evil enemy of the public," and practitioners filed multiple lawsuits against Jiang and other senior leaders overseas.

In addition, Jiang adeptly employed the Central Commission for Discipline Inspection to consolidate power and eliminate his opponents under the guise of corruption. One example was Chen Xitong, the former party chief of Beijing, who reportedly obstructed Jiang's policies with a group of like-minded officials known as the "Beijing clique."

On April 5, 2005, when the deputy mayor of Beijing, a close friend of Chen Xitong, was found shot dead in what was determined to be a suicide near an official guest house after he received news that he would be investigated, Jiang used the shooting as an excuse to take action against Chen. In July 1995, Jiang ordered the Central Commission for Discipline Inspection to review Chen's case and hand its findings to the court. In February 1998, Chen was officially arrested on charges of corruption and dereliction of duty. The Supreme People's Court in Beijing sentenced Chen to sixteen years imprisonment. In the official verdict, the scope of the crime was much smaller than previously reported. He was charged with accepting about US $80,000 worth of gifts from foreigners without declaring or turning it over to the government. Between 1990 and 1992, he used about US $4.2 million in municipal construction funds to build two villas in the suburbs of Beijing, allegedly as investments for the government. He and his friends simply brought their mistresses over for extended stays in the villas, spending US $40,000 on food and entertainment and service charges.

Overseas media concluded that the Chen Xitong's case was politically motivated, an apparent scheme by Jiang to intimidate his political opponents and consolidate his power base. The fall of Chen led to the convictions of more officials inside the Beijing municipal government.

In the years after 1997, with the deaths of Deng Xiaoping and other revolutionary veterans, Jiang safely occupied the paramount leader's seat and elevated many of his supporters from Shanghai to high positions within the party, the military, and the government to ensure his legacy was preserved and his family interests were protected.

At the time of his retirement in 2002, his followers even proposed creating a national security committee to institutionalize Jiang's paramount position. In the end, Jiang reluctantly jettisoned the idea. He understood clearly that the Chinese people, including the 70 million Communist Party members, had long detested the bloody power struggles. People could no longer accept leaders with lifelong tenures. If Jiang dared to go against the current, the gigantic ship of the Communist Party—rotten and riddled with holes—was in danger of capsizing. Thus, Jiang stepped down, continuing the peaceful transition process started by Deng Xiaoping.

Since Jiang's retirement, his name has never failed to appear at the top, right beneath Hu's, at important events. Insiders know the name order is not merely ceremonial. There used to be a popular saying: "Deng Xiaoping's power was felt by his mysterious absence, but Jiang Zemin reveals his power by his constant presence." In 2006, when Hu Jintao ordered the detention of Chen Liangyu, the former party secretary of Shanghai and a Jiang protégé, many thought Chen's downfall was part of a move by Hu to purge the party of Jiang supporters. It did not take long for analysts to realize that Chen's arrest was at the behest of Jiang Zemin, who felt betrayed by Chen, who allegedly had slighted members of Jiang's family on numerous occasions. A team of investigators from the Central Commission for Discipline Inspection was stationed in Shanghai for months collecting and examining the evidence against Chen. In September 2006, Chen was dismissed for alleged corruption related to the misuse of money in Shanghai's social security fund. The state media portrayed him as a corrupt official who had multiple mistresses. In April 2008, Chen was sentenced to eighteen years in prison on charges of dereliction of duty, abuse of power, and accepting bribes.

Such abuse of the power invested in the Central Commission for Discipline Inspection added to a sense of insecurity among the ruling elite. When Bo Xilai was detained for investigation, many people thought of Chen Xitong and Chen Liangyu: both men had headed large Chinese cities and both had been brought down by Jiang Zemin.

Jiang's lingering power was also illustrated by his critical role in the choice of Hu Jintao as president.

In October 2007, when the Party Congress concluded, many political analysts were surprised to note that Xi Jinping, a princeling and party chief of Shanghai, was anointed heir apparent to the country's top post, rather than President Hu Jintao's favorite, Li Keqiang, the party chief of Liaoning province. As time went by, many behind-the-scenes negotiations were taking place, and the media found plenty of leaks. According to sources, Xi Jinping's rise was the work of Jiang and his allies. As conditions for their retirement, several of Jiang's allies forced Hu to compromise and accept Xi Jinping as the next party general secretary. Skeptics refused to believe the story until 2009, when Xi Jinping visited Germany and presented a special gift to German Chancellor Angela Merkel: a collection of Jiang Zemin's writing.

Xi Jinping was not the only princeling who enjoyed the backing of Jiang Zemin. He was also said to have taken Bo Xilai under his wing early in Bo's early career. Though unconfirmed, Bo Xilai's father, one of the party veterans in the Deng era, secretly advised and helped Jiang in the early 1990s, when Deng Xiaoping's confidence in Jiang wavered and he was contemplating whether to fire him; Jiang repaid the support at such a crucial time by helping Bo Xilai.

However, as time went by, Bo Xilai gradually lost favor with Jiang, who disliked his protégé's deceptive personality and unabashed political ambitions. A friend of Jiang Zemin's son shared the following story over dinner at a restaurant in Manhattan:

> In the late 1990s, at the invitation of Mayor Bo Xilai, Jiang visited Dalian. In an effort to please Jiang, Bo Xilai put up many life-size posters of Jiang all over the city. However, the day after Jiang left, Bo had his staff members tear down all the Jiang posters. The news reportedly upset Jiang, who saw Bo as a mere sycophant. More important, Jiang was said to be shocked when he saw the two gigantic white marbled ornamental pillars in Dalian's Xinhai Square—the pillars, symbols of the emperor's imperial power, are only seen in front of Forbidden City in Tiananmen Square.

The Bo Xilai scandal turned into an unexpected opportunity for Jiang Zemin, who many had thought incapacitated by poor health. In April, when Bo was under investigation, the Politburo Standing Committee remained divided on how to approach the Bo issue and President Hu Jintao displayed his trademark hesitancy. Both the anti-Bo and pro-Bo factions looked to Jiang Zemin for guidance. The patriarch did not disappoint. He was one of the first veterans to speak out forcefully against Bo Xilai. His widely circulated words, "Bo has crossed the basic line of human civilization," dealt a devastating blow to Bo's supporters.

In April 2012, Jiang made more and more public appearances. He first met with the chief of the coffee chain Starbucks and then showed up at a musical at the National Center for Performing Arts. The state media carried a big photo and an enthusiastic description:

> Jiang Zemin walked into the theater in big strides. He was glowing with health and radiating vigor. The audience gave the former president Jiang a long-lasting standing ovation.

The message was clear—Jiang was healthy and would play a critical role in the Bo Xilai case. He traveled to Beijing and met with senior leaders within the party and the military to affirm support for the removal of Bo Xilai.

In September 2012, when President Hu Jintao's chief of staff, Ling Jihua, was demoted, Jiang and his protégés jumped at the opportunity to purge Hu's allies in the Politburo. Jiang and his designated successor, Xi Jinping, reshuffled the original lineup and successfully placed reliable allies in the Politburo Standing Committee, extending Jiang's influence for another decade.

Although many political leaders become more conservative in retirement, Jiang seems to have done the opposite and adopted a more radical stance. Credible rumors suggest Jiang intends to protect his legacy by instructing his successors to implement political reform. In October, a close friend of the Jiang family quoted Jiang as warning the Politburo members at a small gathering that "if the Chinese Communist Party doesn't initiate any political reforms, we could be toppled by a coup and end up tragically." According to the same source, Jiang has repeatedly urged senior leaders in August to reverse the party's position on the demands of the 1989 Tiananmen Square movement. "We can't drag it on any longer. We need to have a plan to resolve this issue and approach the issue step by step," he allegedly said.

There has been no confirmation of Jiang's words, or of his intent, but this account shows how Jiang's loyalists are attempting to boost his legacy as an open- and reform-minded leader. Like Emperor Kangxi, Jiang's biggest contribution may well be his effort to afford a smooth path for Xi Jinping's ascension, even if it means eliminating another princeling. By destroying Bo Xilai for good, Jiang not only helps Xi remove a visible challenger, but also deters potential challengers in the future.

THE WINNER IS . . . "HAIL TO THE NEW CHIEF"

IT WAS SUPPOSED to be a winner's celebration, the successful culmination of years of careful planning and sifting of candidates, but it felt more like a wake. On November 8, 2012, the much-anticipated 18th Chinese Communist Party Congress met in Beijing.

More than 2,200 delegates from across the country descended on the capital city for the quinquennial meeting to set new directions for the party and select the party's new leaders. The event marked a happy ending to what the state media called a "golden age" under President Hu Jintao and the beginning of a new era.

To mark this festive occasion, party censors issued directives to TV and radio stations nationwide, urging them to broadcast laudatory pro-party programs and banning any songs that contained inauspicious messages or words. A musician in Beijing tweeted that a radio station had allegedly removed a well-known love song called "Love You to Death" off the air simply because of the word "death."

However, at the opening ceremony, references to death reverberated inside the cavernous Great Hall of the People. First on the agenda, outgoing party General Secretary Hu Jintao asked delegates to observe a three-minute silence to pay tribute to deceased Communist founders such as Mao Zedong and Deng Xiaoping. The somber mood pervaded as Hu delivered, his face fixed in his signature stern expression, a one-hour-forty-minute speech, in which he issued a dire warning to his fellow party officials and made some gloomy allusions:

> Combating corruption and promoting political integrity, which is a major political issue of great concern to the people, is a clear-cut and long-term political commitment of the party. If we fail to handle this issue well, it could prove fatal to the party, and even cause the collapse of the party and the fall of the state.

Reuters and other Western news organizations published revealing photos of delegate reaction during Hu's largely empty speech, which was filled with political jargon from a bygone era. Some delegates, especially the party elders who lined the front row on the podium, yawned, picked their noses, or dozed off; others looked distracted, as if they were listening to some long-winded eulogy that had little to do with them.

"The Party Congress without Bo Xilai is dull and stifling," observed a princeling—the son of a military leader who was reluctant to disclose his name. "Bo had more personality and he was an unpredictable wild horse. His Chongqing model created a healthy dissenting voice within the party. The country's problems need different approaches and models. With his defeat by a small group of narrow-minded dictators, deathly silence reigns."

Such comments made the senior leadership nervous. Outside the Great Hall of the People, thousands of plainclothes police hovered around Tiananmen Square like specters. The Beijing municipal government had reportedly mobilized 1.4 million police and volunteers to prevent any disorder in public places during the Party Congress. Human rights groups claimed dissidents and petitioners were rounded up and many forced to leave the city. Taxi drivers were told to close their windows and remove window handles to prevent passengers from distributing anti-party leaflets when passing sensitive parts of the city. Kitchen knives were said to have been removed from store shelves, and there was even a rumor that authorities were on the lookout for seditious messages on ping-pong balls, which would be tossed out on the streets. Police inside toy stores asked customers to show their ID cards when buying remote-controlled model planes.

Despite the tension outside, the public reaction was a collective sigh of relief when the lackadaisical opening was broadcast on state media—there had been speculation that the Party Congress would have to be delayed until 2013 due to the Bo Xilai scandal.

Over the following week, many Chinese chose to skip the dull proceedings—for example, the party's work report or approving amendments to the party charter, pro forma proceedings required for the bureaucracy but of little interest to the public—and went about their lives. But the key broadcast, the unveiling of the new leadership lineup at the conclusion of the congress, was a must-see because it would reveal the direction their lives would take for the decade. People were concerned about how the leadership would reverse a slowing economy while tackling the party's rampant corruption.

Since the mid-1980s, the Communist Party has installed new leaders every ten years in even-number party congresses, and nominated prospective successors in odd-number party congresses. In theory, delegates select through a competitive election system 390 members and alternates for the Central Party Committee, which is in turn charged with appointing the general secretary and members of the Politburo (twenty-five members), the most powerful decision-making body of the party. The Politburo elects from among its number a group who will form the Politburo Standing Committee, in which is vested supreme power over the country.

All Politburo Standing Committee members are predetermined by party power brokers, including party elders such as former president Jiang Zemin, outgoing president Hu Jintao, and other members of Politburo Standing Committee. Delegates merely rubber-stamp whatever list is presented to them. The Party Congress is not a place for debate, but for validation of decisions by the leadership.

There is no great secrecy about who is being considered. As in previous years, political insiders showed me a list of the leadership lineup for both the party and the military in September 2012, but since then, a number of changes were made. The final list had yet to be determined just days it was due to be endorsed. Names were added, others deleted as the various factions in the party argued for and against candidates.

Before August 2012, the Bo Xilai scandal further perpetuated the public's negative perception of princelings as a privileged, corrupt, and law-defying group and the polarization of views among princelings weakened its bargaining power over the leadership lineup, giving President Hu and his youth leaguer faction the upper hand. However, following the overseas media expose of the Ferrari incident involving the son of President Hu Jintao's chief of staff, Ling Jihua, the princelings had the opportunity to turn the tide. At the same time, Li Yuanchao, another President Hu protégé and strong contender for a seat on the Politburo Standing Committee, was found linked to several of Ling's unpopular initiatives. The loss of Ling and Li seriously damaged President Hu's credibility and undermined the chances of any candidates he put forward. It gave former president Jiang Zemin more clout over the succession, and he was able to fill six of the seven seats on the Politburo Standing Committee with his allies, three of whom are princelings.

For Xi himself, the transition to the top has not been smooth. While President Hu Jintao and Premier Wen Jiabao became the public faces of the anti-Bo faction, Xi remained silent in public, even though he was seen as the true beneficiary of Bo's downfall. Insiders said Xi felt conflicted about punishing Bo, even though Bo directly challenged his status as the "crown prince." Their life experiences were so matched that Xi used to address Bo Xilai as "third brother." In 2011, Xi visited Chongqing and lavished praise on Bo's "Singing Red and Smashing Black" campaign and his social welfare policies. "These activities have gone deeply into the hearts of the people and are worthy of praise," Xi was quoted as saying. "Chongqing's public housing is a virtuous policy, a benevolent effort, and a positive exploration. We have to come up with more concrete measures that bring benefits to the people." His enthusiastic embrace of Bo's Chongqing model prompted Hong Kong media to report in October 2012 that Xi had promised Bo a top seat in his new leadership team. Given his past history with Bo, Xi maintained a stance of cautious detachment. The Bo Xilai scandal caused a dangerous rift among the princelings, reducing Xi's support from this important political resource. Xi had to exclude several pro-Bo princelings in his new military leadership makeup to purge Bo's influence in the army. There were reports that many of Bo's close princeling friends were being investigated for corruption.

In September, Xi mysteriously disappeared from the public for two weeks—he had supposedly hurt his back, but the state media chose not to report it, leaving the foreign media to speculate about his whereabouts, with unsubstantiated reports saying Xi was under attack from party elders and fellow princelings who shared different views about the future of China. The *Washington Post* carried an unverified story, claiming that Xi had been hit by a chair hurled during a contentious meeting of princelings: "Xi Jinping tried to calm them down. He put himself physically in the crossfire and unwittingly into the path of a chair as it was thrown across the room. It hit him in the back, injuring him. Hence the absence, and the silence, and the rumors." Another journalist in Beijing, Gao Yu, wrote in her blog that Xi had submitted his resignation and his mentor, former president Jiang Zemin, had sent several of his friends to get Xi to stay. The rumor swirled around Beijing as preparation for the Party Congress neared completion. What should have been a done deal—Xi's ascension—was now open to question. Later, a source close to Xi said to me that Xi was not sick.

He actually held closed-door meetings with military leaders to strategize transition. But the rumors illustrated the public's nervousness due to the much-talked-about intense factional struggles.

The leadership transition in China was scheduled to take place two days after the 2012 US presidential election, the outcome of which held potentially huge ramifications for China–US relations. Widely covered throughout China, the heated debate in the run-up to the election and the unpredictable outcome due to the closeness of opinion polls generated unprecedented interest among the Chinese public. Even though government censors restricted any online discussions of nominees Barack Obama and Mitt Romney to prevent comparisons between the US election and the imminent leadership transition in China, several media outlets in Hong Kong cited sources as saying that the Chinese leadership might adopt an internal multiple-candidate election for the Politburo and its Standing Committee as a way to resolve factional conflicts over the lineup.

Because I had already obtained what insiders called "a final list"—the result of the usual behind-the-scenes deal-making—I seriously doubted the speculation about a multi-candidate election. I published my list on *Mingjing News* and stated that all talk about a multi-party election was wishful thinking: "If the final outcome is different from what I have released, it proves that I'm wrong."

On the morning of November 15, 2012, the newly "elected" Politburo Standing Committee members, all dressed in navy blue suits, with dyed black hair and tepid smiles, paraded to meet some four hundred Chinese and foreign reporters in the east wing of the Great Hall of the People. All the faces were on the list.

The Politburo Standing Committee would be reduced from nine members to seven. A smaller committee was deemed to be more efficient, by reducing the incidence of factional haggling over decision-making. The idea, which had been in discussion since 2011, prevailed after the Bo Xilai scandal. Zhou Yongkang's seat controlled China's law enforcement, judicial authorities, and national security, and had a budget bigger than that of China's military. It was eliminated and his former responsibilities devolved to other Politburo members, whose decisions and recommendations would require final endorsement of the Standing Committee. The other function cut from the committee was propaganda. There were concerns about the damage its aggressive censorship activities had done to the reputation of the Standing Committee.

Insiders said the loss of two spots in the top decision-making body exacerbated the political bickering. In the end, all competing factions chose to resolve the debacle with a simple hard requirement—that of age. Younger candidates, such as the fifty-seven-year-old party chief of Guangdong, were excluded on the grounds that they still had time to compete in the next round five years later. Those approaching the retirement age of sixty-eight, such as Yu Zhengsheng, the former party chief of Shanghai, made it to the list with the excuse that "if he doesn't join this year, he will not have another opportunity." In the end, the seven-member leadership has an average age of 63.4 years compared with 62.1 years in 2007.

Backroom bickering aside, the spotlight was on fifty-eight-year-old Xi Jinping, who survived much behind-the-scenes political maneuvering, and was officially crowned the party general secretary—he will be made president in the spring of 2013 when the legislature convenes and charged with leading the world's second-biggest economy for the next decade.

When describing Xi's life, many preferred to compare Xi with Bo Xilai, who shared similar upbringings and work experience, though they landed in starkly different places—one leader of China, the other a prisoner number.

Xi was born into the family of a revolutionary veteran in June 1953 and is four years younger than Bo Xilai. His father, Xi Zhongxun, fought with Mao as a guerrilla in northwestern China, against the invading Japanese and the civil war Nationalists. He was appointed vice premier of China in the 1950s. Like Bo, Xi lived a sheltered life before the age of twelve, attending an elite school for children of senior leaders. But his life took a dramatic turn in 1962.

His father was put in charge of a book that chronicled the life of a former comrade who had been killed in battle in 1936. Because the book objectively mentioned another influential political figure purged by Mao, Kang Sheng, China's intelligence chief accused him of using the book, excerpts of which had been published in several state-run newspapers and magazines, to attack Mao and subvert the party. Xi's father was forced to undergo denunciations and was exiled in 1965 to the central province of Henan. His status was reduced to that of a deputy manager of a tractor factory. When the Cultural Revolution started, Red Guards found him, put him on a multi-city denunciation tour, and locked him up for nearly ten years in a Beijing prison. The Red Guards added another charge to his crimes—that of being a Western spy. The basis for the charge was that he had looked at West Berlin with a pair of binoculars when he toured the Berlin Wall during an official visit to East Germany in 1959.

Xi's entire family was affected by his persecution by the Red Guards. Like Bo Xilai, Xi Jinping was excluded from many activities in school for being the son of a purged official. During the Cultural Revolution, he and other children of disgraced party officials roamed the streets after school, engaging in street fights. They were constant targets of the local public security bureau. At the age of fifteen, Xi Jinping joined thousands of young people who responded to Mao's call to settle in the countryside. Initially, he reportedly returned to his father's native village in Shaanxi province, but no relatives dared take him in. Xi and twelve others ended up in a village in the yellow hills of northern Shaanxi, where people lived in caves and electricity was a rare luxury. There was barely enough to eat.

Three months after he arrived in the village, all of his fellow "sent down" youths had deserted because they found it too hard to acclimate. Xi was miserably homesick and escaped by train to Beijing, where he was caught by the street committee for sneaking back to the city without approval. The public security bureau detained him for six months. By the time he was released, both of his sisters had left to become peasants in Inner Mongolia. His mother, a devoted Communist, insisted that he return to northern Shaanxi to complete his "reeducation."

Upon his return from Beijing, villagers noticed that Xi had changed. He was determined to do well. "I ate a lot more bitterness than most people," he recalled in a recent media interview. "I picked up smoking because a smoker was allowed to take a break from the harsh labor every now and then to puff on their cigarettes," he said. "I would sometimes take longer toilet breaks so I could take a rest." In the first few years, his elder sister in Inner Mongolia would frequently save money from her stipend to subsidize Xi's food rations.

He began to thrive in the harsh conditions and joined the Communist Party, despite the rejection of his early attempts because of his father. He was appointed a village chief, the lowest in the party's hierarchy, and taught his fellow villagers how to produce methane from compost for cooking and heating. Villagers remembered him as a quiet, humble person who hated political bickering. "When people had a conflict with each other, they would go to him, and he'd say, 'Come back in two days,'" a peasant from Xi's former village told the *New York Times*. "By then, the problem had usually resolved itself."

His break came in December 1975 when Chinese universities, after lying vacant at the height of the Cultural Revolution, decided to recruit students who were workers, peasants, and soldiers. Recruitment standards would be based on the recommendations of local authorities, rather than academic merit. Through his family ties, Xi entered Qinghua University, China's equivalent in educational standards and merit to MIT in the US. The morning before he left, villagers waited quietly outside his cave so they could say farewell. Many dropped work and accompanied him on the four-mile walk to the bus station. Xi said the scene made him cry, something he had not done for seven years.

"When I came to the land of the yellow hills at the age of fifteen, I was lost and confused," he later told the Chinese media. "When I left seven years later, I had a clear goal in life and I was full of confidence. The experience has etched in my blood, instilling in me a firm belief, what I do for people has to be practical."

Xi obtained an undergraduate degree in chemistry. Later he returned to Qinghua to pursue a doctorate in Marxist theory and ideological education, making him one of the few Chinese leaders educated in the arts rather than engineering during the Hu Jintao era.

While Xi was studying at Qinghua, Mao died and two years later, Xi's father was released, all charges against him were dropped, and he returned to Beijing. In the spring of 1979, Xi's father was made governor of the southern province of Guangdong. On May 6 that year, more than 100,000 residents of Guangdong swarmed to the border with the then British colony of Hong Kong on rumors that the Hong Kong government would grant amnesty to illegal immigrants on the birthday of Queen Elizabeth II and that the Hong Kong border would be open for three days to allow Guangdong residents to enter.

There were scuffles at border checkpoints as border police tried to hold them back, telling them the rumor was untrue. Crowds broke through several entry points and by the end of the day, more than one hundred people were dead, either shot during the riots or drowned while trying to swim across to Hong Kong. There is no estimate of how many made it to Hong Kong to lead what they believed would be better lives. When Xi's father learned about the tragedy, he was said to be shocked, but very sympathetic. Peasants in Guangdong eyed Hong Kong because farmers who had managed to get there earned a hundred times more than they did in the paddy fields. The incident reportedly motivated Xi's father to spearhead a campaign to create China's first special economic zones, first in Shenzhen, a city bordering Hong Kong, and then the whole Guangdong province, offering special concessions to foreign investors to open factories and help build China.

Xi was profoundly affected by his father's liberal views and his reform initiatives, many of Xi Jinping's supporters said. After graduation in 1979, he worked as a low-level official at the State Council and then as an officer in active service in the General Office of the Central Military Commission. During this time, he married the daughter of China's former ambassador to Britain. In 1982, his wife wanted them to migrate to the UK, but Xi refused to leave China, and the pair divorced. In the same year, Xi and another princeling, Liu Yuan, the son of former president Liu Shaoqi, decided to leave Beijing and launch their political careers at the grassroots level.

Considering he had just spent seven years in one of the poorest regions in China, many of Xi's friends failed to understand his decision. Power was in Beijing, and his father was at the pinnacle of his career—elected to the Politburo in 1982 and asked to head the Central Party Committee Secretariat. There was every reason for him to stay and take advantage of his father's rising political clout. Xi's friends said he wanted to escape his father's shadow and create a path for himself, a move his father supported. Xi Jinping took up the post of deputy party chief in Zhengding County in nearby Hebei province, while Liu Yuan went to the central province of Henan. Bo Xilai followed their example two years later when he settled in Jin County near the city of Dalian.

Xi Jinping encountered much the same obstacles as Bo because of prejudiced local provincial leaders who were wary of his true motives. They believed that Xi was merely there to gain some political capital before moving to bigger things. Xi persisted and his achievement during that period included a project to help the local tourism industry by persuading a movie director to shoot a TV period drama in his county. Xi kept the sets constructed for the TV series as a tourist attraction after the movie, which was seen throughout the country, was over. He also won the hearts of local retired officials when he initiated programs to improve their living conditions.

With his own political savvy and his family connection, Xi rose quickly from this first government post and was quickly identified as one of the prospective leaders. In 1985, on his thirty-second birthday, Xi took the first of several posts in the coastal province of Fujian, adjacent to Guangdong. Due to Fujian's close proximity to Taiwan, Xi supported the region's free-market transformation and approved preferential policies to attract investment from Taiwan and actively promoted direct air and sea transportation between the two regions, which had ceased in 1949. Direct contact with Taiwan, which China claims to be part of its sovereign territory—a claim rejected by many in Taiwan as well as its main ally, the US—remains a problem tangled in diplomatic posturing and punctuated by sporadic military saber-rattling. The US keeps an aircraft carrier battle group based out of Japan in the event of military escalation.

In 1987, Xi Jinping met one of China's most popular army folk singers, Peng Liyuan, whose smooth melodious rendition of a pro-party folk song "In the Field of Hope" at a New Year concert on state television made her a household name. The two were married after a few dates. Their wedding was simple—a meal with the attendance of a few colleagues. Friends say fans would mob Xi's wife when they were out together and Xi would always stand aside quietly, even though he was already high up in the government. After Xi's coronation, many commented on Weibo that China finally had the most glamorous-looking and popular first lady since Madame Mao and Wang Guangmei, the wife of Liu Shaoqi, who was president of China from 1959 to 1969.

Xi became the party chief of Ningde, a relatively poor region in Fujian province, in 1988. State media reported his first task there was to tackle widespread corruption. He was considered an amicable person, but lost his temper in public when he learned that several thousand local officials had seized public land to build private houses for themselves. He ordered an extensive investigation and ended up firing or demoting several hundred officials who were found to have violated land occupation rules. He was also said to have returned 600,000 yuan worth of "gifts" in the late 1980s, when he was Ningde's district party chief. The revelation won Xi much praise.

In October 2002, Xi was transferred to China's southeastern province of Zhejiang, home to the country's most successful private enterprises, which have supplanted state-owned enterprises and generate 65 percent of Zhejiang's GDP.

Unlike Bo Xilai, who painted Chongqing red in a dramatic display of his radical approach to the region's social and economic problems, Xi's steps were more steady and incremental. One of Xi's most notable accomplishments in Zhejiang was related to his efforts to change the region's economic structure from the rapid and rough labor-intensive expansion to a higher level of development, emphasizing concern for efficiency and the environment. Xi came up with a slogan: "Green mountains and clean rivers are more valuable than gold and silver." Under his leadership, the provincial government invested billions of yuan on information technology, environmental, and infrastructural projects. Xi actively cultivated relations with private entrepreneurs, allowing them to participate in the decision-making process by appointing them to the local legislature. The central government under Hu Jintao had provided preferential financial policies toward state-run corporations and suppressed the growth of private enterprises. Xi's experience in Zhejiang suggests that the balance can be expected to tilt toward private enterprises. Xi won praise from governors in other provinces by urging the prosperous entrepreneurs to invest in poorer provinces inland.

If there was one program that grabbed national attention, it was Xi's clean-government initiative that encouraged the public to supervise the work of government officials, setting up a hotline for complaints and protecting the media's investigative work on government corruption.

In 2008, a corruption scandal struck the heart of one of China's largest cities, Shanghai. The city's party chief was sentenced to eighteen years in prison for accepting bribes and abusing power. Under normal circumstances, the party chief of Shanghai has a guaranteed seat on the Politburo Standing Committee. There was wide speculation that President Hu Jintao would bring one of his allies as replacement, but he unexpectedly picked Xi to appease his critics. Xi's modest approach and his nonfactional reputation made him an acceptable candidate for all sides, and he governed a province that was in close proximity to Shanghai and understood the city's particular needs as a gateway to China.

Seven months before the 17th Party Congress, when a "crown prince" would be designated, Xi was appointed party chief of Shanghai. President Hu planned to select his protégé, Li Keqiang, a fellow youth leaguer. However, on October 22, at the routine new leadership press conference, the public was surprised to see the shy-looking Xi Jinping—still better known as the husband of one of China's most popular singers—ranked ahead of Li Keqiang. The ranking indicated that Xi would be head of the party and president, and Li the future prime minister. Xi's heir-apparent status was sealed in 2010 when he was appointed vice president and vice chair of the party's Central Military Commission, overseeing China's vast standing army—whose main activities are road and bridge building, local engineering projects, and emergency natural disaster relief, such as filling sandbags to shore up the banks of flooding rivers.

Xi's meteoric rise intrigued many analysts. In subsequent months, insiders revealed that former president Jiang Zemin and his friends had subverted Hu's planned succession strategy and installed Xi to stem the influence of Hu and his youth leaguers. In addition, Xi also enjoyed broad support from the Politburo and many of the party's old guard, who were friends of Xi's father. Before the selection process started, President Hu Jintao conducted several straw polls and Xi's name ranked at the top every time.

After his elevation, Xi was put in charge of the overall preparation work for the 2008 Summer Olympics in Beijing, which became the target of protests by human rights activists and pro-Tibetan independence groups overseas as the Olympic torch was carried around the world from Greece to China. A devastating earthquake had struck China's southwestern province of Sichuan three months before, and that placed considerable demand on the country's attention and resources, both physical and material. As it was, the Olympics proceeded smoothly and drew accolades for its organization and facilities, and the dazzling opening ceremony and China's impressive medal count did much to boost its international image and strengthened Xi's credentials as head of a state.

As presumptive successor to President Hu, Xi made numerous foreign trips. His tour took him across the US, Europe, Latin America, and Australia.

Western leaders who have met and worked with Xi speak highly of him. US vice president Joe Biden, who befriended Xi during his trip to China, said Xi was "absolutely straightforward" and "open." Occasionally, he could be too straightforward. On a visit to Mexico in 2009, he castigated countries critical of China's new economic power by saying:

> Some foreigners with full bellies and nothing better to do engage in finger-pointing at us. China does not export revolution; second, it does not export famine and poverty; and third, it does not mess around with you. So what else is there to say?

His remarks made many observers skittish about the tenor of his future foreign policies. Those around him point out that in no way is Xi an extreme ideologue or a nationalist. He can be expected to be flexible and practical on foreign policy, and identify more with the democratic values than his processor, who spent the better part of his life within the party network, while Xi spent his with the people. When it comes to Western pressure over the issue of trade and human rights, Xi can be expected to use tough rhetoric for local consumption, but on the world stage will display more flexibility and a willingness to make concessions.

After he was made heir apparent in 2008, Xi avoided the media and seldom granted interviews—it was a political necessity in China for a leader in waiting to tread carefully without running afoul of the current party chief. Therefore, details of his personal and family life are scarce. Public optimism was largely built on what has been written about Xi's family and his own personal experiences.

Before his death in 2002, Xi's father had an unassailable reputation for being open-minded and liberal. Because he was banished from the power center back in 1962, Xi's father did not participate in the brutal power struggles of the Mao era, and was well respected by all political factions. In the 1980s, he was credited for supporting Deng Xiaoping's economic reform policies that helped lift millions out of poverty. He was one of the few senior leaders who voted during the 1980s for political reforms and was sidelined after leading reformers, such as Hu Yaobang and Zhao Ziyang, fell from power. He strongly condemned the 1989 crackdown on the Tiananmen Square protest. Those who worked with Xi's father remember him as a devoted official who lived a simple life. An official who visited him in the late 1980s recalled eating a bowl of noodle soup and a piece of bread in his sparsely furnished home. Xi's father was generous with poor villagers who supported him in the early revolutionary years. Every now and then, he sent them money saved from his pension.

Xi Jinping's mother was said to have shared similar qualities. Over the past five years, the matriarch reportedly called two family meetings, strictly forbidding her children to use Xi Jinping's name to engage in business transactions. However, Xi's siblings did not seem to follow their mother's advice. In June 2012, Bloomberg carried an investigative report about Xi's family. The article claimed that Xi's extended family, such as his sister and brother, had invested in "companies with total assets of US $376 million; an 18 percent indirect stake in a rare-earths company with US $1.73 billion in assets; and a US $20.2 million holding in a publicly traded technology company." Even though Bloomberg acknowledged that none of the assets had any immediate link with Xi and his wife, and there is no indication Xi intervened to advance his relatives' business transactions, the report tainted the Xi family's clean image. As usual, the Chinese government immediately blocked Bloomberg's website and a week later, Xi's supporters supplied *Mingjing News* with a meticulously researched article to dispute the Bloomberg report, claiming that most of the assets belonged to his brother-in-law.

Despite Bloomberg's negative report, the overseas media have largely focused on Xi's own record. China observers say he gained a deep understanding of grassroots politics when he worked as county chief and district chairman in poverty-stricken regions and presided over booming provinces in the coastal region that have been at the forefront of China's market reforms. In all of these posts, though he might not have created an attention-grabbing "Chongqing model" that emphasized Maoist egalitarianism or a "Guangdong model" that advocated a freer market and political liberalization, Xi stayed true to his own nature. He was practical and low-key, a trait that made him acceptable to all sides, not so much a compromise candidate but one open to ideas from all sides and prepared to change his position if an argument was convincing. He was a pragmatist, fully aware of the complexities that a country as vast as China required to be governed and led. Xi has broad access to political resources and a broader spectrum of support, all of which will enable him to experiment with new ideas and initiatives.

Xi and many members of his leadership team grew up during the Cultural Revolution, a sensitive issue that previous regimes have chosen to put behind them, and lived in the rural areas as "sent down youths" in the late 1960s and 1970s. People living in the bottom rung look up to Xi as a compassionate leader who is more sympathetic to the predicament. A peasant who used to share a cave apartment in his early hardship days told the Chinese media he was struck with a severe form of bone disease when Xi was the deputy governor of Fujian province. Xi personally arranged for the villager to have surgery in a major city and offered money to support his family. Moreover, the public likes a party chief who loves soccer games and enjoys Hollywood movies. He has popular appeal and is recognized as being in touch with the people, not above them.

Whereas his predecessor was cautious to the point of inaction, Xi's supporters maintain he has sharp political instincts and can weather any political crisis. When authorities in Hubei province banned a symposium on Marshal Lin Biao, whose mysterious death in the early 1970s in a plane crash was still a sensitive political issue, Xi gave permission to move the symposium to Beijing, effectively giving it more prominence, especially to the foreign press corps. Moreover, because Xi's father sustained years of suffering under Mao due to his involvement and support for a banned book, scholars speculated that he might be more sympathetic to freedom of expression. That is yet to be demonstrated.

Xi does not talk like Hu Jintao, who is good at memorizing jargon-filled speeches. In his years as China's vice president, Xi showed more personality, even bluntness. During the Olympic Games, he encouraged officials to bravely face hostile foreign views by comparing countries critical of China to a flock of noisy birds. "If you take the birds out of the cage, it wouldn't be fun anymore."

More important, Xi has the military on his side. As the party chief, Xi also heads the party's top military body, the Central Military Commission, which oversees the armed forces. Throughout history, the Chinese leadership has never allowed the military to interfere with state affairs. But when different factions jockey fiercely for power, the support of the military is crucial. Former President Hu Jintao had no military experience and showed no interest in cultivating relationships with senior military officers. His lack of talent left the military under the firm control of allies of his predecessor, Jiang Zemin. In China, it can be argued that the Communist Party exists so long as the military finds it useful. Loss of military support would be catastrophic. Xi is different. His father's military roots and his three-year stint as an aide to a senior military leader make the generals feel he is one of them. Besides, his singer wife is also a serving high-ranking officer in the army.

A month before the Party Congress, Xi Jinping consolidated his leadership position within the military by placing his allies in key positions and bringing the country's five regional armed chiefs to Beijing to staff the Central Military Commission, which supervises China's large armed forces. Unlike President Jiang Zemin, who held onto the top spot within the military for two years after he relinquished the presidency, President Hu handed over military control upon his retirement. "Xi's advisers know very well that a bumpy ride was awaiting him," said the son of a military officer. "He knows that he has to have the military firmly in his hands so he can weather possible storms from social unrests, power struggles, or instability triggered by his own political reforms."

Still, Xi's priority for the military underscores a disturbing trend: it might be pressed to take a tougher stand in territorial disputes with its neighbors. If a large-scale protest movement should occur, the government would rely on the military to intervene and suppress opposition, possibly in a more brutal way than that in 1989 at Tiananmen Square. The reasoning is simple—when its basic interests are threatened, the party will resort to any means available to protect itself. Fortunately, after 1989, the government has become more sophisticated in dealing with protests and has learned to use arms as sparingly as possible to avoid inflaming public outrage and international condemnation. However, when the situation grows out of control and armed police cannot handle the protesters, there is little doubt that Xi would follow the direction of his generals. He is a pragmatist.

So far, the public has high expectations for Xi, due to what experts said was "deep disillusionment with the inaction and incompetence of the Hu Jintao administration." A week after the transfer of power to Xi, "The Field of Hope," the song made famous by his singer wife, was on the radio and rising on the pop charts. It captured the public mood and helped dispel pessimism. It would not be a mistake to compare this song with the effect "Happy Days Are Here Again" had on the US public with the ascendancy of President Franklin Delano Roosevelt in the early 1930s and his promises of US prosperity.

To the public, especially Westerners, Xi has unlimited power at his disposal—he leads a party that has no opposition and rules the world's most populous nation, a booming economic power inexorably headed toward the top position the US has held since the two great wars of the past century. But—and in China there is always a "but"—such high expectations of Xi may not have taken into account factors that limit what he can achieve.

Xi lacks legitimacy because he is not directly elected by the people he serves. Moreover, within the Politburo Standing Committee, each member represents a vast patronage network and a cluster of interest groups. Xi could no longer dominate the agenda like Mao Zedong and Deng Xiaoping did. On major policy issues, members operate by consensus, involving balancing the political and economic interests of all factions. Committee members might attend different public meetings together, but they seldom communicate or socialize with each other.

The current structure of the Politburo Standing Committee was part of Deng Xiaoping's effort to promote collective leadership and ensure China's stability. "The key to China's stability is to have a good Politburo, especially a good Politburo Standing Committee," said Deng in 1992. "As long as this decision-making body remains united and doesn't go awry, China will be stable as the Tai mountain."

Ironically, this very structure, created ostensibly to prevent one-man dominance, has made it inherently easier for party elders such as Deng Xiaoping to control, because nobody within the committee has absolute control. In 1989 Deng, even though he had relinquished his political power, ordered the military to crack down on protesters against the wishes of a majority of the Politburo Standing Committee. Members who opposed his military action were purged.

After Jiang Zemin was designated party chief, Deng monitored Jiang's every move. If it hadn't been for his Parkinson's disease, insiders said Deng would have deposed Jiang in 1992 because he was unhappy with the slow pace of the country's economic reforms. To ensure that his legacy continued, Deng even designated Jiang's successor.

In the aftermath of Deng's death, Jiang's authority grew rapidly. Following his retirement, he still held sway over the Politburo Standing Committee. President Hu Jintao reportedly consulted with Jiang on all major policy initiatives. Like Deng, he intervened in two succession plans—designating Xi as the crown prince at the 17th Party Congress and influencing the leadership makeup in 2012.

With Xi's installation in November 2012, for the foreseeable future he will have to deal with two king fathers, former Jiang Zemin and Hu Jintao, as well as former premiers Wen Jiabao and Zhu Rongji. "The party elders will constantly call him and send him memos, telling him how he should rule," said Gao Xin, coauthor of *Chinese Princelings*. "If Xi strays too far, they can muster enough support to depose him. The interference could severely restrict what Xi can do." Xi further faces challenges from other princelings, who feel entitled to have their opinions heard. "Both his friends and foes in the princeling group will try to influence his decisions," said Gao Xin. "Considering their political and economic clout, they could cause obstructions if Xi does not handle these interpersonal relations well."

Resistance to change comes as well from officials at different levels of the party and the government bureaucracy. Scholars and journalists in the West erroneously characterize the Chinese leadership with labels such as "conservative" or "reformist." To a large extent, there are no true reformists or conservatives within the Communist Party. As beneficiaries of the current political system, Chinese leaders choose to be reformists only when the reforms advance or maximize their own economic and political interests—they can enjoy lifelong privileges and their children are in control of a vast amount of China's wealth. They all turn into ultraconservatives when any reform initiatives disrupt the power balance and jeopardize their well-being.

The majority of party officials, including Xi and his fellow Politburo members, will publicly agree political or democratic reform is the only solution for China's future, but no one wants it to happen while they are in power. The recent uprisings in the Arab world—the so-called Arab Spring—have made Chinese leaders keenly aware of their own fate should it come to settling political scores. Moreover, there is no apparent motivation for the leadership to engage in large-scale political reform. Internationally, China's vast foreign reserves and real and potential market control can still attract a large group of money-grabbing investors, desperate politicians, and opportunistic scholars, who will cozy up to China for economic gain. Domestically, authorities can still maintain their grip on the masses through extreme means of suppression.

In such a context, there is little to suggest that Xi will be China's Mikhail Gorbachev and steer the country in a sharply different direction and seek to loosen the ropes of one-party rule. Xi's new initiatives will inevitably be limited to stopgap measures to aggressively combat corruption, boost social welfare for the poor, and encourage the development of private enterprises, while temporarily relaxing political controls to regain the trust of the intellectual elite. The party could introduce experimental measures to broaden intraparty democracy by allowing limited elections for certain positions within the party and encouraging greater debate, but stability remains a top concern and one-party rule will be safeguarded. In handling relations with the US and its Asian neighbors, who are wary of China's past belligerent style, Xi might be more conciliatory in settling trade and territorial disputes.

However, no superficial measures can solve China's deepening fundamental social, political, and diplomatic problems.

After more than three decades of market reform, China has reinvented itself, growing from a broken sampan into a luxury cruise ship. The ship of state has been in choppy waters. The pace of China's economic growth has slowed significantly. A bubble created by booming construction and surging real estate prices, and a shaky financial system resulting from irrational lending to corrupted officials at local government and mammoth state-run enterprises could be shoals that sink the ship.

Moreover, the economic reforms have unleashed a strong and deep desire among the masses to get rich, and it angers and frustrates them to see wealth fall into the hands of a small group of party officials and well-connected private entrepreneurs. The gap between the rich and the poor has spawned discontent if not hatred for the rich and powerful. Short-sighted development is depleting natural resources and polluting the environment without consideration for the future generation.

The greed of government officials knows no bounds. Rampant corruption has seeped into every aspect of social and political life—police, the courts, taxation, quality control, and petition handling. One needs to bribe the teacher to get into a better school and the doctor before surgery. Under Hu Jintao, the government launched one campaign after another to purify the party ranks and there are more anticorruption organizations than ever before, but apart from a few high-profile showcase trials, nothing has worked.

Despite the government's tight control of the news media, the public is better informed than ever, as was evident by the way that the Bo Xilai scandal spread by Weibo and mobile technology, subverting government attempts at censorship. The government finds it harder and harder to control the Internet, with hackers bringing down firewalls almost as soon as the government's own hackers put them up. More Chinese are being enabled to think for themselves and make informed decisions about their country's future. The party could lock up all the dissidents in China, but they cannot prevent disgruntled workers and peasants from rising up to rebel against prevalent corruption and social injustices. The government could mobilize its armed forces, or even the military, to put out ten such fires, but if they lose control of just one, it could spark a spontaneous revolution, similar to what has happened in the Middle East and the dictatorial states of the former Soviet Union.

Many in the government might prefer to see the West as the country's main source of potential instability. And it is true that as China has expanded its investments worldwide, exporting not only cheap goods but also trashy ideological and cultural values, its rapidly modernizing military forces and seemingly insatiable quest for resources have led to more tension abroad, especially with its Asian neighbors. China's increasingly arrogant behavior and rhetoric, typical of the nouveau riche, is drowning out its diplomatic objectives. Growing domestic nationalism also makes China's foreign policy more vulnerable to criticism at home, giving the government less room to maneuver amid its global rivals. But unquestionably the greatest danger to the stability of the Chinese government is the Chinese Communist Party—the most vulnerable and volatile elements come from within the party itself. For years, Western analysts have credited Deng Xiaoping for bringing about an orderly institutionalized leadership transition, but the Bo Xilai scandal, brought about by the death of a formerly obscure Englishman, not only scuppered the formula for the 2012 transition but also suggested that the concept of a peaceful transition that ensures the continued dominance of the Communist Party may no longer be possible.

For more than two decades, the party has established a system of supposed meritocracy for all levels of leadership, from the Politburo Standing Committee to state enterprises. The criteria for promotion are based on a candidate's age, academic degrees, and governing experience or accomplishments. But the process is not governed by open and fair rules. Selections of officials are made by a few party strongmen and elders in a back room. As a consequence, the leadership transition is fraught with conspiracies and fierce factional infighting before the Party Congress. The political elite still relies for advancement on family or personal connections, character assassination, persecution, and as we have seen, even murder. Bo's misfortune befell him when he conspired with his friends and allies at the top to seize power, only for his opponents to apply a similar conspiratorial method to bring him down. In the ancient Chinese imperial court, succession-related conspiracies and killings were perpetual themes. It is no different in the twenty-first century, now that the Communist Party has become a kleptocratic monarchy in all but name.

In some respects, however, getting rid of Bo is proving more difficult than many anticipated. Bo's allies and foes are deeply intertwined—sharing common political and economic interests. Under these circumstances it's hard to move against an opponent without harming or offending elements of one's own clique, especially as alliances are fluid and constantly shifting. New rounds of political conspiracies are being fomented by the clones of Wang Lijun and Bo Xilai, and more political earthquakes are likely to strike. Observers of contemporary Chinese court politics might not know in what form and how big future political shakeups will be or who will emerge victorious, but the cascading scandals are revealing the vulnerability of the entire China development model—economic development without democratic reforms. In a country where the rulers reject democracy and the public lacks the ability to rise up against the rulers, political coups are constant threats. Until China ends the one-party system, there will not be stability or safety for Chinese citizens or foreign businessmen, corporations, and governments.

The strange death of Neil Heywood in the provincial backwater of the Lucky Holiday Hotel might have passed unnoticed but for the neurotic vulnerability of China's competing power players and the fundamental rottenness of the system. A police chief with too many enemies and an overambitious politician facing his last chance at the ultimate elevation turned a minor character into a cancer at the center of the body politic, causing the hurried and almost desperate reorganization of its greatest public show. The show—the Party Congress—was kept on the road this time, with the parade of new leaders unfurled, and the overall sense of China's global rise uninterrupted. But the Chinese Communist Party might not be so lucky next time.

INDEX

Pin Ho, a journalist and writer, is the founder of Mirror Media Groups and has covered Chinese politics for twenty-five years. He broke the news on leadership lineups for three consecutive Communist Party Congresses since 2002. His book, *China's Princelings,* was the first to coin that phrase to describe the children of Chinese revolutionaries, and is the source for much that has appeared in the accounts of various Western journalists.

Wenguang Huang is a writer, journalist, and translator whose articles and translations have been published in the *New York Times,* the *Chicago Tribune,* the *Paris Review,* and the *Christian Science Monitor.* He is most recently the author of the memoir *The Little Red Guard* and the translator for Liao Yiwu's *For a Song and One Hundred Songs, The Corpse Walker,* and *God Is Red.*

PublicAffairs is a publishing house founded in 1997. It is a tribute to the standards, values, and flair of three persons who have served as mentors to countless reporters, writers, editors, and book people of all kinds, including me.

I. F. STONE, proprietor of *I. F. Stone's Weekly*, combined a commitment to the First Amendment with entrepreneurial zeal and reporting skill and became one of the great independent journalists in American history. At the age of eighty, Izzy published *The Trial of Socrates*, which was a national bestseller. He wrote the book after he taught himself ancient Greek.

BENJAMIN C. BRADLEE was for nearly thirty years the charismatic editorial leader of *The Washington Post*. It was Ben who gave the *Post* the range and courage to pursue such historic issues as Watergate. He supported his reporters with a tenacity that made them fearless and it is no accident that so many became authors of influential, best-selling books.

ROBERT L. BERNSTEIN, the chief executive of Random House for more than a quarter century, guided one of the nation's premier publishing houses. Bob was personally responsible for many books of political dissent and argument that challenged tyranny around the globe. He is also the founder and longtime chair of Human Rights Watch, one of the most respected human rights organizations in the world.

.   .   .

For fifty years, the banner of Public Affairs Press was carried by its owner Morris B. Schnapper, who published Gandhi, Nasser, Toynbee, Truman, and about 1,500 other authors. In 1983, Schnapper was described by *The Washington Post* as "a redoubtable gadfly." His legacy will endure in the books to come.

Peter Osnos, *Founder and Editor-at-Large*